WITHDRAWN

Valparaiso's First Century

Chancel of the Memorial Chapel
September, 1958

Valparaiso's
FIRST CENTURY

*A Centennial History of
Valparaiso University*

BY JOHN STRIETELMEIER

Published by the University

1959

Preface

THIS HISTORY of Valparaiso University has been written against a deadline, for its primary purpose is to serve as a backdrop to the events of the University's centennial year, 1959. No one could be more conscious than is the author of how much has had to be omitted because of limitations of documentary sources, time, and space. But the history of the University is intrinsically such a fascinating one that even the limitations of a particular writer can not prevent it from coming through and laying its own claim to the reader's attention. Valparaiso has had periods of greatness and periods of profound distress, but it has never yet enjoyed the privilege of being ordinary.

A peculiar disadvantage under which the University historian of 1958 must operate is that there can be little question that the University, in its centennial year, is at the height of its prosperity. It is difficult, therefore, to avoid portraying the past as merely the prelude to the present, and even more difficult to appraise the present objectively. Recognizing these difficulties, the author has attempted to observe the warning of his colleague, Mr. Martin Schaefer, in the October, 1956, issue of *The Cresset:*

The past begins with us, with our parents, with our elders in general. The latter are most noticeably already partly behind us, of the past. But we have no right to consider them as mere means that were instrumental in our attaining the present and our moving on into the future. We owe them an imaginative respect that sees them fully as ourselves and not one whit less important before God. And when occasion presents itself, we must apply this respect to the men and women of the broader and more distant past. That belongs, as a colleague of mine has put it, to the "integrity of Christian personality." It is not merely a matter of "split personality" to honor the present and hold the past in contempt. Respect for the full humanity of both the immediate and remote past enhances our integrity in the present.

Every university—and perhaps uniquely Valparaiso—is built upon the day-to-day work of men and women who, in the nature of their calling, are not likely to attract more than local notice.

It seems unfair that any man may earn the remembrance of history by killing enough people or stealing enough money while the builders and carriers of civilization—the teachers, the scholars, the pastors, the business men, the wives and mothers, the faithful farmers and workers—are all but totally ignored. The author has, therefore, consciously attempted to rescue from anonymity the names of men and women who deserve something better than to be forgotten. Despite this conscious attempt, however, he is aware of the fact that there must be many who deserve mention in this history but who, because of the inadequacy of the records or perhaps because of their own desire for anonymity, have left no record.

The author has attempted to abide by his instructions to tell the story of the University honestly. Few institutions survive for a century without accumulating a fund of memories which they would rather forget. And no institution which has experienced trials and difficulties is without its record of conflicts which are not easily forgotten. No attempt has been made in this history to rewrite the record. As encouragement or as warning, that record is a part of the University's heritage and must be accepted as a mature man must accept the accomplishments and the indiscretions of his youth.

Five sources have been of inestimable value in the writing of this history: *The Story of Valparaiso University*, written and published privately in 1921 by George W. Stimpson, then a student at the University, who obtained most of his information from Miss Mantie Baldwin; "A History of Valparaiso University from 1875 to 1925," an unpublished dissertation submitted to the Faculty of the Division of the Social Sciences in candidacy for the degree of Master of Arts, School of Education, The University of Chicago, by Cecil Loar Bigelow; an unpublished, thoroughly documented history of the University from 1925 to 1940 by Mrs. Lois Sohn Glock; an unpublished history of the Kretzmann administration by George W. E. Nickelsburg, Jr.; and the wealth of materials that have been assembled in the University Archives by Mrs. Katharine Ertz Bowden. So heavily has the author drawn upon these sources that Mr. Stimpson, Mr. Bigelow, Mrs. Glock, Mr. Nickelsburg, and Mrs. Bowden might, without any impropriety, be listed as co-authors. Much of the expense of gathering material for the history, as well as for publishing the book itself, has been underwritten by the Valparaiso University Alumni Association.

Acknowledgments should also be made to President O. P. Kretzmann and Dr. Walter G. Friedrich, chairman of the university committee on the centennial, upon whose insistence the author undertook the writing of this history; and to Dr. Alfred H. Meyer, head of the department of geography and geology, who adjusted the work in that department so as to allow the author time to complete his manuscript.

In some cases, the author has stated conclusions or value judgments which can be found also in his sources. Where this is the case, the author accepts full responsibility for their appearance in print. Records of conversations in Chapters V and VI, as they appear in the footnotes, are to be understood as the work of Mrs. Glock.

J. S.

Acknowledgments

THE AUTHOR gratefully acknowledges the generous cooperation of the many individuals and groups who participated in the search for pictures to illustrate this history. He is especially grateful to Mrs. Katharine Ertz Bowden, the University Archivist, who supplied most of the pictures in this book;

Mr. John Adams, the University's director of press relations, who furnished many of the pictures of the post–1925 period;

The Archives of DePauw University, for the picture of President Sims;

Mrs. C. A. Robbins, for the picture of her father, President Thomas Bond Wood;

Mr. Jacob E. Somsel, for the picture of President Staley;

The Purdue University Libraries, for the portrait of President Smith;

Mrs. Joseph Bartholomew, for the picture of her father, President Roessler;

The Valparaiso *Vidette-Messenger* for pictures of Pastor Schutes and President Kreinheder;

Mrs. Frederick L. Miller, for the picture of her late husband, Pastor Miller; and

Mr. Harry Fox, for pictures of Vice-President Kinsey, President Henry Kinsey Brown, President Bowman, Dean A. A. Williams, and Professor B. F. Williams

Contents

		PAGE
Preface		v
Acknowledgments		ix
List of Illustrations		xiii
Foreword		xv

CHAPTER

I. The Valparaiso Male and Female College, 1859–1871 3

II. Mr. Brown's School, 1873–1900 13

III. "The Poor Man's Harvard," 1900–1919 . . . 48

IV. A Time of Troubles, 1919–1925 62

V. A New Beginning, 1925–1930 77

VI. A Period of Consolidation, 1930–1940 . . . 111

VII. A Lutheran University in America, 1940– . . 133

APPENDIX

A. Officers of the University 180

B. Student Leaders 185

C. Athletic Record of the University 187

D. Officers of the Alumni Association 190

E. National Officers of the Valparaiso University Women's Guild 191

Illustrations

Frontispiece . . . . Chancel of the Memorial Chapel

Following Page 16:

The Old College Building
The Rev. Charles N Sims, M.A.
The Rev. Erastus Herman Staley, M.A.
The Rev. B. Wilson Smith, M.A.
The Rev. Thomas Bond Wood, M.A.
Henry Baker Brown
The Faculty of the Northern Indiana Normal School and Business
  Institute—1873
W. A. Yohn, M.D.
Miss Samantha Elizabeth "Mantie" Baldwin
Professor Martin Eugene Bogarte, M.A.
Oliver Perry Kinsey
Richard A. Heritage
Harrison N. Carver, M.A.
Mrs. O. P. Kinsey
Colonel Mark L. DeMotte, M.A., LL.B., LL.D.
Heritage Hall
East and South Halls

Following Page 80:

The Campus Early in the Twentieth Century
The Old Law School Building
The Auditorium
Altruria Hall
Lembke Hall
Science Hall and the Medical Building
The Arts-Law Building
Henry Kinsey Brown, M.A.
Daniel Russel Hodgdon, A.B., LL.D.
John Edward Roessler, A.M., Litt.D.
Milo Jesse Bowman, A.M., LL.B., LL.D.
Horace Martin Evans, M.D.
Benjamin Franklin Williams, M.A.
Alpheus Americus Williams, A.M., Sc.D.
John Wallace Morland, J.D.
The Rev. William Henry Theodore Dau, D.D.

The Rev. John C. Baur
The Rev. George F. Schutes
Herman A. Duemling, M.D.
The Rev. Paul F. Miller, LL.D.
The Rev. Frederick William Kroencke, Ph.D.
The Rev. Henry Herman Kumnick, A.B., LL.B.
Albert Frank Scribner, M.A., LL.D.

Following Page 112:

The Rev. Oscar Carl Kreinheder, D.D.
Mr. Harry E. Eberline
W. Charles Dickmeyer, LL.D.
Mr. Ralph Richman
Alfred H. Meyer, Ph.D.
The Rev. Karl H. Henrichs, M.A.
Walter Emil Bauer, Ph.D.
Walther Martin Miller, M.A.
Walter George Friedrich, Ph.D.
Mrs. Katharine Ertz Bowden, B.S.
Mr. Fred Wehrenberg
Jacob Melius "Jake" Christiansen
Mr. John A. Sauerman
Mrs. E. W. Schultz
The Rev. Gustav W. Lobeck
The Rev. Frederick Lawrence Miller

Following Page 144:

The Rev. Otto Paul Kretzmann, S.T.M., Litt.D., D.D., LL.D.
Guild Hall
Herbert W. Knopp, M.A.
Herman C. Hesse, M.E.
Allen Edmond Tuttle, Ph.D.
Knute D. Stalland, LL.B.
Mr. Paul F. Amling
Mr. Paul Brandt
The President, the Deans, the Professors, and the Heads of Departments
The Valparaiso Union
The Memorial Chapel
Architect's Drawing of the Henry F. Moellering Memorial Library

Foreword

THE HISTORY of a college always provides a significant glimpse of a fascinating microcosm. This is especially true of an institution established close to the American frontier in the middle of the nineteenth century. In many subtle ways the vast and profound changes which have swept over America during the past hundred years are reflected on the quiet Indiana campus described in the following pages. The story of an educational institution is never a *gradus ad parnassum* in a social vacuum; it is always a path which follows the major highway of the culture of which it is a very important part.

In a sense the life of an institution of learning is always a form of dying. While it lives in the past, the present, and the future, it is continuously dying to momentary ideas and obsolete canons of thought. This dying is a necessary prelude to the constant renewal of life and thought which is the essential mark of all good education. The history of Valparaiso University is an excellent example of this process. It has never used yesterday's eyes to look at today.

The University Editor has caught the life and thought of the University with precision and discernment. It is not a simple task to separate the temporary from the timeless, the minor from the major, the less important tangibles from the more important intangibles. He has done that. In addition he has contrived to make the story eminently readable—a fact which will be greeted with joy by thousands of alumni and friends throughout the world.

It is probably true, of course, that the real history of a college or university lies forever beyond the reach of the historian, however competent. It rests in the singularly unspectacular, day-by-day, mysterious interaction of teaching and learning. It begins and ends in the unsung life and work of teachers who have given their days and years to the strangely unrewarding task of living for the world of tomorrow—a world which they will never see. If they add to their concern for the life of the mind an equally sensitive interest in the life of the spirit and the soul—as the teachers at Valparaiso University have done—they are a truly great and greatly significant line. To these teachers, together with their predecessors and suc-

xv

cessors, this volume is respectfully dedicated. Not all their names appear here. But they are written in the hearts of thousands of students, and the record of their life and work is imperishable.

O. P. KRETZMANN

January, 1959

Valparaiso's First Century

CHAPTER I

The Valparaiso
Male and Female College

1859–1871

VALPARAISO UNIVERSITY as we know it today is the third in a succession of institutions of higher learning that have occupied the hilly site on the southeast side of the city of Valparaiso, Indiana. The nucleus of the present campus was acquired by the Lutheran University Association in 1925 from a board of trustees which acted as custodians of the once-great university which had been created by Henry Baker Brown and Oliver Perry Kinsey. Mr. Brown, in turn, had begun his school, in 1873, in a building which had originally housed the Valparaiso Male and Female College, whose history dates back to 1859.

The origins of the Valparaiso Male and Female College have been described in a history of Indiana Methodism by the first president of its board of trustees, the Rev. J. L. Smith:

In its incipiency the people of the town took a lively interest. After a general consultation among the friends and patrons of education, a public meeting was called to be held in the courthouse on Tuesday evening, March 25, 1859; and after earnest speeches were delivered by S. G. Hass, John N. Skinner, Azariah Freeman, and J. L. Smith, the following gentlemen were requested to act as secretaries for the purpose of taking down the names of donors and amounts subscribed for the erection of a suitable college building. These persons were M. L. De-Motte, Elias Axe, Joseph Pierce, S. T. Cooper, and Lorenzo Freeman. At the close of the meeting, in footing up the subscriptions, it was found that the good people had manifested their interest in the enterprise by subscribing over $11,000. The officers of the first board of trustees were J. L. Smith, president; A. Freeman, vice-president; E. L. Whitcomb, sec't; with Sylvester Smith, agent.[1]

The time was ripe for such a project. Northern Indiana had been

3

settled very largely from New England and the Middle Atlantic states by way of Ohio. For the first generation of settlers and for their children, education was necessarily a catch-as-catch-can proposition. But by 1859 the basic structure of community life had been established in what only a few years before had been frontier country and it was possible to think about restoring the remembered graces of life "back East." There was, however, a very militant opposition to public education at this time, one member of the state General Assembly having gone so far as to say, "When I die, I want my epitaph written, 'Here lies an enemy to free schools.'"[2] By 1850, Indiana stood last in the list of free states and lower than three of the slave states in literacy, and it was said by one contemporary of this period that "the state of common education is truly alarming. Only about one child in eight between five and fifteen years is able to read. The common schools and teachers are few." Of the 300,000 children of school age in the state, less than fifty thousand were in any kind of school,[3] and, according to an estimate made by Caleb Mills, about one man in every seven in Indiana was illiterate in 1850.[4]

Since the state was unwilling to take on the job of education, it was to the churches that people looked for leadership in founding and conducting schools. The primary purpose of the church schools was to train young men for the clergy, but they also assumed the responsibility of training youth for teaching and for other professions as well. In Indiana, two strong incentives to the establishment of church-supported schools were the Dartmouth College Case of 1819, which asserted the freedom of the private college, and a state statute of 1849 which authorized the use of state funds for assisting private schools.[5]

The first of the denominational schools founded in Indiana was Hanover Academy, now Hanover College, which was established in 1827 by the Presbyterians. During the next three decades a number of such schools were founded: Wabash (also Presbyterian), 1832; Franklin (Baptist), 1837; Indiana Asbury (Methodist, now DePauw), 1837; Earlham (Quaker), 1837; Concordia (Lutheran), 1839; St. Mary of the Woods (Roman Catholic), 1840; Notre Dame (Roman Catholic), 1844; Taylor (Methodist), 1846; St. Meinrad (Roman Catholic), 1854; Mooresville (Methodist, now Evansville College), 1854; and Butler (Christian), 1855. The contribution of these denominational schools can hardly be over-estimated. They were the only institutions of higher learning of any consequence in the state prior to the Civil War, and it was from these schools that practically all the educators of the post-war period were recruited.

In Indiana, and indeed throughout the Midwest, the Methodist Episcopal Church was especially interested in education. In the 1850's the Methodists undertook to found, in every congressional district, a college under the auspices of the church.[6] In the congressional district to which Valparaiso belonged, there were a number of towns, LaPorte among them, that hoped to win such a college for their own community. The purpose of the public meeting held in Valparaiso March 25, 1859, was to bring the proposed college to that city.

The site which was selected for the new college was one of the most desirable sites in a section of the state which at that time still consisted very largely of swampy lowlands.[7] Southeast of the town proper was a tract of high and dry morainic hill country, much of it belonging to the estate of Mr. Azariah Freeman, a public-spirited citizen who was one of the prime movers in the college movement and a major influence in re-establishing the College under Mr. Brown's control in 1873. From this estate, fifteen acres were purchased for the college property. At the time there were as yet no streets in the area, but, soon after the College opened, streets were laid out to link it with the town. Appropriately, the street which forms the northern boundary of the old campus plot is called Freeman Street.

The name chosen for the new college offers an interesting insight into an academic dispute that was going on at the time. According to the Rev. Mr. Smith,

At this writing (1892) co-education has become the rule in our best and most popular institutions of learning, but it was the exception in 1859, and this may account to the present generation for what doubtless seems to them a peculiar name for a school—"Valparaiso Male and Female College."

The first of this class of schools was the Thorntown [Indiana] Academy. The founders of that institution, in 1854 and '55, had become thoroughly convinced that, since it was the order of nature for brothers and sisters to be reared in the same family, it was according to the true order of things for them to be educated together in our schools of learning. At first there was a strong public prejudice against the new order; and it was not until years after that date, that, through the persistent efforts of the friends of co-education, the Indiana Asbury, now DePauw, University threw open its halls, admitting without distinction of sex all seeking the benefits of higher education. In order, therefore, that the public might distinctly understand that the college at Valparaiso was not for males nor females as such, but, that it was an institution where all, upon the same terms, were entitled to all the benefits of the school, they gave the institution the corporate name "Male and Female College."[8]

Through all of its subsequent history the College and its successor institutions remained co-educational, and Valparaiso University may, therefore, claim to be one of the oldest co-educational institutions in the country.

The first term of the new college began on September 21, 1859, when six instructors and seventy-five students met for classes in a temporary wooden building which had been built by John N. Skinner on the site of the present Music Hall.[9] A 24-year-old graduate of Indiana Asbury College, Charles N Sims,* had been appointed first president of the college, but he was unable to leave his post as principal of Thorntown Academy until the following year; for the first year, therefore, the Rev. Francis D. Carley, professor of mathematics and natural sciences, served as acting president. During the first year, the total enrollment reached 157, a figure substantial enough to suggest that the founders had not been overoptimistic in hoping for a college which would eventually serve from three to five hundred students. The school year was divided into three quarters: a fall term beginning about the middle of September, a winter term beginning late in December or early in January, and a spring term beginning early in April.

The first problem which faced the new college was that of securing suitable quarters. The estimated cost of $25,000 for an adequate building seemed to be beyond the resources of the community, and there were many who urged that the building of a permanent structure be deferred. But Mr. Skinner insisted that the building could not wait, contributed a thousand dollars of his own money, and organized community support for an immediate construction program. On April 25, 1860, the cornerstone of a new

---

* The "N" in Mr. Sims' name was adopted by Mr. Sims early in life. It was not an initial.

brick building was laid, and by the opening of the fall term of that year the building was ready for occupancy. This building stood on the site of the present old-campus flagpole until 1923 when it was destroyed by fire. Meanwhile President Sims had arrived to take charge and the enrollment had grown to 327. A normal school was founded in that year to train public school teachers, and literary and debating societies were organized, among them the Calliopean Society for women, and the Philomathean and Berean literary societies for men. A few years later a scientific society, the Philological, was added.

Discipline, in the words of the catalogue, was "parental and designed to be at once preventive and corrective." "A mild but firm course of discipline will be maintained," the catalogue of 1864–1865 stated. "The higher and nobler faculties of the students will be appealed to, but should this fail the means will not be wanting to correct the evil." The details of this "mild but firm course of discipline" were spelled out in the succeeding paragraph:

> Students are required to attend church at least once on Sunday, and to be present at the Sabbath Lecture in the afternoon. The promiscuous association of young ladies and gentlemen will not be permitted, and correct social habits, and polite manners will be enforced. Punctual attendance at recitations, public college exercises, and prayers, and the observance of study hours will be required of every student. Unkind treatment of fellow students; disrespect toward teachers; irreverence at church; leaving town without permission; absence from room at late hours of night, without permission; the use of profane or obscene language; card-playing, and gambling of every kind; visiting gambling or drinking saloons; drinking intoxicating liquors; disorderly conduct, such as running, jumping, hallooing, and boisterous singing in the College building; marking or disfiguring the College walls or furniture; all, and each, are strictly and totally prohibited.[10]

Commencement was the big occasion of the college year. Prior to commencement day, public examinations were held at which, after the instructor had asked his questions, textbooks were distributed to the guests who were then invited to ask the students any question that could be answered from the books. People came from all over northwestern Indiana for these occasions. Immediately before commencement the alumni held their reunions, and the trustees held their annual meetings.

Because of the limited accommodations on campus, many of the

students boarded with families in the town, paying from $3.25 to
$3.75 a week. Tuition ranged from twelve to fifteen dollars a
quarter, with extra charges for music, French, and German.
Amusements included skating on Sager's Lake in the winter and
playing ball in the summer.

President Sims was a stern, thoroughgoing Methodist of the
frontier type, unimpressed by titles unless they promised opportunity to make converts. He was, moreover, a strong believer in the
principle of an itinerant ministry, on which in later years he wrote
a book. By 1862, it was apparent to him that the Civil War would
stunt the growth of the college for years to come, and in that year
he left the presidency to become minister of a church in Richmond,
Indiana, where he is credited with having made four hundred converts in a period of two years. Thereafter, for another seventeen
years, he served Methodist churchs in Indiana and in the East, accounting altogether for two thousand conversions. From 1881 to
1893, he served as chancellor of the then young and struggling
Syracuse University and played a major role in making it the great
university which it subsequently became. His last years were spent
in Indianapolis, where he served as superintendent of the newly-
established Methodist Hospital.[11]

President Sims' successor, the Rev. Erastus Herman Staley,
served only a year. The War had, by now, engaged all of the interests of the people, and both students and faculty members were
leaving the campus to enlist in the Union Army. Eventually even
President Staley, who was only in his early thirties, caught the war
fever and enlisted for hospital work with the United States Christian Commission. After the war, he settled in Frankfort, Indiana,
where he served as a local preacher, superintendent of schools,
state legislator, and newspaper editor. His successor as president
was the Rev. B. Wilson Smith, like his two predecessors a youthful
graduate of Indiana Asbury University. Mr. Smith had taught at
Cornell College in Iowa and was highly regarded for his manners
and eloquence. During his presidency, in 1864, the first graduating
class—five in number—received its degrees.

President Smith soon embarked upon a vigorous program of
renovation and expansion. The college building was repaired, "war
orphans" and wounded veterans were given free tuition, a part of
the college was set aside for public school work, children of patrons

were admitted free, and the curriculum was expanded to include such hitherto-ignored subjects as physical education and elocution. But the enrollment continued to decline, finances continued to deteriorate, and by 1867 President Smith had to admit defeat. In later years he served as postmaster at Lafayette, Indiana, and as a member of the Indiana Legislature.[12] His active support of the newly-established state agricultural and technical school in West Lafayette prompted a Methodist church historian to say that "next to John Purdue, Rev. B. Wilson Smith did more for Purdue University than any other man." [13]

What was needed at this juncture was someone who would do for the Valparaiso Male and Female College more than any other man had done, and it appeared that the newly-elected president, the Rev. Thomas Bond Wood, was just that man. A graduate of both Indiana Asbury University and Connecticut Wesleyan University, Mr. Wood was a remarkable, many-sided young man—an amateur astronomer, a talented singer, and the personification of youthful health and vigor. His infectious enthusiasm caught on in the town and inspired a successful campaign for $25,000 which went into the building of a women's dormitory addition to the college building. This addition was especially necessary because the college had by now become almost a women's college, perhaps because its coeducational policy made it suspect to men in a day when coeducation was still a novelty. For a while it appeared that the college might recover from the effects of the war after all. The graduating class, which had numbered only three in 1867, rose to ten in 1868, and to thirteen in 1869. The collegiate department was organized to offer classical, scientific, and English courses leading to the B.A., the B.S., and M.A. degrees. In addition to the collegiate department, there was an academic department, a preparatory department, and a thriving primary department. The faculty, although small, was extremely competent by the standards of that day. It might be noted also that more than half of the instructors were women. But when, by 1869, the enrollment still showed no gain, Mr. Wood also resigned and accepted a call into Latin-American missions. For forty years thereafter he carved out a remarkable career as missionary, educator, and college president in Argentina, Uruguay, Peru, and Panama.[14] Among other things, he helped to organize the public school system of the Argentine Republic. Ironically, at the time of his death in 1922, the University which had risen from the ashes of his old college was passing through a period of trials very similar to those which had plagued his own administration.

By now it was evident that the College stood little chance of survival. In November, 1869, it was decided to have one more try at recouping the situation, and the presidency was entrusted to the Rev. Aaron Gurney, a distinguished lawyer, editor, educator, and clergyman who had served for many years on the Board of Trustees. Mr. Gurney's failure to reverse the tide, despite urgent appeals published in the local newspapers, made it obvious that the declining fortunes of the college were the products of something more than inexperienced or unimaginative leadership. Only later would historians be able to put their fingers on the great changes which the Civil War had wrought in American society and, as a consequence, in American education. But it was these changes which doomed many a small college and forced others, among them the Valparaiso Male and Female College, to suspend operations. For one thing, the northern states emerged from the War much more heavily industrial than they had ever been before, and the social changes which resulted from industrialization made an education very desirable, if not absolutely necessary. But the kind of education most in demand was not a "genteel" education but a practical education. The War had also brought on a period of inflation in which educational costs could no longer be met from tuition and the limited assistance that could be supplied by a small community. Responding to the growing demand for publicly-supported education, the state of Indiana established a system of state-controlled graded schools and, as the Rev. Mr. Smith observes, "the membership of the church being taxed with their fellow-citizens for the support of the public schools could not afford to tax themselves for the support of denominational schools." [15] The public grade schools hit these old colleges at their most vulnerable points, that is, their primary departments, which accounted for the bulk of their enrollments and, accordingly, for the larger part of their incomes. It seemed that the small college could survive only by finding wealthy and public-spirited benefactors who would furnish the support which the churches felt they could no longer provide. DePauw and Northwestern had the good fortune to find such benefactors at critical moments in their history. Their little Methodist sister in Valparaiso did not have the same good fortune. And so, in the summer of 1871, the trustees voted to discontinue classes for one year and to entrust the affairs of the college to a three-man board which was to investigate the possibilities of resuming work on a sounder basis. This board resolved to keep the charter alive and to prevent the disposal of the property for any purposes other than education. Thus, despite the closing of classes, the college remained a corporate entity until the time of its purchase by Henry Baker Brown.

Few of the records of the college have survived the numerous fires that have destroyed the successive offices of the Normal School and the University. But from various fragmentary records it is possible to assemble the names of some of the faculty who served the old college. Among the professors were H. W. Allen, William H. Banta (later superintendent of Valparaiso city schools), Francis D. Carley (mathematics), I. W. McCasky (mathematics and natural sciences), Worthy Putnam (elocution), the Rev. J. M. Davis (mathematics and natural sciences), J. W. Ruggles and G. W. Hewitt (both music), and the Rev. Russel D. Utter (ancient languages and literature). Other teachers on the higher levels included Miss Delia Carley, Miss Helen E. Houghton (French, German, and drawing), Miss Serene H. Hoadley (German), Mrs. Ella F. Jewell (instrumental music), Miss S. P. Winslow (instrumental and vocal music), Miss Estella Eldred (French and German), Miss Julia A. Calkins (instrumental and vocal music), J. Baker Hawkins (vocal music), O. Reynolds (penmanship), Miss Susan E. Hale (French and drawing), the Rev. Henry Shultz (German language and literature), Mrs. R. A. R. Smith (guitar), Miss Rhoda Bates (mathematics, later the wife of Professor Banta), Miss Lizzie Stephens (higher English branches), Dr. James H. Newland (physiology and hygiene), the Rev. C. Morf (German language), Miss Mattie A. Green (French), Mrs. Ellen Wood (music), Miss S. S. Pratt (piano), Miss Clara J. Loomis (piano and organ), Miss Ellen J. Sibley (drawing and painting), and L. I. Gildersleeve (commercial work and telegraphing). The junior faculty and the staff of the primary department included Miss Fannie M. Smith, Miss Nannie E. Keeny, William Johnston, John H. Shultz, Miss C. G. Elvin, Miss Kate A. Thompson, Miss Louise

Forbes, James C. Stephens, W. F. Ware, and Mrs. J. A. Woodson. Few of these served more than a year or two. The women were mostly recent graduates of the college, and the men appear to have been mostly very young Methodist preachers.

NOTES

1. John L. Smith, *Indiana Methodism* (copyright by the author, 1892), pp. 261-62.
2. Richard G. Boone, *A History of Education in Indiana* (D. Appleton and Co., 1892), p. 87.
3. *Ibid.*
4. Edgar A. Knight, *Education in the United States* (Ginn and Co., 1929), p. 228.
5. *Ibid.*, pp. 232-33.
6. Thomas H. Cannon, H. H. Loring, and Charles J. Robb, *The Lake and Calumet Region of Indiana* (Historians' Association, 1927), I, 541.
7. For an excellent description of northwestern Indiana *circa* 1859, see Alfred H. Meyer, "Circulation and Settlement Patterns of the Calumet-South Chicago Region of Northwest Indiana and Northeast Illinois," *Proceedings of the Eighth General Assembly and Seventeenth International Congress of the International Geographical Union* (1952), pp. 538-44.
8. Smith, *op. cit.*, pp. 262-63.
9. Much of the chronology for the first three chapters has been taken from George W. Stimpson, *The Story of Valparaiso University*, published by the author in 1921 and based upon information and documents furnished by Miss Mantie E. Baldwin.
10. Catalogue of Valparaiso Male and Female College for the Year 1864-1865.
11. *Dictionary of American Biography* (Charles Scribner's Sons, 1935), XVII, 185-86.
12. Smith, *op. cit.*, pp. 277-78.
13. J. Milton Williams, "The Monticello Circuit of the Methodist Church: A Hundred Years of Progress," *Indiana Magazine of History*, XXXII, No. 1 (March, 1936), 47.
14. *Dictionary of American Biography* (1936), XX, 473-74.
15. Smith, *op. cit.*, p. 261.

CHAPTER II

Mr. Brown's School

1873–1900

THE STORY of Valparaiso's next half-century is very largely the story of two remarkable men, Henry Baker Brown and Oliver Perry Kinsey. Mr. Brown, or Professor Brown as he was invariably called both on campus and in the town, was the older of the two men, and it was he who, largely on his own, laid the foundations of that strange and wonderful "off-beat" institution which was eventually to be known throughout the world as "the poor man's Harvard."

Henry Baker Brown

Professor Brown was born on a farm near Mount Vernon, Ohio, on October 6, 1847, a son of Thomas and Rachel (Mills) Brown.[1] His father's family was of German descent, his mother's Scottish. Following the familiar pattern of bright young boys of his day, Mr. Brown began teaching country school at the age of fifteen and from his earnings managed to save enough to finance his schooling at Ohio Wesleyan University and later at the now defunct National Normal University in Lebanon, Ohio. At Lebanon he made a number of friends who were later to be associated with him in the work at Valparaiso, among them Oliver Perry Kinsey, Miss Sarah J. Porter (later Mrs. Kinsey), and Miss Mantie Baldwin. One of his instructors was Professor Harrison Carver, who was later to follow him to Valparaiso. In 1871, having received his A.B. degree from the National Normal School, Mr. Brown became professor of mathematics at the Northwestern Normal School at Republic, Ohio, and it was from this position that he came to Valparaiso.

Mr. Brown came upon the educational scene at a time when profound changes were taking place in American higher education. Under the impulse of economic and social changes that had been brought about by the Civil War, reform movements were chang-

ing the face of American education. As Mr. Ernest Earnest has put
it, the Civil War was

. . . a war which had been won not only on the battlefield but by the
factory, the railroad, the technician. The American public understood
this better than did the professors. A large part of the history of higher
education in the sixties and seventies is the story of community pressure
on colleges to meet the needs of a new age. . . .[2]

With the coming of peace, the demand for a more practical kind of
education could not be denied. The returning veterans were mature
men, many of them married, who had immediate vocational aims.
Wealthy industrialists and businessmen were often ready to give large
sums for departments of science and engineering. Faculties, long deaf
to ideological arguments, began to listen to the language of money.
After all, they had almost literally starved during the war.[3]

The great decade of educational re-awakening and reform may
be taken as having extended from 1865, the year when Cornell University was founded, to 1876, when Daniel Coit Gilman was inaugurated as the first president of the newly-founded Johns Hopkins
University. Each in its own way, Cornell and Hopkins came into
being as protests against the traditional pattern of university education: Cornell as a protest against its narrowness, and Hopkins as
a protest against its shallowness. But the protest did not necessarily
take the form of founding new colleges and universities. Some of
the older institutions were practically rebuilt under a generation of
great administrators: Frederick A. P. Barnard, president of Columbia after 1865; Charles William Eliot, whose long tenure as president of Harvard began in 1869; and William Watts Folwell, president of the University of Minnesota after 1869.

Professor Brown had been caught up in the spirit of reform
which was in the air, and he was intensely excited by it. President
Barnard had told his trustees that

it is not an inferior grade of education which the popular voice demands, nor a diminished amount of education. It is rather that education
shall be varied to suit the varying capacities of individuals; and further,
that, in place of limited and necessarily superficial attainments in many
things there shall be thoroughness, or at least the opportunity for
thoroughness, in a smaller number.[4]

Although there is no way of knowing whether Professor Brown
ever actually read these words of President Barnard, it is certain
that they were altogether agreeable to his own view of the nature

and function of education. And what he was looking for was a place to give form and body to the kind of education which he believed the times demanded. The place had to be somewhere in the education-hungry Midwest, it had to be on a reasonably attractive and accessible site, and it had to be available at a cost which the young mathematics professor could afford.

In 1953, Mr. Brown's daughter Ruth (Mrs. Houston) presented to Mrs. Katharine E. Bowden, the University archivist, four pages of notes in her father's handwriting which were apparently intended as an outline for a history of the University which Mr. Brown never found time to write. These notes tell of Mr. Brown's first reactions to the suggestion that he establish his school in Valparaiso:

> Ira Hoops who had been a student in the Valparaiso Male and Female College—a M.E. College which had been closed for three years—told Mr. Brown of these buildings being vacant and urged him so hard to come and see them that he finally consented to come—and did so in May—and went to see Azariah Freeman about the buildings. Stopped at the old Gould House over night. Mr. Freeman had me stay at his house and he went around with me all that day. I talked with him of the possibility of having a school. They thought it a splendid place for a school but I was not impressed with it or the town. I went up to the school alone and went up to the third floor, but still did not think much of it.
>
> They said I could come and take the building and see what I could do, but did not think I could do much. If I could make anything of it or made much money there was a sort of understanding that I would pay something. I was glad when I started home on the train. Then later on we wrote back and forth about the buildings—but no tacit agreement was made. No written agreement made for some 4 years.[5]

Upon his return to Ohio, Mr. Brown discussed the proposition at length with his friends, but secretly, for fear of losing his job at the Northwest Normal School. Finally, he decided to accept Mr. Freeman's offer. On September 16, 1873, he opened the Northern Indiana Normal School and Business Institute in the old building of the Valparaiso Male and Female College.

The last three decades of the Nineteenth Century in the United States were a period dominated by a still-vigorous Protestant ethic which gave an unabashedly economic interpretation to the Scriptural statement that "godliness is profitable unto all things." So generally accepted was the assumption that virtue has its rewards in material success that a whole mythology, best exemplified in the stories of Horatio Alger, grew up around the figure of the serious-minded, hard-working young man who, by pluck and luck, surmounted the limitations of his home environment and made his million in the big city. Professor Brown, himself a deeply religious member of the conservative Christian Church (Campbellite), needed no elaborate philosophical rationale for the kind of practical education that he proposed to offer at Valparaiso. If, as he believed, God helps those who help themselves, the secrets of success were not really secrets at all. What was needed was a serious purpose, hard work, application to the job at hand, and a bare minimum of interference from other people. Accordingly, he proposed to allow his students to come and go pretty much as their inclinations and resources permitted, to keep discipline to the barest possible minimum, and to avoid cluttering up his school with the frills and side-attractions of college life. Drinking was absolutely forbidden and, if discovered, meant immediate expulsion. Dancing was suspect, apparently more on economic than moral grounds, and there were instances of students being asked to leave the school because of dancing. Fraternities and sororities were rigorously banned on the simple, but (to Mr. Brown) sufficient, grounds that they were nests of snobbery; and although secret societies were organized in the late years of Mr. Brown's administration, discovery that a student belonged to one of them was sufficient grounds for immediate expulsion. Intramural athletics were encouraged from the earliest days of the Normal School, but intercollegiate athletics found no place on campus until after Mr. Brown's retirement. He did not seem to be particularly opposed to them. He simply didn't care to divert any institutional funds into what he considered side-shows. (It is one of the small ironies of history that the only physical memorial to Mr. Brown on the modern campus of the University is the athletic field, "Brown Field.")

As early as 1882, one of Mr. Brown's biographers described him as an "autocrat." [6] Certainly there was much of the autocrat in the make-up of this hard-driving, no-nonsense educational entrepreneur. But he was, by and large, a benevolent autocrat. From his faculty he demanded exhausting hours and a high level of performance. In return, he paid them salaries which were very substantial by the standards of the time, and he gave them the widest

The Old College Building. *From a Photograph c. 1868*

The Rev. Charles N Sims, M.A.

*President of the Valparaiso Male
and Female College, 1860–1862.*

The Rev. Erastus Herman Staley, M.A.

*President of the Valparaiso Male
and Female College, 1862.*

The Rev. B. Wilson Smith, M.A.

*President of the Valparaiso
Male and Female College,
1863–1867.*

The Rev. Thomas Bond Wood, M.A.

*President of the Valparaiso
Male and Female College,
1867–1869.*

No picture is available of The Rev. Aaron Gurney, M.A.
President of the Valparaiso Male and Female College, 1869–1871.

Henry Baker Brown
1847–1917

President of The Northern Indiana Normal School and Business Institute, 1873–1900; Valparaiso College, 1900–1907; Valparaiso University, 1907–1917.

The Faculty of The Northern Indiana Normal School and Business Institute—1873.

Front Row, Left to Right: Mr. B. F. Perrine, President Brown, Mr. W. A. Yohn, Mr. Martin Eugene Bogarte.

Second Row, Left to Right: Miss Ida Hutchinson, Mr. Pearly Sherman, Miss Mantie E. Baldwin.

W. A. Yohn, M.D.

Director of Preparatory Department,
Professor of the Natural Sciences,
1873–1886.

Miss Samantha Elizabeth
"Mantie" Baldwin

"She gave her best and in return
demanded your best."

Professor Martin Eugene Bogarte, M.A.

"He never worked for me,
he always worked with me."

Oliver Perry Kinsey
1849–1931

Vice-President of the Normal School, the College, and the University, 1881–1917; Acting President of the University, 1912–1919.

Richard A. Heritage

Professor of Music, 1878–1894.

Harrison N. Carver, M.A.

Professor of philosophy and the classics, 1878–1917. Dean of the Classical Department, 1913–1915.

Mrs. O. P. Kinsey

Professor of Geography, 1881–1919.

Colonel Mark L. DeMotte, M.A., LL.B., LL.D.

Founder and Dean of the School of Law, 1879–1907.

Heritage Hall

The third floor was later destroyed by fire. After 1925 this building became the University Library.

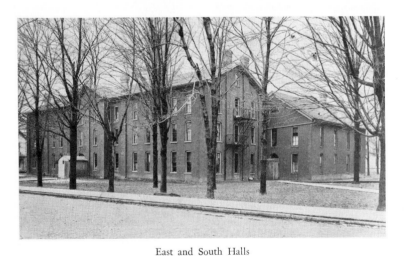

East and South Halls

Dormitories built around 1875 near the south end of Greenwich Street and razed in the early days of the Lutheran administration.

possible freedom of expression. In the most prosperous days of his school he chose his faculty, as far as possible, from among the most promising members of the student body—men and women whose attitudes and performances he had had opportunity to observe for himself. Often he subsidized their further education so as to equip them better for their work. As a result, the turnover rate was amazingly low. Occasionally an instructor would go off to try his luck at founding a school of his own, hoping to imitate Mr. Brown's success, and a few instructors were tempted away by good salaries and easier work in other institutions. But by far most of the members of Mr. Brown's faculty stayed until death or retirement. Some of these, although they spent their entire professional lives at Valparaiso, were well-known beyond the boundaries of the campus, for the faculty of that day was prolific in the publication of textbooks. These textbooks were almost automatically guaranteed financial success by their use in the large classes of the school itself, and their adoption by other institutions brought prestige and additional income.

To the students, Mr. Brown eventually became almost a legend. Basically a shy man, he never quite succeeded in winning the warm affection which his colleague, Mr. Kinsey, enjoyed in his later years. But he was highly respected, almost reverenced, and more than forty years after his death townspeople and alumni still recall him standing at the east door of the Christian Church, greeting student worshippers by name as they entered; taking time out of a busy day of registration to telegraph Chicago to recover an overcoat which a freshman had left on a train; permitting students to register with no better credentials than a worthy ambition and an evident willingness to work towards its realization.

Mr. Hugh Langham Stephens, a member of the class of 1882, says of Mr. Brown:

He was interested in everybody he met, and you knew it was genuine. . . .
Mr. Brown said, "Yes, we will have school on the Fourth of July; we can do our country more service by doing honest work on that day than in idling away our time." Work was Mr. Brown's gospel; he never tired of talking about work.
My liking for Mr. Brown was not all on one side; he early took an interest in me, and many a time and oft did he rap on my window (I roomed on the corner in what was then known as the Commercial

Building), with his cane at two and three in the morning, coming home from Chicago or some other city, and say, "Now quit studying and go to bed. If I return and find you up, I shall give you a good hammering with this stick"—with that twinkle in his eye.[7]

Another alumnus, Mr. W. H. Hawthorne, who attended the Normal School in the late 70's, has written this recollection of Mr. Brown:

> Prof. H. B. Brown was my real friend and staked me for enough to finish a term on my personal note. After I had been absent from the old school for fifteen years I stepped in on Mr. Brown one day unannounced; he wheeled around in his chair and exclaimed at once, "Well, well, W. E., where did you come from?" He always called me "W. E." [8]

But Mr. Brown was no "softie." He was generous in the use of his own money, both for the institution and for students who needed help. But his help to students always took the form of loans, never outright gifts. It was his belief that unearned help damages a person's character. This conviction of his has occasioned some criticism, particularly in our day when most institutions are very generous in their grants of outright aid. But assistance of any kind was comparatively rare in his day, and students who had the opportunity to earn their way through Mr. Brown's school were grateful for the opportunity to do so.

On the American educational scene, Mr. Brown was, to some, an object of contempt, an educational charlatan who was trying to run a university like a business and whose products were little more than narrowly-trained boors. To others he was an object of envy, a successful man (reputedly a millionaire) who had managed to become wealthy in a profession which had never been noted for its financial rewards. To still others, Mr. Brown was an object of respect, a man who had made a necessary and significant contribution to American education in a time of transition when the old inherited pattern of a classical education for the privileged few was giving way to a new pattern of practical, scientific education for the masses. Among those who knew and respected Mr. Brown both as a person and as an educator were two of his fellow administrators, President Nicholas Murray Butler of Columbia and President Woodrow Wilson of Princeton. An even closer friend and admirer was the Great Commoner who so largely summed up in his own person the kind of man Mr. Brown's school admired, William Jennings Bryan.[9]

On one point both friend and critic agreed: that Mr. Brown and his school were scrupulously honest in their advertisements of the kind of education that Valparaiso offered and the kind of facilities that were available to its students. Mr. Brown's school produced neither poets nor captains of industry. (For that matter, very few colleges and universities did during this period.) But it did set the feet of many a young man on the road that led eventually to the circuit bench, the county school superintendency, a comfortable place in the business community, or a secure position in a large office. Mr. Brown was too much of a realist to have any illusions about producing great men and women at his school, but he knew precisely what it took to produce men and women who could be considered moderately successful by the standards of his day. Horatio Alger's literary heroes, if they were fortunate enough to get to attend college at all, attended one of the prestige schools of New England. Young men and women who read the Alger stories as fact rather than fiction attended "The Northern Indiana Normal School, H. B. Brown, Prop."

Early Days of the Normal School

In the twenty-fifth anniversary issue of *The College Current*, its editor, Mr. G. W. Doty, set down his recollections of how it had all begun:

It was in the early summer of 1873, that the writer first heard of the Northern Indiana Normal School. He was walking with Prof. H. B. Brown, then at the head of the Scientific Department of the North-Western Normal School, in Ohio.

We had walked up and down the streets through the rain for an hour, discussing the probable future of the school in which Mr. Brown was then engaged as a teacher, when suddenly he said, as though he thought of it then for the first time, "I shall have a school of my own." He then went on outlining what he thought would be a successful institution, and wound up by saying that he hoped, if he could find a suitable place, and would work very devotedly indeed, that he might possibly build up and sustain a school of 300 students, though he was setting the mark very high. It was soon after this that he heard of the closing of a college in Valparaiso, Ind., and a consequently empty building. He made a journey to Valparaiso, secured a lease of the building from the none too credulous board of trustees, and opened the first session of the

Northern Indiana Normal School on the 16th day of September, 1873, just 25 years ago.

His faculty consisted of four members beside himself: Miss Mantie E. Baldwin, M. E. Bogarte, B. F. Perrine, and Miss Ida Hutchinson.

Mr. Brown taught Greek, German, Mathematics, all the Natural Sciences, History, Vocal Music (!) and anything else his teachers couldn't take, besides attending to his correspondence and office work. His working hours, as well as those of most of his faculty, included most of the twenty-four.

Miss Baldwin taught Geography, Latin, Rhetoric, Literature, and a dozen other branches—always ready to take any class that was organized, assist with the office work, or care for the sick.

Mr. Bogarte taught the Commercial work, Elocution, Mathematics, Penmanship (!) folded and addressed circulars, or did anything else that was to be done.

Mr. Perrine had charge of the boarding department, and in the intervals of his commissarial duties taught Physics, History, and Latin.

Miss Hutchinson had charge of the Musical Department.

The enrollment the first term probably reached two score, but was the small beginning from which has grown the greatest school in the land.[10]

Mr. Doty is just a little generous in his estimate of the size of the first student body. Actually, it was thirty-five, of whom twelve or thirteen had come from Ohio with Mr. Brown. Most of these students were teachers or prospective teachers and were in most cases as old as Mr. Brown and the other members of his faculty. The plan was to offer normal school work in three general areas or departments: a preparatory department, a business department, and a teachers department. It was several years, however, before these departments were at all clearly set off from each other.

No history of the University would be complete without mention of the two members of the "First Five" who contributed so largely to its later success, Miss Baldwin and Mr. Bogarte.

Miss Baldwin was the only child of Judge William H. Baldwin and his wife, Elizabeth.[11] Her Christian name was Samantha, but she was never called anything but Mantie. Her mother died when Samantha was eleven, and her father died three years later, leaving his daughter to the care of a stepmother who proved in every way true to the trust.

At fifteen, Miss Baldwin began to teach in a country school, thereafter alternating between teaching in the winters and attending the National Normal University in the summers. At eighteen, she became a teacher of the common branches in the Northwestern Ohio Normal School, where she both studied and taught for three years until she was graduated in June, 1873. In the fall of that year, she came to Valparaiso and continued as a member of the faculty until 1914.

In 1908, Miss Baldwin broke a hip in a fall, but she continued teaching until November, 1914, when she broke her other hip. Thereafter, until her death on March 14, 1933, she remained an invalid in a wheel chair, but a very lively invalid who retained a great interest in the University and was especially helpful in enlisting the support of friends of the old school for the new Lutheran administration.

Miss Baldwin was a stern and demanding teacher who managed, nevertheless, to win and retain the friendship of her students. One of her former students, Dr. Luther Pflueger, wrote of her in 1930:

I had at sixteen a mild fear of her mingled with much more admiration and affection. No shabby work ever met her approval. No sincere honest effort, even when the results were rather disappointing, ever met her disapproval. Her instinct seemed to tell her unerringly what was our best and what our second best, and with no uncertainty we knew that only the former was acceptable.

Another of her former students, Mr. John I. Stafford, had this to say about her:

Patience, perfect poise, superb qualifications, industry, manifest love of her work and the student, generosity and magnanimity, always present with her, brightened and glorified her every effort. Wherever I have found a student of Miss Baldwin, I get a frank, ready, and unsolicited expression of affection and appreciation of this splendid woman.

The best appreciation of Miss Baldwin has been written by Mrs. Katharine E. Bowden, who was Miss Baldwin's student in her last years as a teacher and her friend for more than twenty years thereafter:

Miss Baldwin never tolerated poor recitations; her lessons were carefully planned, she never met a class unprepared—she gave her best and in turn demanded your best. The knowledge, training, and drill received in her rhetoric was most thorough, and helpful all through life. Sometimes it seemed the teacher was severe when a trembling, choking, almost frightened-to-death lad broke down in the midst of his oration and gasped he could not finish, when the reply firmly came, "Go right on." But Miss Baldwin knew what she was about. She was moulding character.

The students admired her culture and refinement and respected her authority. The attention and response in those big classes was remarkable, for she exercised complete control. It seems now, thinking back over the years, that she was one of the best disciplinarians of the school. She was ever master of the situation and always had the welfare of the student in mind. She was witty, quick at repartee, and she could put an impertinent student "back in the basket where he belonged," most effectively and decisively without sacrificing one bit of her womanliness.

Miss Baldwin was an indefatigable worker. Her eyesight was never of the best, yet she graded thousands of papers, reading every word, and gave many hours to backward students needing extra help. . . .

Miss Baldwin inspired one to love the beautiful, the good, the true. Cannot the former students hear her say: "It is our purpose to do our part in forwarding and uplifting humanity. This is life in life's best sense."

Mr. Bogarte was born on a farm near Republic, Ohio, on May 3, 1855.[12] He attended the academy at Republic where he met Mr. Brown and from which he came to Valparaiso. Shortly after beginning his work in Valparaiso he took a leave of absence to finish his college work at Boston University, from which he received the degree of Bachelor of Arts. While in Boston he married Miss Lillian Chamberlin who was also a member of the Normal School faculty on leave, having succeeded Miss Hutchinson in the chair of music.

Mrs. Bowden has written the following appreciation of Mr. Bogarte:

On one occasion, when Prof. H. B. Brown was introducing Prof. Bogarte to a large audience as the lecturer of the evening, he used these words in the course of his remarks: "Prof. Bogarte and I have worked together many years but he has never worked *for* me, he has always worked *with* me." What a splendid tribute. In whatever capacity Prof. Bogarte served, it was always in sympathy and accord with the principles and policies of the school.

Prof. Bogarte's class in elocution and oratory was for many years one of the most important, and popular, branches of the college, and finally the demand for a department of expression became absolutely necessary; and though Prof. Bogarte's heart was in this work, yet he gave it up when Prof. Brown and the demands of the Scientific Class felt they needed his entire time as a teacher of higher mathematics. And so the expression department lost a wonderful teacher, a teacher par excellence, and the scientific department gained a powerful, masterful instructor.

The college book store needed a loyal, understanding faculty member at its head; and in 1894 Prof. Bogarte took complete charge, and conducted its business in accordance with the ideals of the school, selling everything at as low a price as possible for the benefit of the students. In the rental department there was as low a charge as fifteen and twenty cents a term of ten weeks on some books; the rental on most books averaged about thirty-five cents per term, on a small number there was a fifty cent charge. The rental price a trifle more than paid for the cleaning and repairing of the books. After about the fourth or fifth rental the books were sold as second-hand at a small profit.

. . . One book which always had a big demand, and few of which ever came back for re-rental, was the Manual of Elocution, which Prof. Bogarte had compiled and edited; and there are still requests received for this book [1930].

Mr. Bogarte's best-remembered contribution to student life was in the nature of what would today be called a non-professional interest. Of this activity, his son, Mr. R. H. Bogarte, has written:

Many old students will remember his Sunday School class which he taught for so many years in the upstairs room at the rear of the Christian Church. This was crowded to the rear door every Sunday. It was really a vital part of his work at the University, for thousands of students came under his influence in this class. During the years since his death Bruce and I have had numberless calls and many letters from men and women who have wanted to express to us their gratitude for the inspiration they received from the teaching in this class.

It is claimed by some of the members of this class that, at the turn of the century or thereabouts, Mr. Bogarte's class was second only to Mr. John Wanamaker's class as the largest Sunday School class in the country.

Such, then, were the people whom Mr. Brown brought with him from Ohio. The first task that confronted him was to let people know that there would be a school at Valparaiso, and this he set about doing with a careful program of advertising. During the summer of 1873 the local newspaper, the *Porter County Vidette*, published a series of articles on the advantages of education to the youth of the state. These articles also commented at length on the unnecessary waste of time and money that seemed to characterize education in most of the institutions of higher learning at that time. These articles, although they appeared anonymously, were written by the versatile Miss Baldwin and may therefore be considered official statements of the policy of the school. The first of these articles was published under the title, "Normal Schools," and reads as follows:

Two questions are now engrossing public attention: (1) What kind of an education is adapted to the wants of the whole community? (a) How is it to be made easily accessible to all?

A reply to the first of these questions needs no ingenious argument. We all concede that the present age is one of progression, one of improvement, and especially one of activity. The time has now come when man cannot be idle, cannot wait. So rapidly does the car of progression move forward in its course that for us to stop is most certain ruin or failure. We must work in the age in which we live. The spirit of our age demands an education which will prepare the student for life as it is, real, active life. We may be acquainted with all the mathematics and thoroughly versed in all the classics; yet if we know not how to use this knowledge, what will it avail us? No, we need an education that can be used in everyday life.

How is an education to be made truly accessible to all? This is an important question and demands our most worthy consideration. Is it true that we must devote five, six, or ten years to the purpose of acquiring an education? Is it true that we must be wealthy before we can secure this? If so, then it is not accessible to all. Does it not seem reasonable that there ought to be improvement in this direction? We do not reap our grain with a sickle as did our forefathers; we do not mow our grass with a scythe; it does not require five or six days to go to the mill. Why? Because of improvement! In all the departments of life, except education, we see marked progress. The remark is frequently made by our aged friends: 'Our schools are not in as good a condition as they were when I attended school.' Why do we not see more improvement? Why these remarks? Simply because there is not as much work in the educational field as in other departments of life. We have no schools in which our teachers may prepare themselves for their work. In other words, education is not accessible to all. In our present school system, the poor have not the means to secure the advantages desired, and the rich too frequently buy their way through college; thus the cause of education is retarded. We want a school where both rich and poor may secure a thorough, practical education in as short a time, and with as little expense, as possible.

A school that, we think, will meet the demands of all will be established at Valparaiso. This school will open its first term on the third Tuesday in September, 1873, in the Valparaiso Male and Female College Building, and will be known as the Northern Indiana Normal School.

This school will present many advantages to the young. It will have no endowment, and therefore must depend upon its own merits for its patronage and support, thus causing the teachers to exert every energy in order that entire satisfaction may be given.

A student taking a three years' course in this institution will secure an education equivalent to a six years' course in many of our colleges, hence making it the cheapest and most profitable school in the West.

Superior advantages will be presented to teachers. How shall I teach? What shall I teach? How shall I make the schoolroom a pleasant resort for my pupils? And a host of similar questions will receive special attention.

In short, it is designed to make this one of the most practical and living schools of the age. We hope that its merits and the manner in which it is conducted will be sufficient passports to public attention.

With this hope and claiming only that indulgence and forbearance, which is the common right of all, and which we know a kind and courteous public will grant, we present our views and plans to the candid consideration of the teachers and friends of education.[13]

In addition to these newspaper articles, Mr. Brown had a number of handbills printed in LaPorte for distribution throughout the territory around Valparaiso. Apparently he had the handbills printed in another town so as to keep secret the identity of the new management until the psychologically correct moment.

On July 3, 1873, the following advertisement appeared in the *Porter County Vidette:*

The Northern Indiana Normal School will open its first term Tuesday morning, September 16, 1873, and will continue eleven weeks. Classes will be formed in all the common branches—Algebra, Geometry, Botany, Latin and German. It is designed to make this a thorough training school for teachers as well as those who wish to enter any other professions. Especial attention will be given to methods of teaching and other school government.

Those desiring to take a complete Business Course will find superior advantages in the Commercial Department. We do not propose to be excelled by any other popular Commercial College.

The Principal is making great efforts to render everything as pleasant and home-like, and at the same time as cheap as possible. Arrangements will be made to supply furnished rooms and good table board at $3.00 a week. Furnished or unfurnished rooms and good table board can be had at very low rates. Private board, $3.50 to $4.00 a week. Tuition is $7.00 a term, payable in advance.

While the moral and religious interests of the school will receive most careful attention, yet no sectarianism will be introduced or encouraged. For further information address H. B. Brown, Principal.

Mr. Brown's own account of the beginnings of the school was written just a month before his stroke in 1912 and was printed in the March 28, 1930, edition of the *Valparaiso University Alumni Bulletin:*

I reached Valparaiso the first of September, 1873. Mr. B. F. Perrine had already preceded me; and together we began the work of the school, he taking charge of the boarding department and acting as instructor in history. The county institute was then in session. We gave such time as we had to those sessions in order to become acquainted with the city and county teachers.

The first work I had done in August was to employ some half dozen boys to pull up the weeds in the college campus; then the cleaning of the building began, and looking out for students in real earnest occupied every moment of our time. A Mr. Fifield and myself visited the various families in the county and solicited students. This was done in a most effective and thorough manner. The building was prepared and boarding house opened. . . .

. . . In the music department we had only one piano and, as I remember it now, only two students. Perhaps half of the students on the first morning were from surrounding counties, the other half from Valparaiso. . . .

Perhaps the proudest time of my own life in the school was at the opening of the third term, after the train reached Valparaiso over the Pennsylvania, about three o'clock in the afternoon, this being the only railroad then passing through Valparaiso. I had been busy at the college until after this train had passed. We had, during the day, half a dozen or more students, but I was not expecting very many because of the fact that it was the springtime of the year. After these students had been cared for, I started to town. When I reached where the Commercial building now stands, I looked across the ravine (where no buildings then stood) and saw what seemed to me about a million students coming. The omnibus was filled with students inside and out, and a long row of young people were coming up what was then the old sidewalk crossing the ravine at the corner of what are now Union and Morgan streets. Of course at that time there were no buildings on the "Hill."

I returned to the college building and posted myself where I might meet these students in a way to make them think it was no more than I expected. At that time I had no office except my own private room, the northeast corner of the old college building. I explained to them that we would have accomodations for them at once. We ordered two livery teams and took the students to various places in town where we had been promised rooms if we needed them. In a little while we had everything arranged in a satisfactory manner. Whether I slept that night I do not know; but at any rate we were ready for the opening of the term in the morning at 8:30. There has never been a time since when it seemed that we had so many students as that morning. Over and over I kept thinking how remarkable it was.

At the opening of the school we had as recitation rooms what is now called Elocution Hall. It was two-thirds as large as it is at the present time. The entrance was the same as it is now and on either side of the entrance was a small room. The one on the left was used as the music department and the one on the right was used for an office, but not having any need for an office we used it for the wood house. Above these rooms were small rooms. These rooms together with what is now known as Room 5 were used for recitation purposes. What was later known as Crescent Hall was used by the elocution department and for the "actual business" in the commercial department.[14]

At the beginning of the second term of the first year, Mr. George A. Dodge established a department of telegraphy, the first of several specialized departments which were organized around the nucleus of the Normal School. This department set a pattern which became typical of such specialized departments, a pattern of autonomous schools owned and managed by their deans or heads who collected fees from their students and paid Mr. Brown a percentage of such fees for advertising. Mr. Dodge sold his interests in the school to Mr. George L. Durand in 1882 and Mr. Durand, in turn, sold out to a Mr. Clarkson a few years later. Mr. Clarkson discontinued the school, but it was revived by a Mr. West, who operated it only a short time. In March, 1891, George M. Dodge, the son of the founder, re-established the department of telegraphy; but in November, 1894, disagreements between Mr. Dodge and Mr. Brown led to the withdrawal of the department from the Normal School. Mr. Dodge then founded the Dodge Institute of Telegraphy which, under its present title of Valparaiso Technical Institute, has won an enviable reputation as a technical school for electronics.[15]

By the beginning of the second academic year, Mr. Brown's "very high mark" of three hundred students had been surpassed and he was faced with the problem of providing sufficient accommodations for the anticipated increases in enrollment. Housing, especially, was inadequate, and, according to a report in the August 3, 1876 *Porter County Vidette*, Mr. Brown was so displeased by the apparent lack of co-operation in the community that he threatened to move the school to another location. Meanwhile he got along as best he could, still committed to the expansion of the school, whatever the obstacles. Special emphasis was placed on the preparatory department, and Mr. W. A. Yohn was placed in charge of that part of the work. Boarding clubs were organized under the supervision of Mr. Perrine, furnishing board for less than two dollars a week. Student activities, also, began to develop during the first three years of the school's existence. Several debating societies that were open to any of the students who wished to participate were organized. Earliest of these organizations was the Star Literary Society, which was organized in 1875. This organization, along with the Crescent Literary Society which was founded about a year later, played a major role in student life, providing both a forum for discussion and an opportunity for the development of leadership qualities among the students. It was not unusual in later years for leaders of these societies to move up, after graduation, to positions on the faculty. There was also a baseball team which played games with various town teams but did not compete against other schools.

In 1874, the school established a collegiate department consisting of the Scientific and Classic classes, each offering fifty weeks' work.[16] The Scientific year offered work in languages, history, natural sciences, and English literature, plus some work in parliamentary law, debating, penmanship, and vocal music. The Classic Class offered all of the courses of the Scientific Class plus work in the classics. As time went by, still other courses were added. Indeed it appears that a new course was added at any time, even in the middle of a term, if there was sufficient demand. One of the best examples of this effort on the part of the school to meet the demand for additional subjects is the fact that phrenology, which was a pseudo-science based upon the supposition that a person's mental capacities could be gauged from the conformation of his skull, was added to the curriculum and was continued until 1888. (Before anyone casts any stones at Mr. Brown on this score, it might be noted that the great Horace Mann was much excited by phrenology and considered an interest in it one of the marks of a progressive educator.)

Expansion of courses and enrollment made physical expansion essential by 1875, and in that year two new buildings were erected: East Hall, a dormitory at the south end of Greenwich Street which continued to serve as a dormitory and dining hall until it was demolished in 1928; and Flint Hall, better known to students of the Old School as Heritage Hall and to students of the Lutheran era as the University Library. In October, 1875, Mr. Brown also bought the old college building for twelve thousand dollars from the trustees of the Valparaiso Male and Female College. This enforced expansion left Mr. Brown in need of money, and he turned to the town for assistance.

Once again John N. Skinner, who had played such an important role in the founding of the Male and Female College, "came through." At this time mayor of the town, Mr. Skinner persuaded the city council to buy back the old college building from Mr. Brown for twelve thousand dollars, the price he had paid for it, allowing him the privilege of redeeming it within ten years—a privilege which, needless to say, he exercised. This gave Mr. Brown sufficient working capital to continue his program of development. A little later, at the urging of Mr. DeForrest L. Skinner, the county government gave the Normal School ten thousand dollars in ten annual payments of one thousand dollars each. So far as the records show, these two contributions by the city and the county were the only outside help that Mr. Brown received during his long administration as president of the Normal School.

Mr. Brown's own account of these measures by the city and the county is contained in hitherto-unpublished notes which were found in his desk after his death by his daughter, Ruth:

. . . I went over to Michigan City with Mr. Bloch. He said he knew I was in trouble and would help me. He would see Mr. DeFoe Skinner. $12000 from city $10000 from county } $22000

Mr. Skinner got a law passed allowing the county to pay $10000 towards the school.

Then the $12000 came from the city as a loan because I was in debt and had to either pay up or close the school. Rather than lose the school the city borrowed $12000 and paid these debts. And then in ten years I was to pay the city this amount.

Then when the ten years were up the city had collected $28000 on account of students tax—or tax on ac of students.

I said now you can take the $28000 which was really more than I owed without interest, and give me the buildings, or I will take the $28000 and pay for the buildings. I remember Mr. DeFoe Skinner said "My God! take the buildings, and Mr. Gotleib Bloch said take them. So they deeded the buildings to me."[17]

By 1877, the enrollment had climbed to 970, the faculty had increased to fifteen, and the number of departments had increased to eight. In 1878, the enrollment stood at 1050, and by 1880 the number had increased to thirteen hundred. Departments in 1880 included the preparatory department, the collegiate department, the teachers department, and the departments of business, engineering, music, fine arts, medicine, elocution, law, telegraphy, and phonography. These departments were open to all students. Additional classes in German and penmanship could be taken by the students without extra charge. The faculty in 1880 numbered twenty-eight.

Such success did not, naturally, go unnoticed, and one of its unhappy concomitants was a rash of rumors about the alleged inferior quality of facilities and teaching at the school. Leaders of the community, including the mayor, a number of prominent businessmen, all of the clergymen, and the superintendent of schools, therefore, drew up a declaration of confidence which they permitted Mr. Brown to circulate over their signatures in combating these rumors. (Incidentally, the pastor of the local Lutheran church, who did not otherwise participate in community affairs, signed this statement.) In addition, Mr. Brown offered to pit his classes against classes in the same subject in any other normal school in the country in an examination, the losing school to pay the winner a thousand dollars. This offer stood through all of Mr. Brown's administration, but there is no record of any school's having accepted the challenge.

That the success of the school was not merely a fortunate accident may be deduced from the fact that in Indiana alone fifteen "independent normal schools" were founded between 1870 and 1890.[18] Of that number, only the Northern Indiana Normal School survived the century. The success of Mr. Brown's School must be ascribed in large measure to two things: 1) his vigorous and sustained program of public relations, involving much direct mail advertising and, on the part of Mr. Brown personally, an exhausting round of public appearances at teachers' meetings and, indeed, at any other kind of meeting where teachers were likely to be present; and 2) his careful choice of exceptionally gifted teachers for the School's faculty.

Among the notable figures of this early faculty were J. W. Holcombe, a Harvard honors graduate, who was appointed professor of Latin and Greek in 1876 and became Indiana state superintendent of public instruction a few years later; C. W. Boucher, who became head of the commercial department in 1877 and later served for many years as superintendent of Valparaiso city schools; and Richard A. Heritage, who was appointed professor of music in 1878 and later established a conservatory of music of his own in Helena, Montana, which was adopted by the Montana Wesleyan University and the State University of Montana as their school of music.

Special mention should be made of Professor Harrison N. Carver, who joined the faculty as professor of Greek, Latin, and philosophy in 1878 and served until his death in 1917. Professor Carver had been one of Mr. Brown's instructors back in Ohio, and he seems to have remained a respected mentor to his former student through all of the years of their association at Valparaiso. Professor Carver was what might be called a "compulsive teacher." His whole life was spent in reading and teaching, his class load in his earlier days at Valparaiso running as high as ten hours a day. The great love of his life was the Greek and Latin classics, and he was impatient with those who considered the classics a kind of ointment to be spread thinly over young gentlemen to give them a patina of culture. His own views of the place of the classics in a practical education are set forth in a description of the Classic Course which he prepared for the silver anniversary issue of *The College Current:*

> Although called the Classic Course it is not to be understood that the work is not eminently practical and thoroughly up to date. In the Mental Sciences care is taken to interest the student in the questions of the day, to introduce him to the great scientific thinkers, but especially to put him in the way of thinking carefully of these things for himself. We want him to read Herbert Spencer as well as Homer, and to know how to use his Psychology and Logic while he is enjoying Shakespeare.
>
> . . . we try not to make the literature of Horace and Cicero, nor the great tragedies of the Greek poets a mere stamping ground. All this the student must have, of course, but we want him to realize that parsing is not reading Homer and that there is more in Virgil than in dactyls and spondees. In a word the whole work is designed not so much to drill things into the members of the class as to lead them out of themselves, to open to them the best that lies hidden in the works of great thinkers of all ages and to give them an introduction to that culture which comes from "higher companionship of books" and from one's own habits of careful thought.[19]

Within five years from the establishment of the Normal School it had become evident that it could not restrict itself to the modest offerings authorized in its original charter. Accordingly, in 1878, it applied for a new charter under the terms of which it was authorized to organize itself into the following departments: preparatory, teachers, business, collegiate, law, medical, engineering, music, fine arts, phonographic, telegraphic, and review. Not all of these departments were immediately established (although, as has been noted, most of them existed in embryonic form by 1880), but by the end of Mr. Brown's administration the School included all of these departments and more. The articles of incorporation were signed by Mr. Brown; John N. Skinner, the mayor; Joseph Gardner, a prominent contractor; Azariah Freeman; DeForrest L. Skinner; Marquis L. McLelland; Artillus V. Bartholomew; John C. Flint, also a contractor and builder of several of the older buildings on campus; and Gotleib Bloch. The seal of the Normal School was also described in these articles: an open book with the name of the institution along the margin of the seal. This remained the seal of the School and the University until 1925.[20]

The present school of law traces its history back to November, 1879, when Colonel Mark L. DeMotte founded the Northern Indiana Law School with Judge Hiram A. Gillett as principal instructor and a student body of one senior and fifteen juniors. Like the Normal School, the N.I.L.S. was committed to a policy of reducing the expenses of professional education without reducing standards. As for credentials, it was Dean DeMotte's contention that "There is no reason why *any person*, regardless of age, sex, or condition, who has a good moral character, should not be allowed to acquire a profession if he can. There are no requirements for admission to the junior class, the student must earn his degree before he gets it." [21] This policy may account for the criticism, common in the early days of the law school, that it was "too easy to enter, and too hard to get through." [22]

Of the numerous buildings constructed on the campus in the late seventies, only one remains. This is the Old Engineering Building, built around 1880 and known originally as Commercial Hall. It was built on the site of an earlier dormitory known as The Temple, which had burned down, and it was designed to accommodate the large classes of the commercial department.

Despite the large enrollments of these days, the Normal School was essentially a regional school drawing its students mostly from the Midwest, especially from Indiana and Illinois, although there were significantly large numbers also from Ohio, Michigan, Wisconsin, and Iowa. Most of the students were straight off the farm. Many of them were barely literate. However limited their background, the Normal School offered them a chance. The only restrictions that were made by the School in the way of entrance requirements were that the student must be at least sixteen years old and not a Negro. Although it was recommended that the prospective student be able to read in common school books, the ability to do so was not made an entrance requirement. If he could not read, there were facilities for teaching him that, too, at the Normal School.

The whole tone of campus life reflected the poverty and the limited backgrounds of the students. Amusements were simple ones, and even these occupied only a very small portion of the student's time. For one thing, the kind of student who came to the Normal School was not inclined toward what he would have called "frivolity;" for another thing the occasional student who did show any such inclinations was not allowed to stay around long enough to make any converts; and for a third thing the work at the School bore all of the earmarks of what would today be called a "cram" course. Some idea of life on campus at the time may be had from an account of the School which the editor of the *Rantoul* [Illinois] *News* published in his paper after a visit to the campus during the winter of 1877:

Our visit at the Northern Indiana Normal on Friday, Saturday, and Sunday last was a rare treat. This college is located fourteen miles south of Lake Michigan, near the northern line of Indiana, some forty miles east of Chicago, on the Pittsburgh, Fort Wayne, and Chicago Railroad, in a locality sparsely covered with timber but not far from prairie and good farming lands. A beautiful lake [Sager's Lake] covering an area one by two miles, supplied with all kinds of sailing boats and steamers for pleasure seekers, is only some two miles from the city and college. The city has a population of between five and six thousand inhabitants, is some forty years old, and bears the name Valparaiso. . . .

Mr. H. B. Brown, principal, founder, and sole owner of the college, received his education at Delaware and Lebanon colleges in Ohio; is a single man, of middle age, medium stature, social, conversational, attractive, and very practical and determined. To know him is to admire him; to hear him is to be convinced; and to see what he has accomplished in three years is to wonder at his pluck and energy. From sixty-one students during the first term, it has continually increased until they now number over thirteen hundred. The curious and wonderful feature of Professor Brown's success can be all or nearly so attributed to the fact that he has no rules or set of rules to hamper in its progress. The students can do as they please, study just what they please, and have perfect freedom to room, eat, visit or sleep when and where their own inclination dictates, so long as that is inside of respectability and conforms to the rules of society. The only requirements are perfect lessons, prompt pay and a proper respect for the rights of others. In our three days' visit we never saw a more jolly set, better decorum, better manners, more quiet at the table, more real social intercourse than is displayed by that vast army of 1,300 students.

We conversed with many students and heard no complaints about the board, rooms, or treatment of the teachers, other than some thought that there was a little too much push for perfect lessons. The school is so large that scholars can always find classes to suit their tastes and qualifications. All kinds of books are used, thus saving much expense on that score. Good board is furnished at $2.00 and $2.40 a week. Tuition, including German and drawing, $8.00 a term, everything furnished except lights and fuel, which are as reasonable there as at most other places. . . .

There are some fifteen or sixteen different societies acting in competition with each other, each striving to get ahead of the other, and all without dictation or molestation by any of the principals, who, in fact, enter into contests with the students, seemingly with as much animation as any. There are five large rooms occupied by these societies each evening, so that there is no time for anything only push ahead in different branches. Another singular feature is that a student's clothes and purse are not taken as a standard by which extra treatment is meted out. The poorest is in the eyes of the teachers as good as the richest, and commands as much attention, which fact is always claimed for professors in all schools, but which, we are sorry to say, is seldom the case in any. . . .

"Push ahead!"—that is exactly what Mr. Brown had been doing ever since his arrival in Valparaiso. By 1880, his venture had become an undoubted success both educationally and financially. But the burden of work involved in managing an operation of the size and complexity of the Northern Indiana Normal School had become too great for one man to carry, particularly for a "middle-aged" man who was well into his thirties. Someone was needed to assist in the management and especially to deal with the still-vexing problem of boarding and rooming facilities. The right man for the job should be more than a paid employee; he should have a share in the ownership. Mr. Brown knew whom he wanted, and in the winter of 1880 he asked him to come to Valparaiso to discuss buying a half-share in the School. That man was O. P. Kinsey.

Oliver Perry Kinsey

Mr. Kinsey was descended on both sides of his family from Scottish Quakers who had come to Pennsylvania with William Penn.[23] The family name was originally MacKinsey or Mackenzie. From Pennsylvania the family eventually moved to Ohio, and it was on a farm near Freeport, Ohio, that Oliver Perry Kinsey was born on December 7, 1849.

Mr. Kinsey attended the Harlem Springs Academy, near his home, for about thirty weeks, then taught for two years in country schools. He completed his schooling at the National Normal University in Lebanon, Ohio, working his way through, first as a janitor and, in his last year, as an instructor. Upon graduation, he became professor of English literature at the Normal School.

At Lebanon, Mr. Kinsey met Miss Sarah J. Porter, a strikingly handsome and intelligent young woman who was also interested in a career in education. It was not until some time after their graduation, however, that they were married, Miss Porter having accepted a position as principal of a high school in Des Moines, Iowa. Upon their marriage in 1876 they settled in Lebanon, where Mr. Kinsey was, by now, head of the department of English.

The Kinseys were good friends of Mr. Brown and his associates at Valparaiso and were very sympathetic to Mr. Brown's ideas about practical, low-cost education. When the invitation came, therefore, to buy an interest in the Northern Indiana Normal School, it did not take them long to accept the offer. But they had planned to tour Europe, and so they asked Mr. Brown to give them a year before expecting them to take up the work in Valparaiso. Their travels in Europe took them through Great Britain and the continent, and Mr. Kinsey made a particular point of studying the colleges and universities of the countries which he visited, gathering information which he hoped would be useful to him at Valparaiso.

In 1881, the Kinseys moved to Valparaiso, making their home in the large house at the corner of Greenwich and Monroe Streets, directly across Monroe Street from the present President's House. From the house a broad lawn swept down to College Avenue, and this lawn became, as the years went by, a favorite site for the many parties and receptions which the hospitable Kinseys liked to give. Mr. Kinsey now became co-owner and vice-president of the School and took charge of the Scientific Class and boarding and rooming facilities. Mrs. Kinsey organized courses in physical and descriptive geography, acted as matron of East Hall, and, in later years, taught grammar. Her sister, Miss Luella Porter, joined her in Valparaiso soon after and became the School's first librarian.

In a very short time, Mr. Kinsey had the boarding and rooming problem well in hand. He was a natural-born administrator who managed to reduce costs to the bare minimum while maintaining a relatively high level of comfort in the halls which he supervised. Some idea of how Mr. Kinsey operated may be had from Mr. George W. Stimpson's account of his methods:

Mr. Kinsey always tried to give the students the greatest possible variety in menu, which he watched very carefully, paying close attention to the various conditions which affect appetite and food consumption, such as weather, temperature, and amount of outdoor exercise. He owned a large orchard in Ohio, had under cultivation several gardens worked by students under the direction of hired gardeners, and sought co-operation with the local farmers and gardeners, effecting a profit to them by furnishing student help and supplying a sure market for their product before the seed is sown, and receiving his sweet corn, celery, potatoes, or whatever the crop might be, at less than half the cost in the open markets. He was so well acquainted with crop conditions that he knew just what foods would be high at a certain time of the year, just when and where to buy them, and just how long they would keep. His knowledge of the relative values of different foods placed him in an advantageous position over those who did not have such knowledge. He knew a good apple, pear, peach, potato, or beet when he saw it, and he knew under what conditions it must be kept to preserve it with the least possible deterioration. This scientific knowledge of the value and conservation of foods, combined with his wide acquaintance with crop conditions and the economic status of different parts of the country, enabled him to purchase large quantities of supplies without taking the risks commonly accompanied with like enterprises, such as decay in storage, changes in the market value, and fraud in the transaction.

Besides making all purchases and contracts, Mr. Kinsey supervised in person the repair of the buildings, the work of the gardeners, cooks, and student helpers. He worked out many devices whereby small economies were effected, such as the disposal of waste products, the prevention of unnecessary labor, and the easy and economical distribution of supplies. The work of the student helpers was of a highly specialized character, some were operators of the different machines, some waiters, janitors, dishwashers, and others looked after the secretarial and supervisory work of the boarding and rooming business. Wherever labor and time could be saved, provided it did not involve unnecessary waste, machinery was used. The dishes were washed, potatoes peeled, fruits pared, meats cut, and bread was sliced, with machinery adapted for the purposes. Nearly every week Mr. Kinsey would make a little talk to the students at the boarding halls. He would advise them to economize, to aid him in keeping down the cost of going to school. They were told not to take more food on their plates than they could eat, and not to waste butter, sugar, and other expensive foods. "If you have eaten two or three slices of bread," he would say, "and feel that you would like some more, but not a whole slice, break off half a slice and leave the rest on the plate." Simple, clean, nutritious, and wholesome food in sufficient quantities, and good service, were the result of Mr. Kinsey's constant application of his energy, intelligence, and business capacity to the problem of reducing the cost of living.[24]

But Mr. Kinsey was no dyspeptic fanatic with the soul of an accountant. Mr. Brown had his critics, some of them quite violent in their criticism. So far as the records show, Mr. Kinsey was universally liked and respected. He took an active part in public affairs, serving as a member of the city council, the county council, and the library board of which, for many years, he was chairman. He helped to organize the city water company and did considerable traveling at his own expense to study water companies in other cities. He was also a member and regular attendant at the Methodist Church. With Mr. Brown he shared a strong interest in the campaign for women's rights and in the prohibition movement. Politically, however, the two friends were on different sides of the fence, Mr. Brown being a fervent Democrat and Mr. Kinsey an equally fervent Republican.

Mr. Kinsey was highly respected among educators. In his later years he served as president of the Northern Indiana Teachers Association and of the State Teachers Association of Indiana.

So far as records or recollections show, Mr. Kinsey and Mr. Brown never had any serious disagreements during their almost forty years of close, day-by-day association. Indeed, the complete faith which each reposed in the other makes it difficult for the historian to document the record of these years for it resulted in very few records, and these records are mostly in the form of sketchy memoranda. The two men complemented each other. As their students used to say, "Henry Baker Brown brought the students to Valparaiso and Oliver Perry Kinsey took care of them after they arrived." The affection in which Mr. Kinsey is still held in the community was clearly evidenced when, in 1940, townspeople predicted a bright future for the new president of the University (whom they had not yet seen) just because his initials were O. P. K., and he was, like the earlier O. P. K., a redhead.

The Good Years

Mr. Kinsey's assumption of the business side of the administration freed Mr. Brown for the work that was his first love, the building of a large, academically strong school. One of his first moves was to reorganize the calendar to include five ten-week terms, thus putting the School on essentially a year-'round basis. At the same time, tuition was increased from the former seven dollars to eight dollars per term, and a number of departments were added.

As the School was organized at that time, the law school, the phonographic department, the telegraphic department, and to a certain extent the fine arts department were actually affiliated schools, although the fine arts department did not have a separate corporate identity.[25] Work in fine arts included drawing and painting under what was known as the "Smith System." The complete course ran for six months and included hand drawing and designing, drawing from the flat, model and object drawing, light and shade sketching from nature, portrait painting, China painting, oil painting on silk, etching, and engraving. The tuition for the course was fifty dollars.

The department of elocution and oratory was added at this time, using the Boston University School of Oratory methods and the Delsarte system of gestures. This course was recommended for all teachers, law students, and pre-ministerial students. For many years it was possible for students to earn the Bachelor of Oratory (B.O.) degree at Valparaiso.

It has already been noted that, in the early years of the Normal School, departmental lines were only very vaguely defined. This was partly because of the small faculty, but it was also partly the result of Mr. Brown's insistence upon instructors who had the specific gift of teaching. Even when the larger size of the faculty made it unnecessary for individual instructors to be jacks-of-all-trades, Mr. Brown continued to insist that his instructors should be prepared to teach any subject that they had ever studied. This was obviously no way to encourage profound research, but it did force members of the faculty to keep a high polish on the techniques of teaching.

As enrollments grew, a certain amount of departmentalization became inevitable, and by the turn of the century certain departments were well-defined and were staffed by men and women who were specialists in their disciplines. The "and women" deserves special emphasis, for throughout Mr. Brown's administration women held key positions as senior professors and department heads, and this at a time when women found it difficult to find positions even in the lowest instructional ranks at most colleges and universities. One of the most influential positions on campus, that of secretary to the president, was held by Miss Catherine Corboy, who served in that capacity from 1885 to 1917. (Miss Corboy succeeded Miss Neva Axe, who had resigned to accept an even more influential position as Mrs. Henry Baker Brown.)

The first department to show clear signs of a separate departmental identity was the business department. In 1877, Professor Chauncey W. Boucher was appointed head of what was at first called the commercial department, serving until 1883, when he resigned to open his own normal school in Muncie, Indiana. Mr. Kinsey succeeded Professor Boucher as head and brought in Professor Charles W. Benton as instructor in a course called "Actual Business." After a few years Professor Benton became head of the commercial school and continued in that position until 1918.

A little later, music became, for all practical purposes, a separate department. The man who did more than anyone else to establish music as an important part of the School's work was Professor Richard A. Heritage, who served as professor of music from 1878 to 1894. Professor Heritage was an indefatigable worker. In addition to his regular academic duties, he taught music classes in Hebron and Hobart, Indiana; directed the choir at the local Methodist church; conducted the School orchestra; took part in numerous plays presented under the direction of Professor Bogarte; for a year or so around 1885 edited and published a little magazine called *The Musical Ideal;* ran a dormitory for two years (1882–1884); and, to top it all, organized sight-seeing excursions. When Professor Heritage left the School to open his own conservatory in Montana, he was succeeded by a Professor Gottschalk who, in turn, was succeeded by Professor William Wade Hinshaw. Professor Harold L. Butler became head of the department in 1899, serving thereafter for about five years. Officially, however, music did not become a department until about 1904, when Professor Edmund W. Chaffee, who had been appointed professor of piano in 1894, became the first formally-appointed head of the department.

The largest of the original departments, the normal department, was not organized along formal departmental lines until 1896, when Professor Sanford Bell was appointed head of a "department of psychology and pedagogy." Work in this department included thirty weeks of adult psychology, twenty weeks of genetic psychology, ten weeks of general method in the common branches, thirty weeks of history and philosophy of education, ten weeks in the science of education, and a thesis on some phase of educational thought. Before a student could be graduated from this department, he was required to have completed the Scientific Course or its equivalent in academic work. Work in the department led to the degree of Bachelor of Pedagogy, and it was possible for the student, by remaining one year longer and doing special work under the direction of the department head, to earn the Master of Pedagogy degree.

In the natural sciences, specialization of courses developed gradually from the core of the old Scientific Class. Professor Bogarte and Professor Yohn were the principal instructors in the natural sciences, Mr. Bogarte being especially interested in mathematics. Work which was later offered in engineering can also be traced back to Mr. Bogarte's classes in higher mathematics and surveying, which were included in the earliest course offerings of the Normal School.

When Professor Yohn resigned in 1886, Professor Horace Martin Evans was appointed to succeed him. Professor Evans, in 1892, organized a class in pharmacy which, in the following years, developed into a department of pharmacy under Professor A. E. Hiss. Shortly after the establishment of the department, Professor J. N.

Roe became its head, serving in that capacity and later as first dean of the School of Pharmacy until 1912.

To an even greater extent than is usually true of colleges and universities, the heart of the Normal School was its faculty. Apart from the original faculty and Professor Carver, probably no member of the faculty contributed as much over as long a period of time to the Normal School and its successor institutions as John E. Roessler, who for more than forty years played an active part in the affairs of the School as a student leader, a member of the faculty, and, in the early Twenties, as president of the University. Born in Shelbyville, Illinois, on February 28, 1859, Mr. Roessler came to Valparaiso as a student in the fall of 1879, withdrew after four terms, and then returned in 1882 and completed his work. During his student days he was what would today be called a "wheel" on campus, occupying all of the most important student offices. His prominence in campus affairs made his romance with Miss Anna Harbor, whom he married in 1885, a matter of general interest and of good-natured joshing which, one suspects, must have become a bit tiring to its principals. Upon his graduation, Mr. Roessler became professor of German and mathematics, a position which he retained until his election to the presidency. He also conducted the *Männerchor*.

Although the Northern Indiana Law School did not become officially a part of the University until 1906 or 1907, its founder and first dean, Colonel Mark L. DeMotte, must be included among the major figures of the campus during this period. Colonel DeMotte (the title derived from his service in the Civil War) was a member of a distinguished pioneer family of clergymen and educators of French descent. His training had been in the law, and he was senior partner in one of the most respected law firms in northwestern Indiana when, in 1879, he founded his law school. Shortly thereafter, he was elected to Congress and served for one term, after which he returned to Valparaiso and directed the law school until his death in 1908. Shortly before his death, he transferred his interest in the law school to the firm of Brown and Kinsey and retired from the deanship. The original law building was the south addition to the west wing of the Old College building. Some years later, Colonel DeMotte bought a house which had been built as a private home by Professor Felix Ecblad who had been head, for a while, of the fine arts department. This building remained the home of the law school until the early days of Lutheran administration, when the law school was given quarters in the present Arts-Law building.

Three other men who joined the faculty in the later years of this period remained in the service of the School for periods of more than a quarter of a century. These were Professor Edgerton William Agar of the commercial department, later mayor of Valparaiso; Professor Mason Locke Weems, for thirty years professor of physiology; and Professor Calvin S. Hoover of the history department.

Classes in these years began at 6:30 in the morning (Mr. Brown had one at that hour) and continued until 9:30 in the evening. Since courses were numerous and physical facilities were limited, class sizes were necessarily large, and members of the faculty might find themselves teaching in several departments during the same term. There was no prescribed order of courses, and it was not unusual for a student to take calculus without having had college algebra or analytical geometry. It should be pointed out, however, that the student assumed full responsibility for any inadequacy in his background. If he wanted to by-pass what would today be called the prerequisites, he could. But he had to keep pace in his work with those who were better prepared.

Dependable enrollment figures for these years are difficult to arrive at. For one thing, as has been noted, only rather rudimentary records were kept, and, for another thing, enrollments were customarily stated in terms of total enrollments for the year. This meant that a student who enrolled for three terms would be counted three times. With the great amount of coming and going that characterized the student bodies of these days, the only way of arriving at any reasonably accurate estimate of the actual number of different students enrolled in any given year is to count the students listed in the catalogues, eliminating the duplications. But for the later years of the period, Mr. Cecil Bigelow was able to compile a table of enrollments from the handwritten records of Mr. Kinsey.[26] This table is interesting not only because it is the best available record of total enrollments but also because it shows that even at this rather late date the School was still primarily a regional school.

State or Foreign Country	Year			State of Foreign Country	Year		
	1895	1896	1897		1895	1896	1897
Alabama	3	2	0	New York	5	6	7
Arizona	2	0	0	North Dakota	13	37	35
Arkansas	15	7	10	Ohio	208	201	191
California	3	4	5	Oregon	1	2	1
Colorado	9	3	2	Pennsylvania	110	81	67
Connecticut	1	1	1	South Carolina	1	1	1
Dist. of Columbia	3	1	0	South Dakota	43	38	34
Florida	1	2	4	Tennessee	6	6	15
Georgia	9	2	2	Texas	17	23	20
Idaho	4	6	8	Utah	4	2	2
Illinois	940	824	842	Virginia	5	2	5
Indiana	1058	915	962	Wisconsin	204	189	198
Iowa	184	147	150	Wyoming	2	0	1
Kansas	11	12	15	Washington	8	5	2
Kentucky	98	89	78	West Virginia	12	10	5
Louisiana	6	3	3	Indian Territory	1	2	0
Maryland	3	3	4	Alaska	0	1	0
Michigan	268	220	165	Canada	3	4	4
Minnesota	76	70	57	England	0	2	1
Mississippi	6	9	3	Germany	2	1	0
Missouri	58	58	45	Italy	0	1	0
Montana	20	22	18	Persia	0	0	1
Nebraska	10	6	10	Russia	1	0	1
New Jersey	2	1	0	Sweden	1	3	1
New Mexico	3	0	1	Not Given	12	41	24
North Carolina	0	1	1				
Total					3443	3066	3002

Mr. Brown and Mr. Kinsey were both insistent upon prompt payment of student accounts, but there are several instances in the records of tuition receipts being issued with no record of any money's having been received. It is very probable that these tuition accounts were either worked out or perhaps never paid at all. The administration is known to have accepted mortgages, notes, watches, jewelry, and other collateral in lieu of tuition payment, but there is no record of any such transactions. As an example, Mr. Brown was known to have held title to some very valuable oil land in Texas, and the supposition is that he secured it by accepting mortgages as security for tuition and student loans. In two different instances, tuition receipts show that men paid tuition and then, for some reason, withdrew from school. Miss Corboy is authority for the statement that in these two cases the men sent their sons to the School thirty years later and that Mr. Brown accepted the old receipts as payment for the sons' tuition.[27]

Of the buildings built during this period, only the old building which houses foreign language classrooms and offices still survives. Built by Mr. Perrine in 1892 as a bookstore, it was sold to Mr. Bogarte in 1894 and became Bogarte's Bookstore. A year later a part of it was let to Wade Brothers and Wise, commercial printers, who did a considerable textbook business and, until the Second World War, printed *The Torch*, the campus newspaper. The grandest of the buildings on the old campus, the Auditorium, was built in 1892 to relieve the crowded classroom situation, to accommodate the crowds that came to the campus for concerts and recitals, and to provide a suitable setting for the weekly chapel exercises. The fire which destroyed the old Auditorium in November, 1956, burned out the heart of the old campus.

As the century closed, it was obvious that the Normal School was a great success, at least from the financial standpoint. That it was successful also in the judgment of its students is apparent from an editorial which appeared in the silver anniversary edition of *The College Current:*

From the beginning *whatever from necessity may have been omitted,* the students were satisfied as to *these* points, and were confident that they could always depend upon their faithful and conscientious fulfillment. One was that they would always be in charge of *thoroughly competent instructors,* the other that the accomodations would be *precisely as advertised,* and that the *expenses would be the very lowest possible.* Even before the Institution could afford to employ *special instructors,* the best *general teachers* were employed. As prosperity came *specialists* were employed for each department, thus affording equal, and with the methods used, we believe, superior advantages to the older and endowed institutions. Upon the character of its work the School depends for its prosperity. The best evidence that it has accomplished its purpose is in the success of the students who have gone out from it and the continued increasing demand for those trained here. Also in the fact that those who, at the beginning, were its bitterest opponents are now its warmest friends. City Superintendents, County Superintendents, Presidents of Colleges and Universities, and State Superintendents *from whom we have the most flattering testimonials,* have visited the school and investigated the work. As the Institution has grown and could afford it an *abundance of the best apparatus* has been secured, a *very complete library* has been purchased, and every appliance that would in any way advance the interest of students supplied.

So that now the Institution is not only one of the most *thoroughly equipped in the land,* but has the respect and confidence of the most popular educators everywhere.

The very fact that the School has been *compelled to pass through such tests and such poverty,* we believe has proven *one of its strongest elements.* Being compelled to do with so little, the inventive powers of the instructors were developed to the fullest extent, and the greatest possible use was made of the material at hand. The same spirit has gone out with the students, and is an invaluable aid to them, and as there have been very few changes in teachers, except as new ones have been added to the list, this same experience is continued and the peculiar training puts those connected with the school in a condition to enter into the sympathies of those who are *struggling against adversity in order to secure an education.*[28]

The same edition of *The Current* contained advertisements for the third edition of Practical Bookkeeping, by Professor C. W. Benton; an excursion to Macinac [*sic*] arranged by Professor Agar with the Lake Michigan Transportation Company; a copy of the "N.I.N.S. March" for piano, fifteen cents, and a notice of

> *The 16th Annual Excursion to Niagara Falls.*
> *Via the Nickel Plate Ry.*

On August 15th, 1898, M. C. Kelly will conduct an excursion to *Niagara Falls, Toronto, Canada,* and *Chautauqua Lake, New York,* fare for the round trip *$9.00.*

He will also furnish a coupon ticket including railroad fare, hotel bills, and all necessary expenses for $20.00. The following is included in the $20.00 ticket: railroad fare to Niagara Falls and return, hotel bills at Niagara Falls, trip down Great George Route, ride to Whirlpool Rapids, Whirlpool, ride on ferry boat from Lewiston, N. Y., to Canada, trip from Chippewa to the great International Bridge, across the bridge to Prospect Point, down the incline Plane to the Maid of the Mist landing, and a trip on the steam boat, "Maid of the Mist," up the Incline Plane, a carriage ride around Goat Island and the Three Sisters Islands, admission to two of the museums at Niagara Falls and admission to the Tower, round trip to Toronto, hotel fare at Toronto, carriage fare around the city of Toronto visiting the parks, government buildings, colleges, schools, churches and exhibition grounds, admission to the gate at Chautauqua assembly grounds and boat ride on Lake Chautauqua. This ticket dates from 9:45 Monday morning until 6:02 Saturday morning. Dinner and supper on the trip going down is not furnished with this ticket.[29]

The only thing wrong with the Northern Indiana Normal School was that it was no longer really a normal school. It had grown to a full-scale college and, following its policy of honest advertising, it took steps to call itself what it had become.

The Normal School had been in existence only a little more than a quarter of a century by this time, but it had produced a surprisingly large number of graduates who would later distinguish themselves in public life and in the professions. Greatest of them all was George W. Norris, '82, destined to be one of the greatest senators in the history of the country. Three contemporaries of Mr. Norris who were also to become senators were John J. Blaine (Wisconsin), Alpheus A. Jones (New Mexico), and Samuel Ralston who, in addition to his senatorial service, served also as governor of Indiana. Other distinguished alumni of the period include Robert J. Aley, '82, later president of Butler University; Bernard G. Cigrand, '86, later for many years a member of the faculty of the University of Illinois but better known as the father of Flag Day; and J. E. Hagerty, '87, later dean of the College of Commerce and Journalism at The Ohio State University.

NOTES

1. Biographical data on Mr. Brown are available in *Counties of Porter and Lake, Indiana* (1882) and in Stimpson's *Story of Valparaiso University*.
2. Ernest Earnest, *Academic Procession* (Bobbs-Merrill, 1953), p. 138.
3. *Ibid.*, pp. 139-140.
4. *Ibid.*, p. 161.
5. Holograph in the Archives of Valparaiso University.
6. *Counties of Porter and Lake, Indiana* (1882), p. 137.
7. *Valparaiso University Alumni Bulletin*, I, No. 11, 3.
8. *Ibid.*, I, No. 18, 4.
9. Older residents of Valparaiso remember that Mr. Bryan was often a guest in the Brown home. Mr. Brown's friendship with President Wilson is attested to by Mr. J. W. Larrew of Valparaiso. It is possible that Mr. Brown and Mr. Wilson were distantly related by marriage, their wives being members of the Axe family. Mr. Brown was also on close terms with President Eliot of Harvard who is reported to have said, after he had addressed the Valparaiso student body, that if Harvard had Valparaiso's students it would be the best university in the world, and if Valparaiso had Harvard's equipment it would be the best university in the world.
10. *The College Current*, August 6, 1898, p. 2.
11. A biography and several appreciations of Miss Baldwin can be found in the *Valparaiso Alumni Bulletin*, Vol. I, No. 8. Dr. Pflueger's comments and Mr. Stafford's comments are from this source.
12. A biography and several appreciations of Mr. Bogarte can be found in the *Valparaiso University Alumni Bulletin*, Vol. I, No. 7. Mrs. Bowden's appreciation and Mr. R. H. Bogarte's comments are from this source.
13. *The Porter County Vidette*, June 12, 1873.
14. *Valparaiso University Alumni Bulletin*, Vol. I, No. 10.

15. Stimpson, *op. cit.*, pp. 73-74.

16. For a record of the development of departments, see Cecil Loar Bigelow, "A History of Valparaiso University from 1875 to 1925," an unpublished dissertation submitted to the faculty of the Division of the Social Sciences in candidacy for the degree of Master of Arts, School of Education, The University of Chicago, 1937.

17. Holograph, Valparaiso University Archives.

18. Richard G. Boone, *A History of Education in Indiana* (D. Appleton and Co., 1892), p. 437.

19. *The College Current*, August 6, 1898, p. 10.

20. These articles of incorporation are preserved in the Valparaiso University archives.

21. *The College Current*, August 6, 1898, p. 9.

22. *Ibid.*

23. Biographical data on Mr. Kinsey are available in *Counties of Porter and Lake, Indiana* (1882) and in Stimpson, *op. cit.*, p. 55 f.

24. Stimpson, *op. cit.*, pp. 87-88.

25. Bigelow, *op. cit.*, p. 25.

26. *Ibid.*, p. 29.

27. *Ibid.*, pp. 28 and 30.

28. *The College Current*, August 6, 1898, p. 5.

29. *Ibid.*, p. 19.

CHAPTER III

"The Poor Man's Harvard"

1900—1919

THE Northern Indiana Normal School and Business Institute was a peculiarly American institution. Nothing like it existed, or could have existed, in any other country. Privately owned and managed, it was an educational business dependent, like any business, upon the satisfaction it gave its "customers." To keep its customers, it had to offer what they wanted. And as these wants changed, the School changed. By 1900 the public school system had so far developed in almost all of the states that students who came to Valparaiso had had at least some elementary education, and many were high school graduates.[1] There was thus a demand for more truly college-level education and less need for the kind of work which had heretofore been offered by the Preparatory Department. Curricular changes in the last decade of the Nineteenth Century were, therefore, directed largely toward strengthening and expanding the offerings in the higher-level courses.

The period from 1880 to about 1915 was also a time of large-scale immigration. In the thirty-five years after 1880, almost twenty-five million immigrants entered the United States, a few of them religious or political refugees, but most of them ordinary folk from the overcrowded towns and farms of Europe, drawn to the New World by the lure of open lands and expanding industries. Most of these immigrants were poor, but what they lacked in money they more than made up for in ambition to get ahead. Many of the younger immigrants, and some not so young, recognized that the passport to opportunity in their new homeland was education. But lack of satisfactory academic credentials or difficulties with the English language or limited funds made it impossible for many of them to meet the entrance requirements of most colleges and universities. As a result of Mr. Brown's policy of widespread advertising, many of these people heard about the institution in Valparaiso, Indiana, where education was available at every level and at low cost. During the first decade and a half of the Twentieth Century a large number of the School's students, including a number who were to become some of its most distinguished alumni, came from this immigrant group.

Valparaiso College

Recognizing the radical changes which had taken place in the structure and function of the institution, the administration rechartered the School in 1900 under the name of "Valparaiso College." This remained its corporate name until 1907, when it became Valparaiso University.

Valparaiso College was something unique in American education. Its total enrollment, including duplications, increased from around two thousand in 1900 to five thousand in 1907, placing it next only to Harvard in enrollment and far above the state institutions, which have grown to mammoth size only in recent years. Its income derived almost entirely from tuition which, as late as 1906, was only fifteen dollars per twelve-week term. And its student body was perhaps the most cosmopolitan in the country.

The College was organized into seventeen distinct departments: preparatory, teachers, psychology and pedagogy, penmanship, scientific, biology, Latin and German, English, civil engineering, elocution and oratory, classical, pharmacy, medicine, music, fine arts, business, phonography and typewriting, and law. Work in the preparatory department still consisted of common school subjects, but after 1905, when Mr. Joseph Melvin Lien established the elementary department, attention was directed primarily to foreign students. High-school work in the department was designed to allow the student to complete the standard high-school program in two years, and special provisions were made for rapid advancement.

In the other departments, the trend during these years was distinctly toward greater specialization and higher standards. The most notable example of this trend is the law department which, in 1907, became the School of Law. Professor Milo Jesse Bowman, who succeeded Colonel DeMotte as dean that year, patterned the curriculum after the offerings of the best law schools of the time.

The faculty of the College more than doubled during this period, from sixty-one in 1900 to 166 in 1907. (These figures include a considerable number of senior students who assisted in laboratory work or did some teaching. The line between faculty member and student assistant was not a sharp one in those days.) Most of the members of the faculty had been students at the institution, a fact which occasioned some unfavorable comment in educational circles because of the danger of in-breeding. Faculty teaching loads were still heavy both in terms of hours and in terms of students, but, in spite of what were perhaps less than ideal teaching conditions, the turn-over rate was very low. In equipment, library accommodations, laboratory facilities, and other material necessities, the College ranked high.[2]

Financially, the College was in excellent shape. There is no evidence of any indebtedness against it, although both the present Biology Building and the present Music Hall were built during this period, that is, in 1906. These, along with Science Hall (1900) did much to alleviate the problem of overcrowded classrooms. Housing, on the other hand, remained something of a problem, and many of the large boarding houses that surround the present old campus date from this period.

The College Becomes a University

By 1907, it would seem, Mr. Brown and Mr. Kinsey were contemplating the gradual and orderly development of a full-scale university which would carry on under a self-perpetuating board of trustees after their death. With the re-chartering of the College as Valparaiso University, a structure was set up which would permit colleges to be established one by one as resources and demand permitted. But events were shaping up which would block the fulfillment of these plans and engage the University in a struggle for survival from which it escaped only by the narrowest margin.

A portent of one unhappy chain of events was the sudden and unexpected death, in 1911, of Professor Bogarte. One of the "First Five," Professor Bogarte had become practically a campus landmark. He had taught almost every course on campus, he had run the bookstore, he had helped out from time to time in the business management of the University, and he had played an active part in the extra-curricular life of the campus. His death was a reminder that time was running out for the veterans who had built the institution from a local normal school to a national university. More than that, it was the first in a series of deaths which, within less than a decade, took all of the old veterans except Miss Baldwin from the scene. And even Miss Baldwin was forced to retire in 1914 when she became an invalid.

To this change and decay within the University itself must be added changes that were taking place on the American scene generally. By the turn of the century higher education was well on its way to becoming big business and the lack of any generally-accepted standards encouraged a proliferation of institutions, some of which can only be described as diploma mills. To remedy this situation, regional accrediting associations were being established, having as their purpose the setting of minimum standards of institutional respectability. At the outset these standards were, of necessity, largely quantitative, having to do with such readily-measurable criteria of soundness as endowment, length of term, number of volumes in the library, percentage of earned doctorates in the faculty, student-teacher ratios, and faculty teaching loads. Alumni of the University might decry these "mechanical standards" and insist that there was no better education available anywhere in the country than at Valparaiso. The fact remained that the new standards were being applied, and those institutions which could not or would not meet them found their enrollments dropping off and their faculty members leaving for the greater security and prestige of the accredited institutions.

Equally significant changes were beginning to appear in the attitudes of the college-going population. A college degree had always been a prestige symbol, but, as more and more young people were graduated by the colleges, the degree itself lost some of its significance. In the older schools out East, prestige was a matter of having been tapped for the right clubs. In the Midwest, prestige went with pledging the right fraternities and sororities. Mr. Brown, as has been noted, considered such organizations antithetical to everything that his School stood for and rigorously suppressed them. But as the enrollment grew, it was impossible for him to be everywhere, and secret societies were organized, the earliest of them as far back as 1903. In themselves, these societies did little to bring on the troubles which the University later experienced. But

as symptoms of a new generation which did not consider egal-
itarianism a virtue, they prophesied trouble for an institution which
had always been proud of its democracy of poverty.

Meanwhile, in Europe, events were shaping up toward a climax
which not even the most pessimistic considered a real possibility in
the bright new century of progress and enlightenment. Confronted
by the rising power of the new German Empire, France and Great
Britain had composed ancient differences and were prepared to
contest any additional growth of German power on the continent.
The saber-rattling in Europe meant nothing, of course, to Ameri-
cans insulated from the Old World's alarums by the broad Atlantic,
but, the Atlantic proved to be narrower than it had seemed.

These events (except for Professor Bogarte's death) were not
immediately reflected in the fortunes of the University. To all
appearances, everything was going much as it had been going, perhaps even better than ever before. The University was famous, so
famous that national magazines sent reporters to see whether the
"educational miracle" at Valparaiso was real or a figment of over-
imaginative advertising. The great S. S. McClure (a graduate, incidentally, of the Valparaiso high school) sent one of his reporters,
George Kennan, to find out the truth about the University and,
in view of his delight in "muck-raking," must have regretted having to report that

One would hardly think it possible to furnish board, room, and higher
education for the small sum of thirty-eight cents a day; but the Valparaiso University gives a student an abundant, well cooked, and well
served dinner for ten cents, a breakfast for four cents, a supper for four
cents, a good bed in a single funished room for five cents, and tuition
for fifteen cents a day. . . .

The first supper that I had at Valparaiso was in the East Hall dining-
room. It cost four cents, and consisted of hot tea biscuits, French fried
potatoes, boiled or steamed rice, baked apples, with sugar and milk,
stewed peaches, gingerbread, and tea. Everything was good as it would
have been in a well managed private household. The tables in the
Valparaiso dining halls accommodate ten or twelve persons each, and
are decorated with flowering plants furnished by a local florist at fifty
dollars a year. These plants are changed from table to table every three
or four days, and, as they go out of blossom, are taken away by the
florist and replaced with others. Food is brought to the tables by student
waiters, who are working their way through the University and receive
their board for their services. . . .

Students are housed in Valparaiso almost as economically as they are fed. In the older dormitories a single furnished room costs sixty cents a week, and a double room one dollar a week. Both are intended for two occupants, but the latter consists of a sitting room, bedroom, and closet. In the new Lembke Hall the rooms are all double, with hot and cold water, and the rental, including heat, is two dollars a week, or one dollar each for two. Lembke Hall tenants, however, have superior accommodations, and pay about forty-five cents more a week for board. At these rates the dormitories yield a revenue of from six to eight per cent on the sums invested in them. In each of the buildings for women there is a matron; and students who wish to economize by doing their own washing may have the use of a well equipped laundry for five cents a day.[3]

That was in 1908. In 1914, in response to an inquiry by a reader who had read one of the University's advertisements and had concluded that there was a "bit of graft about this institution," *Collier's Magazine* sent a reporter, William T. Walsh, to investigate. He reported that

With modifications not sufficiently serious to invalidate them, I found the claims made by the management of the University to be substantially correct.

An hour after my arrival in Valparaiso I had "dinner," the noon meal, in Heritage Hall, where 240 students are accommodated with table board. This was the menu: White, or Irish and sweet potatoes, slaw, two kinds of bread, butterine, pork sausage, cornstarch pudding—everything unlimited in quantities. The quality of all was the best. The food was well cooked, cleanly served, on white-clothed tables. The cost of this sort of fare to the students is $1.40 a week, a trifle less than 7 cents a meal! In three other halls 900 more students were dining at the same hour but not at the same price. Though they were paying $1.75 and $2, there was no difference in the fare, at least in quality; only in variety. At the $1.75 per week tables, the addition of beef gravy and substitution of apple pie for pudding chiefly seemed to warrant the increased price; the surroundings here were less severe, the furniture less plain. Creamery butter accounted for the $2 rate.[4]

Enrollments continued to rise during this period, reaching what Mr. Kinsey called the all-time high in the 1914–1915 academic year, when a total of 4977 different students were listed in the catalogue. Of this number, 548 were registered in the preparatory department, leaving 4429 university-level students. The largest enrollments were in medicine (600) and dentistry (449), both of which were taught in Chicago. The largest departments on the

Valparaiso campus were education with 497; the scientific department, 495; the teachers department, 439; commerce, 362; higher
courses of the preparatory department, 331; engineering, 280;
music, 239; pharmacy, 142; and law, 137.[5] Classes at this time were
limited to forty-five, additional sections of the same course being
set up when necessary. More than three hundred classes, including
the classes in Chicago, met each day.

Three buildings that were constructed in the years between 1910
and 1915 still stand on the old campus: Altruria Hall (built by
private interests) and Lembke Hall, both of which date from 1912;
and the Domestic Science Building (now Arts-Law), 1914.

The ultimate test of the quality of an educational institution is
the quality of the men and women it sends out into public and professional life. By this time, Mr. Brown had given leadership to
Valparaiso for more than forty years. What did the University
have to show for all of those years of dedicated leadership?

It is very difficult to assemble a complete list of alumni who
"made good." This should not be surprising, for one of the contributions which the School made to the educational pattern of its
day was that of serving as a kind of "half-way house," a place to
which young men could come without formal qualifications and
pick up the basic backgrounds and skills which they had to have
before they could hope to be admitted to institutions organized
along more traditional lines. Some of those who benefited from
this service of the School were quite reticent about mentioning it
in later years, especially after the University came upon hard days
after Mr. Brown and Mr. Kinsey had passed from the scene.

But the Old School also had its full quota of distinguished alumni
who remembered their alma mater with gratitude and pride. Those
who were in attendance before 1900 have already been mentioned.
Distinguished alumni of the period 1900 to 1912 include Gov-
ernors Gordon Browning of Tennessee and Flem D. Sampson of
Kentucky; Lt. General Walter Bedell Smith, who served as chief
of staff to General Eisenhower during the Second World War;
Judge Green H. Hackworth, for many years a member of the
International Court of Justice in The Hague and, since 1955, its
president; Claudis H. Huston, chairman of the Republican National
Committee during the Hoover administration; David B. R. John-
son, former president of the American Pharmacy Association; and

Angus Ward, veteran career diplomat who, after several years in Communist internment camps, was appointed U. S. ambassador to Afghanistan.

Perhaps the best known living alumnus of the University is Lowell Thomas, '09 and '11, world traveler, radio commentator, author, and movie producer. Mr. Thomas has taken an active interest in the development of the University, and is presently serving as co-chairman of the Alumni Centennial Crusade. Not so well known, but highly respected in his own field, was Dr. Reuben L. Kahn, a graduate of the Scientific Class of 1909, who devised the test which has come to be the accepted test for venereal diseases. In the business world, two alumni of this period who made especially notable achievements are W. L. Moss, founder, first president, and present board chairman of the Suwanee Life Insurance Company; and Fred W. Keller, leading realtor and former mayor of South Bend. In education, an outstanding alumnus is Dr. Forrest R. Polk, president of Wisconsin State Teachers College at Oshkosh.

Reputation and position are, of course, only superficial indicators of real success. The mentioning of alumni who have won recognition in their own generation may serve to indicate that the School had something to offer the young man or woman of unusual ability, but it must be remembered that the School was not designed for exceptional people. Stimpson says that "Mr. Kinsey used often to admonish the students of the dangers and pitfalls lying in the path of the man who conceives himself an exception to the rule, the man who thinks it is unnecessary to regard the laws which govern the ordinary individual. Valparaiso University grew up with the people, was supported by the people, was managed by men who were of the people, and was eminently adapted to the needs of the people."

In October, 1912, Mr. Brown went to Boston, where he was to receive the 33rd degree of the Masonic order. While there, he suffered a stroke which did not prove immediately fatal, but from which he never recovered. For five years he lingered on, busying himself with small details of administration. (Mrs. Katharine Ertz Bowden, the University archivist, who joined the faculty in 1913, remembers Mr. Brown trimming the grass, just to have something to do.) But he was forced to withdraw from the active management of the University. This left Mr. Kinsey in charge as acting president, although he refused to accept the title until after Mr. Brown's death in 1917. Thus, at an age when he had already begun to anticipate retirement, Mr. Kinsey was forced to assume the hardest job of his life.

Mr. Kinsey and the War Years

The full effects of Mr. Brown's enforced retirement were not immediately felt on campus. Plans which he and Mr. Kinsey had made for the orderly expansion of the curriculum were put into effect one by one, enrollments continued to rise, and finances remained sound. In 1914, a high-school department was established, shortly thereafter winning accreditation by the State. In that same year, a domestic science department was founded and given quarters in the newly-completed Domestic Science Building (now Arts-Law). In 1915, a department of agriculture was established under Professor Earl Price, using the W. E. Pinney Farm (now the Pinney-Purdue Farm) as an experimental farm. In 1916, a School of Bible Study was established under the direction of the minister of the local Christian Church, Mr. Pendleton. And, in 1917, work in engineering was expanded with the organization of a three-year school of engineering which offered courses in civil, electrical, and mechanical engineering. As far as the records show, the University was completely debt-free in 1915 except for the small debt that had been contracted in connection with the building of the Domestic Science Building.

Student life, too, was beginning to reflect a greater measure of sophistication. Sometime around 1910, brown and gold achieved the status of unofficial school colors, a symbol of "school spirit" which had apparently not been needed by the rugged individualists of earlier days. In 1911, the first yearbook, the *Record*, was published. In 1914, a monthly literary magazine called *The Torch* was founded. The magazine suspended publication after a few issues, but in the following year its name was taken over by a new weekly newspaper which managed to survive the many subsequent changes in the fortunes of the University and still serves as the campus newspaper. The year 1915 also saw the creation of a Students' Council which became a very influential body and played a major role in the confused events of the early Twenties.

In addition to these officially-recognized student activities, secret societies were being organized despite the strong disapproval of the administration. The first of these, founded as early as 1903, was the Alpha Epsilon fraternity, now a chapter of Tau Kappa Epsilon. In 1914 Phi Delta Psi fraternity, now a chapter of Phi Kappa Psi, was founded. Women students, who were more closely supervised than were the men, seem not to have been able to maintain any permanent secret organizations, although it would appear that there were a few ephemeral sororities during the period. More typically, the women organized clubs. Two of these clubs later developed into recognized sororities: the Owl Club, which became Alpha Phi Delta sorority, and the Roselle Club, which became Sigma Theta.

Intercollegiate athletics, which by now had become a consuming interest of students in most other American colleges and universities, were still under a ban at Valparaiso, but there was a well-developed program of intramural athletics, and occasionally teams from the campus played teams from the town or even from the surrounding area. The administration approved of athletics as such, as witness Mr. Kinsey's co-signing of a note by the Students' Council for a new gymnasium (1916). But both Mr. Brown and Mr. Kinsey felt that sound scholarship and intercollegiate athletics could not thrive side by side on the same campus.

In spite of all these outward signs of progress and prosperity things were not as they had been.[6] Shortly after Mr. Brown's enforced retirement, Mrs. Brown had called their young son, Henry Kinsey Brown, back to the campus to represent the family's interests in the management and to prepare himself for the day when he would take over the presidency. Kinsey Brown had no interest in educational administration and no great desire to become a college president. His interests were in banking and, at the time of his father's illness, he was just getting well established in the banking profession. It is likely that he knew of the plans which his father and Mr. Kinsey had made to turn the University over to an independent board of trustees, a plan which, if it were carried out, would probably leave him no place in the administration of the University. But in the circumstances, with his father ill and his mother anxious to have him come home, he had little choice and he joined Mr. Kinsey in the management of the University.

From the very outset there were frictions, probably inevitable in view of the great differences in age and outlook between the two men. Mr. Kinsey was concluding a career which had been eminently successful, and he naturally attributed his success to his adherence to principles which had been tested by the experience of more than thirty years. Young Mr. Brown, on the other hand, was convinced that higher education was entering a new era, an era for which the old University was ill-adapted and in which it could not survive unless it adjusted to the changing times. Although reluctant at first to have any part in the administration of the University, Mr. Brown became more and more convinced of the rightness of his views and more and more determined to re-shape the University in accordance with them.

Mr. Brown's determination to play an active role in determining University policy was encouraged by his mother, who had never favored the idea of turning the University over to a board of trustees, and by Miss Catherine Corboy, his father's long-time secretary. Mrs. Brown's attitude is understandable when it is remembered that the millions which her husband and Mr. Kinsey were said to have accumulated over the course of the years were almost wholly invested in the University property. Apart from this property, neither Mr. Brown nor Mr. Kinsey had any considerable private fortune—a fact which did not mean so much to the childless Kinseys but which meant quite a bit to Mrs. Brown, who had four children to consider.

Meanwhile, in 1914, war had broken out in Europe, and with each passing month its effects were felt more strongly on campus. Shortly before the outbreak of the war, some thirty-five foreign countries were represented in the student body. As one nation after another became involved in the war, students left to join the armed forces of their countries or were left stranded without funds on campus. Mr. Kinsey is reported to have spent several hundred dollars of his own money to help foreign students who were unable to get help from home. As the war dragged on and the finances of the University ran short, Mr. Kinsey spent still more of his private means on the University until, by the time of his retirement in 1919, he had only a very modest personal fortune left.

Despite the internal frictions and the war in Europe, there was a general atmosphere of hope on campus until 1917, "the year when everything happened." That year began hopefully enough—indeed it began on a note of high optimism. For after many years of opposition to the reorganization of the University, Mrs. Brown, in late 1916 or early 1917, gave her verbal consent to papers which would have conveyed the Brown and Kinsey interests in the University to a self-perpetuating board of trustees. In order to meet State requirements for accreditation, the management of the University then conducted a campaign to raise an endowment, and this campaign resulted in pledges of thirty thousand dollars, an amount sufficient at that time to win accreditation. On the strength of the success of this campaign, a tentative list of trustees was drawn up, and there remained only the formality of signing the transfer documents. This Mrs. Brown refused to do.

That, however, was only the beginning of trouble. In April of 1917, the United States declared war on Germany, and the war which had seemed so remote soon changed the whole atmosphere of the campus. Within six months after war was declared, more than thirteen hundred students left campus to enter the armed forces, and students in a government training program were quartered and drilled on the campus. In July, two dormitories, Eiss and Vineyard Halls, were destroyed in a spectacular fire. And on September 16, forty-four years to the day after he had assumed the presidency of the Northern Indiana Normal School, Mr. Henry Baker Brown died.

After the elder Mr. Brown's death, the conflicts of policy between Mr. Kinsey and Mr. Henry Kinsey Brown could no longer be altogether concealed. Secret organizations, while not yet officially sanctioned, functioned openly, and, in 1918, two new ones were founded: Gamma Phi sorority and Sigma Delta Kappa, a fraternity for law students. Although Mr. Brown's death had left the presidency vacant, Mr. Kinsey was not made president but acting president, the obvious intent being to elevate Mr. Kinsey Brown to the presidency at the opportune time. And all the while the University was losing enrollment.

By 1919, the enrollment was down to nineteen hundred students, the faculty had been decreased from 220 in 1916 to about a hundred, the number of departments had fallen to twelve, and two schools—the Agriculture School and School of Bible Studies—had been closed. Not all of these losses were the direct consequence of the War. Some of them, at least, must be ascribed to the failure of the University to satisfy state requirements for accreditation. But the declining fortunes of the University accentuated the differences between Mr. Kinsey and Mr. Brown. Finally, on May 1, 1919, the following note was sent to each member of the faculty:

To the Faculty:

Father Time keeps throwing on the screen of the moving picture of my life the shadow of the coming "seventy." I heed the warning and retire.

Your loyalty has been most noble, generous and devoted. No two people ever had more or better friends than Mrs. Kinsey and I. We could pay you no greater tribute.

Most respectfully,
OLIVER PERRY KINSEY

On the same day public notice of Mr. Kinsey's retirement was given in a short statement:

This is to advise you that the firm of Brown and Kinsey has been dissolved by mutual consent, Mr. Kinsey retiring from the firm and from the University.

It would be impossible to express in words your many kindnesses and favors in the many years of our association.

Henry Kinsey Brown, son of the former President Henry Baker Brown, assumes charge of the business and we bespeak for the University the continuance of your good will.

Yours very truly,
BROWN AND KINSEY
Per Oliver P. Kinsey

Mr. Kinsey was now past seventy years of age, and his personal fortune had been largely depleted in his attempts to keep the University going through the war years. Although the terms of the dissolution of the firm were never made public, it appears that Mr. Kinsey gave his half-interest and whatever money the firm owed him to the Brown family in return for their agreeing to negotiate a loan to cover whatever indebtedness the firm owed to third parties. Shortly after leaving the University, Mr. Kinsey established homes in Freeport, Ohio, and in Florida. In later years he periodically returned to Valparaiso for visits. He died in Florida on February 21, 1931, but in the summer his body was returned to Valparaiso for burial in Graceland Cemetery, near those of Mr. Brown and Professor Bogarte and Professor Carver, his associates in the days of Valparaiso's greatness. His last service to the University was an endorsement of the then-new Lutheran administration.

Of the faculty and staff who served the University in Mr. Kinsey's day, only five are still actively associated with the University: Mrs. Katharine E. Bowden, who was first appointed to the faculty in 1913 and later returned to serve as librarian for many years until her retirement in 1949, when she was appointed to her present position of university archivist; Mr. and Mrs. Jay Garrison, who began their long association with the university restaurants in 1917; Professor Virgil E. Berry, who served as professor of law from 1918 until his appointment as emeritus professor in 1958; and Dr. John W. Morland, registrar of the University, 1919–1921, professor (1925) and dean (1928–54) of law, now professor and dean emeritus. Three other veterans of Mr. Kinsey's administration who gave many years of service to his successors and to the Lutheran administration were Mr. Myers E. Zimmermann (appointed 1915, died 1954); Miss Catherine Corboy, Mr. Brown's secretary, who served the Lutheran University Association at first as office manager and later for many years as alumni secretary; and Miss Elizabeth Anna Marie Rechenberg, now retired, for many years instructor in botany and German.

NOTES

1. Cecil Loar Bigelow, *A History of Valparaiso University from 1875 to 1925*, p. 32.
2. *The Boston Transcript*, November 28, 1903.
3. George Kennan, "Cost of Living," *McClure's Magazine*, XXX (March, 1908), 639-650.
4. *Collier's Magazine*, March 14, 1914.
5. University Catalogue, 1914-1915. Compilations by Mrs. Bowden.
6. Even at this writing (1958) there is still much disagreement on the causes of the difficulties which developed in the administration of the University. Stimpson, whose history of the University up to this time is an excellent and unbiased account, was deeply involved in the events which grew out of these difficulties and must be read in the light of this involvement. The author has interviewed more than a dozen townspeople and members of the faculty who recall these days and the account which he gives is an attempt to approximate the truth.

CHAPTER IV

A Time of Troubles

1919–1925

THE UNIVERSITY as Mr. Brown and Mr. Kinsey had fashioned it was, perhaps, too perfectly adapted to the needs of a particular age to survive the passing of that age. It would, therefore, be something less than fair to ascribe all of the University's difficulties in the years following Mr. Kinsey's retirement to inept leadership. But there can be little doubt that the men who succeeded Mr. Kinsey in the presidency were inadequate to the needs of the University in the critical years between 1919 and 1925. Two of the presidents during this period were, however well-intentioned they may have been, simply incompetent. Two of them were elderly men who lacked the vigor to spark a reorganization of the University. The ablest of them was, in effect, an interim president. And over all of them hung the uncertainty of a confused proprietorship situation which was not finally resolved until the Lutheran University Association acquired what was left of the University in 1925. The story of these years is, therefore, the story of a painful lingering illness which came close to proving fatal.

Henry Kinsey Brown, President
May, 1919–July, 1920

Mr. Kinsey had managed his retirement from the administration so tactfully that few people were aware that his withdrawal had been precipitated by deep and irreconcilable differences between him and his successor, Mr. Henry Kinsey Brown. The new president, accordingly, took office in an atmosphere of good will and great expectations.[1] Although still very young, the new president was well liked and, by some, highly respected. "Without a doubt," said his father's long-time secretary, Miss Corboy, "the new president's most prized inheritance from his distinguished father is the forward looking thoughts that are so necessary in the make-up of the head of a university."

It was President Brown's conviction that the University which he had inherited could be restored to its former greatness if it abandoned its "off-beat" policies and practices and modeled itself after the more prestigious state and private universities which appeared to be enjoying such vigorous growth in the years immediately following the war. Physically, this meant renovating the campus, which had become shabby and run-down during the war years when money had simply not been available for proper maintenance. One of his first projects as president, therefore, was a program of campus renovation. Necessary as this project was, it could not be financed out of current income. Its cost increased the debt which the Brown family had incurred in its settlement with Mr. Kinsey.

But it seemed to Mr. Brown that it would take more than physical improvement to make the University attractive to the kind of student that was shopping about for an education after the war. There was a considerable number of mature veterans who appreciated the democratic spirit, the lack of class distinctions, the simple social life, and the no-nonsense atmosphere which had been the pride of the University in the days of its greatness; but the tone of the college-going generation of that day was set by the better-educated, more sophisticated young men and women who were later to find their prophet and apologist in Mr. F. Scott Fitzgerald. It was to this group that Mr. Brown attempted to appeal, and, in the hope of bringing them to Valparaiso, he abandoned or reversed many of the most honored policies of his father. What Mr. Brown apparently did not realize was that, in attempting to compete with institutions supported by huge endowments or by appropriations from the public treasury, he was accepting an impossible handicap.

To Mr. Brown's credit, it must be said that he realized, as some of his critics did not, that the University could not survive without changing to meet the new conditions of a new age. Some of the criticism which was later directed against his administration would seem to have been motivated not so much by disagreement with the nature of the changes as by the very fact of change.

On May 10, 1919, shortly before Mr. Kinsey left the campus,

President Brown appeared at a meeting of the Alpha Epsilon fraternity, the oldest of the illegal secret organizations, and gave official recognition to fraternities and sororities.[2] The question of the value of such organizations on a college campus is one which has been debated for more than a century, and it will not be argued here. But the act itself, and especially its timing, were profoundly significant both on campus and among the alumni, for it reversed one of the most vigorously enforced policies of the former administration and clearly revealed a radical change in the philosophy of the University. As a direct consequence of this act, five sororities and eight fraternities were organized or officially recognized within the following year. Among those which had been organized previously but now received official recognition were Alpha Epsilon and Phi Delta Psi fraternities, Sigma Delta Kappa legal fraternity, and Alpha Phi, Gamma Phi, and Sigma Theta sororities. Of the newly-founded organizations, four have survived until the present: Alpha Xi sorority, Kappa Iota Pi fraternity (now a chapter of Phi Delta Theta), Kappa Delta Pi fraternity (now a chapter of Pi Kappa Alpha), and Sigma Delta Chi fraternity (now a chapter of Theta Chi).

The establishment of Greek-letter organizations effected a notable change in the tenor of student activities on campus. The old literary and debating societies disappeared, and student social life came more and more to center on the fraternities and sororities. Dancing, which had been forbidden under the former administration, came to be the favorite social activity; and, since most of the dances were fraternity or sorority affairs, the unorganized student began to suffer a degree of social ostracism. And in the absence of any regulations or requirements governing the Greek-letter organizations, some of these organizations set no particular requirements either of character or scholarship.

A second major reversal of traditional policy came with the appointment of Mr. George E. Keogan as director of athletics. This was not quite so radical a break with the past as was the recognition of secret societies, for the University had been edging toward a more elaborate athletic program for several years. As early as 1916, a basketball team had been assembled from among the more talented intramural players for the first intercollegiate game in the University's history, against the Chicago YMCA

Training School, and, by the 1917–1918 season, the basketball team was playing a full schedule of games. Mr. Keogan's appointment, however, signified a new emphasis upon athletics and aroused immediate opposition from most of the faculty, the greater part of the student body, and many alumni. And the program which Mr. Keogan initiated, whatever its success may have been in terms of school spirit and favorable advertisement, added to the financial problem of the University by running a deficit of several thousand dollars.

At first, the new policies seemed to pay off. Enrollments showed a gratifying increase at the beginning of the 1919–1920 school year and, with the government engaged in a program of rehabilitation for wounded veterans, there appeared to be good prospects of a still greater rise, since Valparaiso was one of the institutions to which veterans were being sent for rehabilitation training.

But, under the surface, new troubles were brewing. The enrollment resumed its decline in the second quarter. Since nothing substantial had been done to improve faculty salaries or instructional facilities, trouble developed with the accrediting agencies. The University was rapidly losing prestige and was in danger of losing all recognition in the academic world. Two factions began to contend for control of policy, the one favoring the new president's "reforms," the other favoring a return to the policies of the former administration.

President Brown spent much of his time off campus, and there was much speculation as to the reasons for his absences. Some thought that he was trying to secure financial aid from men of wealth, some thought that he was trying to sell the University to some sectarian group, some thought that he was negotiating with the government for more veterans in the rehabilitation program. The effect of these rumors was to shake public confidence in the financial condition of the University and to raise questions about the possibility of imminent bankruptcy. Students became concerned about the acceptability of their credits in other institutions if the University should be forced to close, and members of the faculty began to cast about for positions in other institutions which promised greater security.

President Brown's efforts to interest men of wealth in the institution or to sell the property were unsuccessful, and the indebtedness continued to increase. Meanwhile, Mr. Brown had antagonized the alumni by his policies; he had lost the confidence of his faculty; and he had lost faith in his own abilities to cope with the crisis into which the University had been plunged. In the hope of salvaging the situation, he secured the services of a man who was reputed to be an able educator and a brilliant administrator—Daniel Russel Hodgdon, A.B., M.A., M.S., Sc.D., LL.D., M.D., Ph.D., at that time president of the Hanneman Medical College.[3] Dr. Hodgdon became dean of the faculty in the summer of 1920.

By that summer, the University's indebtedness stood at almost a quarter of a million dollars, an increase of $125,000 since Mr. Kinsey's retirement. There seemed to be no prospect of liquidating this debt or of avoiding additional indebtedness under the proprietorship arrangement, and so, on July 20, 1920, plans were released for a reorganization of the University.[4] Under these plans, a board of trustees consisting of prominent business men was created, with an executive committee consisting of three prominent citizens of Porter County. Mr. Brown resigned as president and became business manager and registrar (later bursar), Mr. Hodgdon succeeding to the presidency.[5] Provisions were made to conduct a campaign to raise one million dollars among townspeople and alumni, of which $150,000 was to go to the Brown family for their interests in the University; the balance was to be set aside as an endowment. Arrangements were also made at this time to give Mrs. Henry Baker Brown an annuity of five thousand dollars. It was provided that, when these conditions were met, the University would cease to be the property of the Brown family. It would become what Mr. Brown and Mr. Kinsey had long ago hoped to make it: a self-perpetuating, self-governing institution. The hope was that under this new arrangement alumni and townspeople would be willing support the University, since it would no longer be a private corporation, operated for profit.

Daniel Russel Hodgdon, President
July, 1920–April 23, 1921

President Hodgdon began his administration under two almost insurmountable handicaps: he had no understanding at all of the history and traditions of the University which he had been called to serve, and he was generally believed to be a kind of "front man" for Mr. Brown. Under the best of circumstances these handicaps might have proved fatal to a president. But Mr. Hodgdon did not take office under the best of circumstances.

From his predecessor, Mr. Hodgdon inherited a feud with the alumni which had developed over athletic policy and a quarrel in which Mr. Brown had involved himself with the state department of public instruction. One of the department's inspectors had written a report which was critical of the way the University was being run, and Mr. Brown had threatened to make an issue of the report in the next election. Soon after he assumed office, Mr. Hodgdon became involved in an argument with Professor Neet, the head of the education department, and Mr. Edward Anderson, the acting registrar, over the advanced standing of a student. This argument resulted in the resignations of Professor Neet and Mr. Anderson.[6]

Mr. Hodgdon succeeded in weathering these early difficulties, however, and by a series of wise faculty appointments restored a measure of confidence in his administration. Among the new members of the faculty whom he appointed were Mr. G. J. Borst, who succeeded Professor Neet as head of the education department; Mr. Hugh C. Muldoon, who succeeded Professor Wisner as dean of pharmacy; and Mr. John W. Morland, who resumed the registrar's office after a summer in the East. The announcement of these appointments, together with a fair rise in enrollment and the announcement of plans for an endowment campaign, created a new atmosphere of optimism on the campus.

President Hodgdon had great ambitions for the University and hoped to make it a great industrial institution. His plans included a very ambitious building program involving the purchase of the property around Sager's Lake as the site of a new campus. It was his hope that wealthy industrialists would become the major supporters of his new industrial university.

President Hodgdon continued the athletic program that had been initiated by his predecessor and counted heavily on the advertising which he hoped would result from a successful season. He also continued President Brown's social program and, in the process, became involved in a violent dispute with the Student Council. Feeling became increasingly bitter, and the two factions that had developed during the previous year became irreconcilable.

On January 1, 1921, Mr. Brown resigned as bursar of the University. With his resignation, the last official connection between the Brown family and Valparaiso University was severed. The family retained a financial interest in the University, however, for the terms under which they had agreed to turn the University over to an autonomous board of trustees had not yet been met. But it was hoped that with the withdrawal of Mr. Brown from the management there might be better prospects of raising an endowment. The campaign for endowment funds was placed in the hands of Mr. Frank Converse, who came to Valparaiso to manage the campaign. He did not have much success in organizing the alumni, but the board of trustees did succeed in launching the campaign. An enthusiastic meeting was held in East Hall and more than $100,000 was pledged to the endowment fund.[7] Mr. Brown announced at this meeting that the Brown family had withdrawn their claim of $150,000 and would give their interests to the University. President Hodgdon announced that the board of trustees had secured an option on the Sager's Lake property as the site for future campus development. Mr. Kinsey sent a telegram from his retirement home in Florida, approving the plan to make the University an endowed institution. All in all, it appeared that the University was finally on its way.

The auspicious opening of the endowment campaign was misleading, however, as the hoped-for pledges from industries failed to materialize. Mr. Converse repeatedly announced that the million-dollar goal had practically been reached, and President Hodgdon brought back glowing reports from the East about money that would soon be coming in from wealthy industrialists. But very little actual money came in, and it became increasingly obvious that the campaign would fail. Meanwhile, nothing was being done educationally, socially, or financially to ensure the future of the University if the campaign should fail.

Campus life during Mr. Hodgdon's administration was one big ball for the more irresponsible element in the student body, which was harried by protests, criticisms, and jockeyings for power among the student leaders. For many of the students, the big event of the year was the football game with Harvard, an account of which has been written by the late Myers E. Zimmerman, for many years faculty manager of athletics:

Valpo electrified the athletic world and telegraphic wires sizzled throughout the whole nation when 13 Valpo footballers held 35 Harvard men to a scoreless tie to the end of the third quarter. Our lack of reserve strength, plus injuries to our great and highly-respected Thomas Dandelet, lost us the game in the fourth quarter 21 - 0.

Immediately after the Harvard game, our coach contacted the Harvard coach to extend his congratulations on winning. The Harvard coach reached into his pocket and handed our coach a telegram, adding that he had received it several hours before the game but did not like to divert his attention from the job at hand. The telegram was signed: "A Valpo Student," and briefly it stated that two men on the Valpo team were not students at Valpo but were picked up enroute from the steel mills in Gary, Indiana.[8]

But bread and circuses were not enough to divert the attention of the faculty and the more serious-minded students from what was happening on campus. Investigations conducted by some of the student leaders disclosed that Mr. Hodgdon's impressive list of degrees boiled down to a respectable A.B. from Bates College and a residue of doubtful degrees from institutions which gave degrees on slight pretext or none at all. Attempts by Mr. Hodgdon to silence his critics in the student body provoked almost open rebellion and aroused the concern of the faculty. Finally, the Student Council prepared a resolution requesting that the president be asked to resign and sent it to the Board of Trustees.

Meanwhile, in March, 1921, the *Moline* [Illinois] *Daily Dispatch* had carried a report on the possible relocation of Valparaiso University in Rock Island, Illinois. According to this report, the people of Valparaiso had failed to subscribe sufficiently to the University's endowment fund and, as a result, the management of the University had decided to plan its removal. This report came as news to the trustees and, taken with the troubles on campus, constituted the last straw. On April 23, 1921, the executive committee of the board dismissed President Hodgdon from office.

Had this been the end of the story, the Hodgdon administration could be written off as one unfortunate year in the history of the University. But the discharged president retaliated with attacks upon the integrity of the University of which the following paragraph from a letter to the Board of Trustees may be taken as a fair sample:

There has existed a wide difference of opinion among both trustees and teachers as to these activities [fraternities and sororities], and in addition to this, there has been fostered by faculty and outsiders, bolshevism, communism, and other cults, the practice of which is destructive to American ideals and principles. Unsigned letters have mysteriously come to my desk, warning me against the principles I have preached; namely, loyalty to Americanism and American industrial life as the basis of American citizenship. I have been visited by so-called "Reds" and foreign-born members of organizations claiming to be backed by strong outside and inside influences in the attempt to force me to proclaim myself against doctrines of Americanism and industrial education. Such representations, undoubtedly, are part of a deeplaid plan to make Valparaiso the center of radical teaching. It is possible that much of the unrest of college life today is due to these destructive outside influences, aimed to destroy the basic principles upon which this government is founded.

These lurid charges created a sensation in the press and were widely reported. Naturally, they found many willing believers, for this was the heyday of the reconstructed Ku Klux Klan, and the excesses of Attorney-General A. Mitchell Palmer's Red-hunt were still a very recent memory. The Valparaiso post of the American Legion and veterans studying on campus under the government's rehabilitation program issued statements certifying to the University's ideological chastity, but the damage had been done. Many of the alumni, who heard only the charges and not their refutation, turned against their alma mater and thereafter had little or nothing to do with her. Even a Republican administration's renewal of the University's contract for the rehabilitation of veterans did no more than assure those who were already favorably disposed toward the University that charges of disloyalty were groundless. Thus to the heavy burden of debt and the discouragement produced by two unsuccessful campaigns for an endowment was added the popular impression that the University had been taken over by a crowd of bolshevist rowdies. For leadership in this almost desperate moment, the trustees turned to the most respected member of the faculty, Dr. John E. Roessler.

John Edward Roessler, President
April 23, 1921-May 25, 1922

Milo Jesse Bowman, President
May 25, 1922-Jan. 1, 1923

President Roessler was already looking forward to retirement when he was called upon to restore the damaged fortunes of the

University. Quietly and without fanfare, he proceeded to restore confidence in the administration and pride in the accomplishments of the institution which he had served for more than a quarter of a century. Operating as first among equals, he directed the faculty back to its proper work of teaching. To the students he gave assurances that there would be no reversal of the policies of his two predecessors. The athletic program would continue, but in a deemphasized form, and fraternities and sororities would not be forced to disband, although they would have to accept reasonable control from the administration. The old policy of democracy was to be restored, and economy was again to be the rule at Valparaiso.[9]

Everyone recognized that, in the long run, the only hope for the survival of the University lay in finding some large and dependable source of financial support. The Board of Trustees, therefore, announced that an effort would be made to float a bond issue among alumni and business men to take the debts of the University out of the hands of the Brown family and others who were not particularly interested in the welfare of the institution, and place them in the hands of the alumni. At the same time, a more vigorous search was undertaken for a possible buyer. Nothing came of either of these efforts, however, and the financial deterioration of the University continued through Dr. Roessler's administration, carrying with it not only the short-run difficulty of maintaining staff and facilities on an inadequate budget but also the long-run threat of collapse in the face of what had become, by now, an urgent need for accreditation.

Dr. Roessler had no illusions about his financial acumen. He had been called upon to re-establish internal peace and quiet, and by the end of the academic year he had succeeded in doing so. He therefore went ahead with his delayed plans for retirement, despite the urgings of the faculty that he remain in office. While the trustees searched for a new president, the able dean of the law school, Professor Milo Jesse Bowman, served as president, continuing through the remainder of 1922 the conciliatory program of Dr. Roessler.

Dean Bowman was different in several ways from the usual Valparaiso faculty member of his day. First and most significantly, he was not an alumnus of the University. Secondly, he was a native-born Hoosier. And, thirdly, he insisted, as dean of the law school, upon conforming to the accepted practices of other respected institutions. Born in Madison, Indiana, in 1875, Dean Bowman earned both his A.B. and his M.A. at Hanover College, a highly-respected Presbyterian liberal arts college. Following the usual practice of his day, he read law in preparation for a legal career. After several years as a practicing attorney, he succeeded Dean DeMotte in 1907 as dean of the school of law, a position which he continued to occupy until 1928, when he joined the faculty of the Indiana University law school. As president of the University in 1922 and as vice-president from 1922 until 1925, Dean Bowman played a major role in the struggle, at times apparently hopeless, to keep the University intact until a purchaser could be found. Years later, after his retirement from the Indiana faculty, Dean Bowman returned to Valparaiso to spend his last years as a member of the law school faculty.

Two other men who stood faithfully by the University in its time of troubles should also receive special mention. These men were A. A. Williams and B. F. Williams.[10]

There have been few more colorful figures in the history of the University than Professor Alpheus Americus ("A-Square") Williams. He had come to the Normal School in the dual capacity of student and instructor in 1890. For five years he taught in the commercial department. Then, in 1895, he became president and owner of the Southern Iowa Scientific Institute. In 1902 he returned to Valparaiso as professor of mathematics. Professor Williams was thoroughly committed to Henry Baker Brown's philosophy of hard work, democracy, and economy, and it was largely because of his well-known loyalty to these ideals that he was appointed vice-president of the University at the same time that Dr. Roessler was appointed president. Later Professor Williams relinquished the vice-presidency, but he served as dean of the college of arts and sciences until after the transfer of the administration to Lutheran control in 1925. By the students of his day, Professor Williams was highly respected as an able teacher and a firm disciplinarian. It was the unconventionality of his dress and his casual attitude toward his academic rank that furnished the material for the legends which have gathered around his memory. Older alumni recall the tall, husky dean of the college of arts and sciences striding up College Avenue to his classes, still wearing the overalls that he had been wearing at work in his orchard.

Quite different from "A-Square" in everything but name was Professor Benjamin Franklin Williams. Born in Turney, Missouri, in 1866, B. F. Williams came to the Normal School in 1891, finished high school, and was graduated in the Scientific and Classic courses. President Brown had been much impressed by his energies and abilities and helped him to finance postgraduate work at Harvard, from which he received the A.B. degree in 1898. For a few years after his graduation, he served as professor of literature at the University, then resumed graduate work at Cornell and Harvard. In 1909 he returned to campus as professor of English and served in that capacity until 1924. For years, Professor Williams, Professor Carver, and Professor Hoover constituted a small core of scholars in a faculty which was more noted for teaching than for scholarship. Professor Williams was also genuinely interested in student activities, and his obvious respect for student interests won him a special place in the affections of the student body.

Of the present faculty, two men trace their service to the University back to the Roessler-Bowman era: Moses W. Uban, professor of mechanical engineering, and Dr. Albert F. Scribner, vice-president for business and finance. Dr. Scribner became assistant registrar in 1922, registrar in 1925, business manager in 1934, and vice-president in 1956. His contributions to the growth and development of the University have been many, significant, and largely anonymous.

Horace Martin Evans, President
Jan. 1, 1923-Jan. 3, 1926

Dr. H. M. Evans had been a member of the Normal School faculty in the 1890's. Later, he had served for a number of years in the United States Public Health Service. Primarily, though, and despite his degree in medicine, he was a business man, and the job which he was called upon to do as president was a business man's job: to keep the University going while efforts were made to find a buyer.

Hardly had the new president settled himself in office when tragedy struck the campus. On February 20, 1923, the Old College Building was ravaged by a fire which reduced it to a mass of rubble. There is considerable evidence to suggest that the fire was of incendiary origin. So nearly bankrupt was the University that it could not afford to clear away the rubble, which remained as an ugly blot on the campus until 1926. And although the Board of Trustees authorized the immediate building of a new administration building, nothing came of it.

The campus was hardly the sort of property a president would want to try to peddle to potential buyers in those days. In addition to its deplorable physical condition, there was the uncertainty of its financial condition. Henry Kinsey Brown still held a lien on the property as a result of the failure of the University to pay off its indebtedness to the Brown family. Some of the dormitories were not University property in any sense of the term, for they were held by Mr. Brown through the Valparaiso Realty Company. And since the University was unaccredited, it had no standing at all on the American educational scene.

Nevertheless, attempts were made to interest various churches and fraternal organizations in acquiring the property, among them the Elks, the Moose, and the Presbyterian Church. Late in 1923, the campus was startled by reports that the national organization of the Ku Klux Klan had taken over the University and planned to make it the official educational institution of the Klan.[11] But the excitement soon died down when it became apparent that Indiana Klan officials had acted without authorization from the national headquarters. Unfortunately, for years to come the University had the reputation of having once been a Klan school, and even today the report persists. The truth of the matter is that the University did come very close to becoming a Klan school, for officials of the University and state officials of the Klan had reached agreement on terms of sale. But the deal was never consummated, and the University never actually became the property of the Klan.

In the early part of 1925, it seemed that the future of the University had finally been settled in an eminently satisfactory way when the State Legislature approved a bill to make the University one of the state normal schools. Northwestern Indiana, despite its growing population, had no state-supported teachers' college, and there was much support of the idea of the state's adopting Valparaiso for that purpose. But Governor Ed Jackson killed the bill with a pocket veto, and morale on campus hit its all-time low.

The remarkable thing about these years is that, despite the difficulties that plagued the University administration, the morale of the student body did not seriously deteriorate until about 1925. The faculty, of course, knew more about what was going on, and from 1924 onward there was a steady exodus of faculty members as pessimism gave way to a growing feeling of hopelessness. But the students still had the social life of their fraternities and sororities, the possibility of getting an adequate education from competent teachers if they wanted it, and the extra-curricular activities which went on irrespective of changes of administration.

Perhaps the single most important morale booster during these difficult years was the basketball team. In 1923, William Shadoan had succeeded Earl J. Goheen as athletic director and head coach of basketball and football. Prior to his coming to Valparaiso, Shadoan had served as assistant coach of the famous "Praying Colonels" of Centre College and, upon coming to Valparaiso, he proceeded to build the athletic teams up to the level of Keogan's day. The most famous of Shadoan's teams was the "Victory Five."

Starting a twenty-eight-game schedule after the Christmas holidays, Shadoan's men took on the best teams in the Midwest. Under the leadership of Captain Millard Anderson, the team won twenty-four of its twenty-eight contests, twenty-two of these in a row. This established a consecutive winning record in inter-collegiate basketball for one season—a record all the more amazing because the same five men performed in almost every minute of every game.[12]

But winning basketball teams could not cure the radical illness from which the University was suffering. Teetering on the verge of bankruptcy, discredited as an educational institution by the events of the past six years, faced with the probability of losing most of its faculty, and likely to lose the greater part of its enrollment, the University might not have opened its 1925–1926 academic year had it not been for the sudden and unexpected appearance of a purchaser. That purchaser was the Lutheran University Association, a newly organized association of Lutheran pastors and laymen, mostly from Fort Wayne, who had a great deal of faith, a few thousand dollars, and no idea of what they were getting into.

NOTES

1. *The Valparaiso Messenger*, Nov. 4, 1919.
2. *The Valparaiso Vidette*, May 11, 1919.
3. *Ibid.*, June 15, 1920.

4. *Ibid.*, July 20, 1920.

5. *The Valparaiso Messenger*, Aug. 10, 1920.

6. *Ibid.*, May 8, 1921.

7. *Ibid.*, Jan. 26, 1921.

8. Richard P. Koenig, ed., *The Crusaders*, Athletic Yearbook of Valparaiso University, 1948, pp. 19-20.

9. Bigelow, *op. cit.*, p. 57.

10. Biographical data on Professor A. A. Williams and Professor B. F. Williams were supplied by Mrs. Bowden.

11. *The Valparaiso Vidette*, August 15, 1923.

12. Koenig, *op. cit.*, p. 18.

CHAPTER V

A New Beginning

1925–1930

VALPARAISO UNIVERSITY officially became a Lutheran University when it opened its first academic year under Lutheran administration on September 28, 1925. But for the first year or two, it was Lutheran in little more than name. Two streams of history met in the reorganized University and, until the eddies calmed, the Lutheranism of the institution was to be more of a hope than a reality.

The first of these streams was the still-vigorous tradition of economy and democratic education which the University inherited from the Old School. The more dedicated students and instructors who remained on the dismal campus of 1925 were those who still believed that poverty need not inhibit learning, and that it was the impression of teacher upon student that really counted. The less dedicated realized the dollar value of a college diploma—any diploma—in this post-war period. And in the town, interested spectators waited patiently for signs of life at the institution which had brought fame and business to the community.

The other stream can be traced back to the founding of a little Lutheran college in Perry County, Missouri, in 1839. The fathers of the "Evangelical Lutheran Synod of Missouri, Ohio, and Other States" (now The Lutheran Church—Missouri Synod) had hoped that their little college would attract general students as well as theological candidates.[1] But their hopes did not materialize, and the college ultimately became Concordia Seminary in St. Louis.

The hope that some day the Church would have a university of its own never quite died, but through all of the second half of the nineteenth century and the first decade of the twentieth century the Church was so involved in serving the thousands of German immigrants who were pouring into the United States that it

77

could spare neither time nor funds for higher education. Instead, it concentrated on the establishment of a strong parochial school system. Even in urban centers it was impossible to muster support for academies which might have been a step toward higher education. In St. Louis three academies were established in the course of time, but each lasted only a short while. Walther College (1887–1917), which was really an academy, lasted a little longer, but it never received any considerable amount of support.

The ferment of higher education for the laity boiled briefly to the surface again in the 1870's in connection with the founding of the confederation of synods known as the Synodical Conference. The Conference was to be an expression of unity in faith and of co-operation in educational and charitable endeavors.[2] A scheme was considered for uniting in erecting a university in the neighborhood of Chicago. But the Conference became involved in doctrinal controversies and took no action on the proposal.[3]

Serious interest in the establishment of a Lutheran university began to develop around the time of the First World War as increasing numbers of young Lutherans began attending state colleges and universities. These young people constituted a serious problem to the church, a *Lutheran Witness* editor declared. Their close association with others of different faiths or no faith at all was, in his judgment, detrimental. He considered the typical university teaching of that day unsettling to religious convictions, and he asserted that a professor could undo in half an hour what it had taken years to build up.[4]

To cope with this growing problem, efforts were made in two directions: on the one hand, Lutheran chapels were erected on or near the campuses of the state universities, and pastors of nearby Lutheran churches were appointed to care for Lutheran students on small campuses; on the other hand, the idea of establishing a Lutheran university was revived. In 1913, the Atlantic District of the Missouri Synod resolved to recommend to the 1914 meeting of Synod that it send two or more graduates of the St. Louis seminary to some university "here or abroad, to continue their studies so as to better fit them for teaching at our higher institutions of learning."[5] General sentiment within the church, however, is indicated by Synod's response that, while it recognized the need for highly trained professors in its institutions, it could not recommend the manner in which these men should be secured. The same convention declined to designate for the establishment of a Lutheran university the funds from a proposed offering to celebrate the quadricentennial of the posting of the Ninety-Five Theses by Luther.[6]

By the end of the First World War, however, two centers of activity in behalf of a Lutheran university were breathing new life into the old hope—one in the Atlantic District of Synod and the other in the Iowa District. In the Atlantic District, a Lutheran Education Society had been formed. Two of its leaders were Dr. G. Sihler, professor of Latin at New York University, and the Rev. William Schoenfeld of New York City. In a paper before the Atlantic District convention at Schenectady in May, 1919, Pastor Schoenfeld suggested that "we seriously keep before us the task of establishing at the earliest possible opportunity a Lutheran university."[7]

Others in the church were less enthusiastic about the idea. Most articulate of the critics was Dr. Theodore Graebner, one of the editors of *The Lutheran Witness* and a professor at Concordia Seminary, St. Louis. In rebuttal to Pastor Schoenfeld's paper, Dr. Graebner questioned the propriety of the church's sponsoring an endeavor for "social betterment." Preaching was the mission of the church, he pointed out. It would also be discriminatory to maintain educational opportunities from which many of the young people of the church would have to be excluded because of poor intellectual ability.[8]

By way of practical difficulties, Dr. Graebner listed the cost, which he estimated at five million dollars plus another five million for endowment; the barrier of distance if only one university could be established in Synod; the slight benefit Lutheran university training would confer upon the student whose morals had already been damaged by attendance at a non-Lutheran secondary school (hence, the priority of secondary schools as an educational effort); a doubt as to whether "academic freedom" could be maintained in a Christian university; the problem of securing a faculty which would conform to "our standards"; the difficulty of meeting state standards in the fields of biology, psychology, and other areas where science and religion seemed to disagree; and a possibly disappointing enrollment since Lutheran students could not be compelled to attend a Lutheran university. Assuming, however, that these hurdles could be surmounted, Dr. Graebner felt that free associations of pastors and laymen ought to be encouraged to establish schools of higher learning, just as such free associations had established Lutheran hospitals.[9]

One such "free association" had already been formed by a group of pastors and laymen in the Midwest, chiefly from Iowa and Minnesota. Of the 114 men who met in Mankato, Minnesota, on June 19, 1917, twenty-nine signed up as members of the association about to be created. On July 26, eleven of their number received a Minnesota charter as incorporators of the National Lutheran Education Association.[10] The purpose of this association was "to establish an activity which would foster and promote educational interests under the auspices of the church, similar to the organization known as the National Education Association in the public schools, but looking especially to the education of Lutheran youth." [11] The N.L.E.A. proposed to construct, establish, maintain, operate, and conduct Lutheran educational institutions in the United States; to organize the course of study, set tuition fees, acquire property, and solicit funds for the institutions.[12] Membership could be held by any member of the Synodical Conference over twenty-one years of age upon payment of a five-dollar annual membership. The president of the Association, and for many years its guiding spirit, was Mr. Bernhard P. Holst, of Boone, Iowa.

The Association received official endorsement from Synod at the triennial convention in Detroit in June, 1920. Already by January, 1919, the Association had listed 2,750 members and the treasurer reported $16,500 in Liberty Bonds and a total of $100,000 in cash and pledges. In the following two years, membership increased to 5,880 through the efforts of the Rev. W. F. Georg, the association's field manager. Subscriptions amounted to $140,000 and activity was begun on the Pacific Coast and in the East.[13] Strangely, though, no definite action was ever taken toward the establishment of a school. In 1919, the Association was offered the chance to acquire Bethany College in Mankato, but the matter was dropped.

The history of the N.L.E.A. is not, in itself, a part of the history of the University. But the solicitations of the N.L.E.A. among thousands of Lutheran people for several years undoubtedly stirred

The Campus Early in the Twentieth Century

The Old College Building (in the center of the picture) stood on the site of the present Old Campus flagpole.

The Old Law School Building

This building, which stood at 355 Greenwich Street, was razed around 1940.

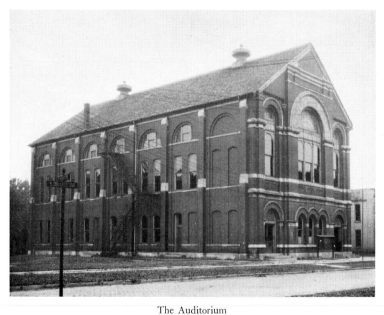

The Auditorium

Built in 1892, the Auditorium was destroyed in a spectacular fire in November, 1956.

Altruria Hall

Lembke Hall

This picture also shows some of the weathered frame buildings which were razed in the early years of the Lutheran administration.

Science Hall and the Medical Building

The Arts-Law Building (originally the Domestic Science Building)

Henry Kinsey Brown, M.A.
President of the University, 1919–1920.

Daniel Russel Hodgdon, A.B., LL.D.
President of the University, 1920–1921.

John Edward Roessler, A.M., Litt.D.
President of the University, 1921–1922.

Milo Jesse Bowman, A.M., LL.B., LL.D.
*Dean of the School of Law, 1907–1927,
and President of the University, 1922.*

Horace Martin Evans, M.D.
President of the University, 1923–1926.

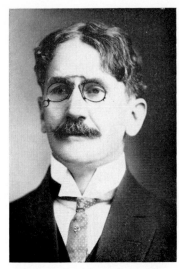

Benjamin Franklin Williams, M.A.
Professor of English, 1909–1924.

Alpheus Americus Williams, A.M., Sc.D.
*Professor of Mathematics and Dean of
the College of Liberal Arts, 1924–1927.*

John Wallace Morland, J.D.
Dean of the School of Law, 1928–1955.

The Rev. William Henry Theodore Dau,
D.D.
President of the University, 1926–1929.

The Rev. John C. Baur
*Business Manager of the University and
Acting President, 1926, 1927–1928.*

The Rev. George F. Schutes

Herman A. Duemling, M.D.
*President of the Lutheran University
Association, 1925–1927.*

The Rev. Paul. F. Miller, LL.D.
Long-time secretary of the Lutheran University Association.

The Rev. Frederick William Kroencke, Ph.D.
Professor of Philosophy and Religion. Dean of the University and of the College of Liberal Arts, 1928–1936.

The Rev. Henry Herman Kumnick, A.B., LL.B.
Dean of Students, 1927–1941, later head of the Department of Religion.

Albert Frank Scribner, M.A., LL.D.
Assistant Registrar, 1922–1925; Registrar, 1925–1958; Business Manager, 1934–1957; Vice-President for Business and Finance since 1956.

a grass-roots awareness of the need of a Lutheran university and thus prepared the way for the work of the Lutheran University Association. In addition, the prestige which the N. L.E.A. enjoyed as a Synodically-approved association was shared by the Lutheran University Association in its earliest and most difficult years.

But the social situation in 1925 was perhaps as important as were any organized efforts within the church in consolidating support of the idea of a Lutheran university. The decade after the first World War was a time of revolt against traditional norms and values. Parents, teachers, and clergymen were alarmed at their young people's apparently casual attitude toward the moral code. Evading the prohibition law had become an accepted form of excitement. The automobile had widened the radius of an evening's adventure-seeking. The pastor who preached against the evils of the modern dance was sometimes embarrassed to learn that his own daughter was the "It" girl of the high-school crowd.

Furthermore, skepticism had replaced the religious beliefs which the older generation had hoped would stabilize the post-war era. "There was an undeniable weakening of loyalty to the church and an undeniable vagueness as to what it had to offer [its young people]—witness, for example, the tone of the discussions which accompanied the abandonment of compulsory chapel in a number of universities." [14] Synodical Conference Lutherans, particularly, were disturbed by the doctrines of heredity and environment, the theory of evolution, and the new science of psychology. Finally, the Scopes trial brought public humiliation to fundamentalist theology. "The sort of religious faith which William Jennings Bryan represented could not take the witness stand and face reason as a prosecutor." [15]

Church papers were full of exhortations to young people and their parents to "notify your pastor . . . write to our pastor at the university [16] . . . let the church go with them to college. . . ."

But in spite of misgivings, more and more Lutheran parents had to consider a university training for their children. The War had jarred the tight social pattern of the "German Lutherans" to its foundations. Military and civilian service left many of the young people of the church with a taste for urban life and a preference for careers other than farming—careers for which a college education was necessary. The anti-German excesses of the war years served to hasten the trend within the church toward adopting American ways. The acquisition of the new culture included a broadening of interests into fields of public service and into ways of bettering one's material lot. University education had been a step up the ladder into a higher social class for these people in Germany, and it seemed a natural step to take in the United States. The church itself had grown to a strong and respected body of more than a million members and was already operating the most ambitious educational program in American Protestantism in its elementary-school system.

In many ways, therefore, the Church was ready for a university of its own. But the decision to establish that university on the campus of Valparaiso University was so sudden that, if one rules out Providential guidance, it would seem to have been almost an impulsive decision.

The Purchase

The early Twenties had been busy years for the Rev. John C. Baur of Fort Wayne. One aftermath of the War had been a number of attempts to outlaw parochial schools as "un-American institutions," and, largely to combat these attempts, the laymen of the Lutheran church had organized the American Luther League. As executive secretary of the League, Pastor Baur had been a leading figure in the battle against the Ku Klux Klan and other groups which were attempting to legislate the parochial schools out of existence. He had also headed a committee which had directed a five-million-dollar fund-raising campaign for Synod's building program in 1923 and 1924.

By 1925, Pastor Baur was back in Fort Wayne, directing the League's program of assistance to parochial schools. In the spring of that year he had a visitor, the Rev. George F. Schutes, pastor of Immanuel Lutheran Church in Valparaiso. Pastor Schutes presented the interesting possibility that at last the church might acquire a full-fledged university of its own—Valparaiso University.[17] "But," he added characteristically, "you will have to act quickly!"

Pastor Baur, not yet recovered from complications following a tonsillectomy, was not greatly interested in Pastor Schutes' idea but, as a matter of courtesy, promised to arrange an appearance for Pastor Schutes before the executive board of the Fort Wayne council of the A.L.L. To Pastor Baur's surprise, the board was interested and decided to bring the proposition before the convention of the Central District of Synod which was soon to be held in Fort Wayne.[18]

On June 19, a committee of the Valparaiso Chamber of Commerce went to Fort Wayne to present its plan to the District convention. A meeting was scheduled for the noon hour of June 22, and invitations were sent to all pastors and delegates who were interested in organizing a Central States district of the National Lutheran Education Association with a view toward acquiring Valparaiso University for the Lutheran Church. Under the chairmanship of Pastor Schutes, resolutions were adopted to organize such a district, and a committee was chosen to present nominations of candidates for an incorporating committee. Late in the afternoon candidates for the incorporating committee were announced and full power was voted to this committee to take such steps as might be necessary to acquire the properties of Valparaiso University.

Elections the following morning resulted in the choice of the executive committee of the Central States district of N.L.E.A.: Dr. Herman A. Duemling, president; Mr. W. Charles Dickmeyer, vice-president; The Rev. Paul F. Miller, secretary; and Mr. Charles J. Scheimann, treasurer. All were Fort Wayne residents. In addition to these officers, Pastor Schutes, Pastor Baur, and Herman Sievers, of Valparaiso, were asked to serve on the incorporating committee. The executive committee was empowered to determine the name of the university; to have the Rev. Martin F. Kretzmann of Kendallville, Indiana, and Professor H. D. Mensing of Fort Wayne draft a constitution; to engage Mr. Martin Luecke of Fort Wayne as counsel in the incorporation proceedings; to direct a membership campaign; to begin considering candidates for the presidency and the faculty of the University; and to prepare promotional literature.

The treasurer was instructed to forward to the national office of the N.L.E.A. a note (endorsed by men of Fort Wayne, Valparaiso, and other places) to secure a loan of $16,500 to cover the first payment for the University property. The committee was instructed to go to Valparaiso on Friday, June 26, to take care of matters requiring immediate attention.

Meanwhile, Pastor Miller and Professor Mensing had brought

the matter of the purchase of the University to the floor of the District convention where it provoked a spirited debate. Decisive support for the university movement came from District Vice-president Francis J. Lankenau of Napoleon, Ohio, and from Dr. Jacob W. Miller, pastor of historic old St. Paul's Church in Fort Wayne and, at that time, fourth vice-president of Synod. Finally, the convention resolved to endorse the purchase of the University with "the ultimate view to offer the institution to the Church"; to encourage members of the District to support the institution "provided proper safeguards were made to keep it under control of our Synod for all time"; and to appoint a District advisory committee to work with the Central States district of the N.L.E.A.[19] These resolutions were the first of a long series of supporting measures which were officially adopted by the Central District during the following quarter-century in behalf of the University.

The organizing committee lost no time, but set out for Valparaiso on June 26. They negotiated a price of $176,000 for the property, provided that Henry Kinsey Brown could give legal assurance that this sum covered all outstanding indebtedness. A sum of sixteen thousand dollars was to be paid immediately, the remainder over a period of ten years at five per cent interest. The local Chamber of Commerce committee had hastily secured cancellation of $331,000 owed by the University to various creditors[20] and the Chamber promised to raise fifty thousand dollars during the ensuing ten years. It also co-operated by helping to negotiate options on property adjacent to the University.[21]

Next morning Pastor Baur, Pastor Schutes, and Mr. Scheimann met with Dr. Evans, President of the University, and explored the condition of the University.[22] It appeared that several old houses on private property should be bought to unify the campus. Several gaps in the faculty had to be filled, and some faculty salaries would have to be raised. Since it was late in the season, it was decided to go ahead with the printing of the fall catalogue. Pastor Baur also called President Evans' attention to the need for a discussion with the faculty of such controversial matters as secret societies, dancing, and the teaching of evolution.[23]

Headquarters for the infant Lutheran university movement were established at the offices of the A.L.L. in Fort Wayne. Consequently, Pastor Baur was drafted into action on many of the organizational details. Attorney Luecke, meanwhile, proceeded to draw up articles of incorporation. He was instructed to use the name "Lutheran University Association" rather than "Central States district of the N.L.E.A." in these articles.[24] On July 15, 1925, articles of incorporation of the Lutheran University Association were filed with the Indiana Secretary of State and with the Porter County recorder. According to these articles, the association had been established to "acquire, own, and control real estate and personal property for universities and colleges as well as for religious, charitable, and educational purposes." Thus, in essence, the L.U.A. was a holding company. On July 17, the board of directors of the Central States district of the N.L.E.A. organized a second corporation, the Valparaiso University Association, to "construct, establish, maintain, operate, and conduct schools, colleges, and universities operated and used for educational, literary, scientific, and charitable purposes." This dual corporate structure was made necessary by the fact that the L.U.A. had no way of making certain that all of the debts owed by the Old School had actually been cancelled, in spite of the recent efforts of the Chamber of Commerce. Claims arising out of these debts, if any should turn up, could not under this structure be charged against the operating funds of the University. The V.U.A. articles of incorporation were notarized in Fort Wayne and in Valparaiso on July 27, 1925. Signers of both incorporating documents were Messrs. Charles J. Scheimann, W. D. Holtermann, Herman Sievers, Martin Luecke, and W. Charles Dickmeyer; Pastors Schutes, Paul Miller, and Baur; and Dr. Herman A. Duemling.

On July 19, representatives of the N.L.E.A. and the L.U.A. met in Valparaiso to work out terms of co-operation. Under these terms, the L.U.A. was to have the entire field east of the Mississippi River and the Minnesota state line for its membership solicitation, in return for which it would pay the N.L.E.A. ten per cent of all hundred-dollar life memberships and five-dollar memberships which it collected, but no share of gifts over a hundred dollars. It was stipulated, however, that the L.U.A. could receive gifts from all parts of the country which it solicited on a national basis.[25]

Three days later, on July 22, the first meeting of the L.U.A. board of directors was held at Valparaiso, followed by the first meeting of the Association itself. Dr. Duemling was elected president, and Pastor Baur secretary, of the Association. Board officers chosen for the following years were Dr. Duemling, president; Mr. Dickmeyer, vice-president; Pastor Baur, secretary; and Mr. Scheimann, treasurer. The Board consisted of the incorporators plus H. C. Letz of Crown Point, Indiana; E. Lothman of Louisville; Byron P. Holst, president of the N.L.E.A.; and O. C. Lemke of Wausau, Wisconsin. Membership on the Board was also offered to A. H. Ahlbrand of Seymour, Indiana, and William Schlacke of Chicago. By unanimous vote, the directors were authorized to "purchase all or any part of the real estate or personal property, or both, of the Valparaiso Realty Company . . . comprising the present Valparaiso University as now constituted and other real estate and property as may be in their judgment necessary for the purposes of the enlarged University as contemplated by the members of this corporation." [26] The corporation also voted $176,500 in non-existent funds to the officers for the purchase of the University. Finally, the L.U.A. as a corporation made itself responsible for the $16,500 note which some of its members had executed as security for the N.L.E.A. loan, and approved borrowing seventy-five to one hundred thousand dollars from the Lincoln Life Insurance Company of Fort Wayne. [27]

After the meeting, the Board met with representatives of the Brown family to arrange a thirty-day option on the property. Mr. Henry Kinsey Brown accepted five hundred dollars as earnest money. The purpose of the option was to allow time to make sure that all complicating legal technicalities and claims were cleared before the actual purchase was consummated.

Despite the fact that the deal had not yet been finally settled, a University convocation was held the next day at which the University choir sang the Hallelujah Chorus; President Evans conferred honorary doctorates upon Pastor Schutes, the Rev. C. W. Wharton, and Mr. E. L. Loomis, the trio who had directed local efforts to such a successful conclusion; and Pastor Schutes delivered an address in which he proved from the Scriptures that there was no conflict between science and the Bible. President Evans wound up the occasion with the afterthought that it was fortunate that Governor Jackson had vetoed the bill that would have made Valparaiso a state school, since its future under Lutheran ownership promised to be so much greater. [28]

Despite the rejoicing, however, it was not until August 11 that word finally came that "the L. U. A. has gone through with negotiations for the purchase of the Valparaiso property." It took half an hour to rouse the sexton of Immanuel Church, after which town and campus celebrated until rain doused the proceedings at two o'clock in the morning. Actually, the formal action which touched off this celebration was only the attorneys' mutual approval of the contract for the sale of the University property. It was not until September 12 that the deed of conveyance was filed with the Porter County recorder.

The Price

The first task which faced the officers of the L.U.A. after they had secured ownership of the property was the herculean task of securing funds—funds to make the initial payment; funds to assemble students and faculty for the September opening; funds to buy essential equipment and to rehabilitate the run-down campus; and funds to provide a $500,000 endowment for accreditation and financial stability. With admitted trepidation, the Board applied to the First National Bank of Fort Wayne for a loan of $100,000. The president of the bank, a Roman Catholic gentleman named Charles Niesser, invited the Board to borrow more than they had originally asked for, since expenses often rise above estimates. His generosity was prompted, he said, by the fact that he had never known Lutherans to fail to pay their debts.[29] With this money in hand, the Board could definitely set the date for the opening of the University under Lutheran auspices: September 28, 1925.[30]

The next major problem facing the Board was the problem of administration. No member of the L.U.A. had had any experience in university administration and, for that matter, no one in the Church had had any such experience. So, largely by default, the whole burden of administration fell upon Pastor Baur. From the summer of 1925 on, he commuted weekly from his home in Fort Wayne to Valparaiso. (He refused to move to Valparaiso because he wanted to make it clear that his work at the University was strictly of an emergency nature. The emergency lasted ten years.) On campus he applied all of his energies and abilities to the myriad problems that faced the new owners: hiring a faculty, paying salaries, reorganizing business, taking inventory, surveying the curriculum, and regulating campus life to conform to Lutheran standards. He himself remembers these as days of such complete absorption that he was not aware of the passing hours or mealtimes, nor of the day's end until exhaustion caused his mind to stop functioning.[31]

The most immediately pressing job was to organize a program of information and solicitation throughout the Synodical Conference.[32] On August 24, the Board engaged Dr. O. H. Pannkoke [33] of New York City as campaign director and set a goal of $883,000, of which $176,500 was to cover the purchase price and $500,000 was to go into endowment; the balance was to be used for meeting current expenses. A campaign committee consisting of Pastors Baur and Miller and Professor Mensing was appointed to assist him. The deadline for the campaign was to be November 29.

Among the endorsements for the campaign was one from the International Walther League, through its board of directors, expressing joy at the founding of a Lutheran university.[34] The Synodical Board of Directors stated that, "While we cannot identify ourselves as a Board of Directors with the movement, we do not wish to interfere in any manner with the endeavors of any private organization in our midst to establish an institution of higher learning on a soundly Lutheran basis, but wish them God's blessing." [35]

In spite of these expressions of good will, however, the Lutheran university movement was anything but a snowball rolling downhill in these early winter days of 1925. Perhaps the greatest single obstacle was sheer indifference. Added to this were misgivings about the Lutheran nature of the university, resentment over the frequency of Synod-wide collections, and clashes of personalities. But there were also notable examples of generous response. The Peter Meyn family of Hammond, Indiana, pledged $15,000 toward the endowment fund. Shortly thereafter the Henry Wehrenberg family of Fort Wayne pledged $25,000 toward that fund. And some of the larger congregations pledged substantial amounts. By December 14, Dr. Pannkoke could report to the executive committee of the Board that $645,000 had been received in cash and pledges and that a total of $750,000 seemed to be in sight. It became necessary now to plan the follow-up on the campaign and, with the release of Dr. Pannkoke, Pastor Baur was appointed fiscal agent to finish off the campaign. Pastor Baur thereupon relinquished the office of L.U.A. secretary to Pastor Paul Miller and assumed the office of business manager of the V.U.A.[36] Thus these two men began their services in positions which they were to hold for many years.

The Prize

The University which the L.U.A. acquired in 1925 was little more than the corpse of the institution which Henry Baker Brown and Oliver Perry Kinsey had built. So run-down had it become that one newly-appointed instructor delayed for a month letting his bride see the campus.[37] Houses and classroom buildings were scattered about helter-skelter, rooming houses and university buildings alternated down the side streets, and chickens and rabbits and debris were all over the place.[38]

The center of the campus was a mass of rubble, the remains of the Old College Building, which had burned in 1923. Pastor Baur claims to have worn out two trucks carrying the debris away in 1925.[39] Soon it became a grassy plot, the center of University Park. Near this point, College Avenue dead-ended in University Place, a cross street which connected Locust Street with Greenwich Street. On the south side of University Place stood two of the more imposing buildings, Science Hall and the Medical Building. The entire third floor of Science Hall was the home of the School of Pharmacy. The basement of the Medical Building was filled with electrical engineering equipment. Across the street stood the Auditorium, into the front part of which the registrar's office was moved in 1925. Across College Avenue from the Auditorium was Music Hall. After the fire of 1923, this building had become the quarters of the Latin department and the location of offices for the president, the business manager, and several deans. Just south of Music Hall stood the M. E. Bogarte Book Store, the basement and upper story of which housed the Wade and Wise Printing Company and Bindery.

From the corner to the east could be seen East and South Halls, dilapidated structures which the new owners scheduled for early removal. Between them and the book store was the Y.M.C.A. building, a cafeteria which was a relic of the war years when temporary buildings had been thrown up to accommodate soldiers. It, too, was soon razed. Part of the women's housing at the time was provided in the relatively new Lembke Hall. Between Lembke

and College Avenue, along Mound Street, were houses and lunch-
rooms which continued in motley parade around the corner on the
east side of College Avenue to Freeman Street.

Next to the Auditorium stood gray-brick Heritage Hall. Shortly
after the War, it had been pressed into service as a machine shop
for the rehabilitation of veterans, and its floors were therefore
bathed in oil. In 1925, it became the University Library, a new
home for the books rescued from the library which had been destroyed with the Old College Building in 1923. Estimates of the
stock vary, ranging from thirty thousand bound volumes and ten
thousand pamphlets [40] to scarcely eight thousand books.[41] The
foreign language, law, engineering, and pharmacy libraries were
scattered over the campus in the respective departments.

To the north of the library, beyond several rooming houses,
stood the newest of the campus buildings, the Domestic Science
Building. Domestic science laboratories occupied the ground floor.
The upper floors provided housing for the Commerce Department
and the Teachers' College. Continuing north, away from the
campus and past intervening eating establishments and drug stores
on both sides of College Avenue, was the gray stucco Engineering
Building at Union and College. One block farther north stood
Altruria Hall, built by a private corporation and acquired by the
L.U.A. in a separate transaction in 1926 for $35,000. It was a
women's dormitory. A block east of Altruria stood an old yellow
frame house, the home of the Law School. Several blocks farther
east, at the end of Union Street, was the large former army barracks
which now served as a gymnasium. Adjacent to it were a ball park
and a grove.

Almost every crack and corner of this property needed a thorough cleaning. Roofs and gutters had to be repaired, rubbish re-
moved, and hasty coats of paint spread over the dingy walls. Large
classrooms had to be partitioned for smaller classes, equipment had
to be cleaned and inventoried, plumbing and wiring had to be
repaired or replaced. And it all had to be done immediately,
if not sooner.

The Interregnum

Negotiations for the purchase of the University had been completed so shortly before the beginning of the 1925–1926 school
year that it had been impossible to set up a Lutheran administration

or to assemble a Lutheran faculty. For the time being, therefore, the University continued with its pre-Lutheran faculty and administration, headed by Dr. Evans. The faculty consisted of forty-one full-time members plus nine critic teachers and nine student assistants. With the exception of two medical doctors (Evans and Douglas) and two members of the law faculty (Bowman and Morland), none held an earned doctorate.[42] The University still operated both a high school and an elementary school.

For the time being, life went on very much as usual. Student organizations were expected to conform to the policies of the new administration, but the implementation of these policies was left to the "mature good sense of the students."[43] Since very few of the students, and fewer still of the faculty, were Lutherans, the devotional part of the chapel program was omitted.

Gradually, however, the Lutheran imprint began to be noticeable on campus. The first pastors' meeting was held in Recital Hall on October 7, 1925. Walther League meetings began to be held on campus early in the fall. And by December, the official publications were beginning to display the seal of the Valparaiso University Association.

On January 3, 1926, President Evans presented his resignation to the V.U.A. and received a vote of thanks for his assistance in bridging the gap between the old administration and the new. Pending the election of the first Lutheran president, Pastor Baur was asked to take on the additional duties of acting president.

No one knew for sure what kind of a president the University needed, but it was agreed that the man should be a clergyman, an attractive personality, and a man well and favorably known in the Church. Of the numerous candidates suggested, the most prominent were Dr. H. B. Hemmeter, a Rochester, New York, pastor; Dr. Walter A. Maier of St. Louis; Dr. F. J. Lankenau; and Dr. William H. T. Dau, professor of dogmatics at Concordia Seminary, St. Louis. The choice finally fell upon Dr. Dau, who accepted the appointment in the spring of 1926 and moved to Valparaiso the following June.

Dr. Dau was born in Lauenburg, Pomerania, on February 8, 1864. He was thus 62 years old when he accepted the heavy burden of the presidency. For almost twenty years he had served in the parish ministry and for seven years (1892–1899) he had been president of Concordia College in Conover, North Carolina. For four years he had edited the infant *Lutheran Witness*, the official English paper of Synod, and then had taught for twenty years at the St. Louis seminary. While at the seminary, he wrote prolifically and served as managing editor of the *Theological Monthly*. He was thus one of the best-known American Lutheran churchmen of his day.

Inauguration Day

The inauguration day for the first Lutheran president of the University, which had been set for Sunday, October 3, 1926, provided a deadline toward which the summer's program of intensive renovation could be directed. By the time the mammoth crowds descended upon the campus for the inauguration, the area where the ruins of the Old College Building had lain could truly be called the "University Park," the gloomy interiors of the old buildings had been brightened up with paint, and the auditorium had been thoroughly scrubbed by some of the Lutheran faculty men who had been pressed into service.[44]

A full (not to say exhaustive) account of the inaugural proceedings appeared in the October 4, 1926, issue of the *Valparaiso Daily Vidette*, from which the following has been excerpted:

The motley [*sic*] crowd, Lutherans for the most part, was estimated at between 9,000 and 10,000. . . . Figure experts, by accurate count, declared 4,000 automobiles had rolled into the city by 2 o'clock. . . . Every available seat in the far too small auditorium was taken long before the official program opened at 3:30. . . .

Rev. O. C. Kreinheder, of Detroit, delivered a powerful address entitled "The Aim of Our University Enterprise." "The highest ideal of a noble life is the Christian ideal and the Christian ideal is the ideal of service," said Rev. Mr. Kreinheder. . . . "Our school voices morality, Christian character, and is certain to exert a noticeable influence for good on youth, church, and country," he said. "It will instruct our boys and girls along the proper channels; it will aid the church by helping to conserve the flower of youth, by furnishing an educated laity, and it will serve the country by inculcating righteousness and Christian character."

Dr. Kreinheder's address was followed by an address in Latin by Dr. Franz Pieper, president of the St. Louis seminary: "De amicitia inter scientiam humanam et religionem Christianam colenda"— "On the Friendship which Should Be Cultivated between Human Science and the Christian Religion."

Dr. Pieper stoutly denied that this present existing strife [between science and religion] was necessary and claimed it was possible for peace and friendship to replace war and enmity. . . .

"However," said the speaker, "we must not forget that there are matters of the greatest moment, in which philosophy or human science is unavailing. These are the matters that pertain to the finding and practicing of the true religion. I say, of the true religion by which man is guided to the life eternal after this life. In these matters human reason, when left to itself, chooses false religion. For, after the fall, all thoughts of every man concerning religion tend to this, that they attempt, by works of the law, to get back into favor of God. That this attempt is futile, not only scripture but also the experience of men teaches.

"Let human reason, then, cease waging war against the Christian religion, for by so doing it goes beyond the proper limits of human science, and commits what learned men call 'metabasis eis all genos,' the blunder of trespassing on forbidden ground."

Dr. Dau, having been charged with the responsibilities of his new and untried office by Board President Duemling, responded to Dr. Pieper's remarks with an address of reassurance on the compatibility of "true" science and Christianity:

Back of the venture which the body of Lutheran churchmen that is now operating Valparaiso University has made in the field of higher education for laymen lies the conviction that the Good Book is, as it always does, speaking truth, when it says: "The earth is the Lord's, and the fullness thereof; the world, and they that dwell therein"; Ps. 24:1. According to the conviction of these men the study of this great universe with its wonderful powers and mysterious workings, also the study of man, who is a small world in himself, of his physical organism and its operations, of his mind and its functionings—all these studies can, yea, should be pursued as in the presence of the All-wise Creator and Ordainer of all that is. The student inwardly attuned to this solemn truth enters the far extending plains of science and art, walks through their valleys and scales their heights, in a spirit of reverence. As he pursues his studies and research he is made ever more conscious of the majesty, the sublime beauty, the consummate wisdom, and last but not least, the incomparable goodness of that infinitely great Power which designed, called into existence, shaped, and ordered this multitude of wonders, and then handed them over to man as his legitimate sphere of activity with the words: "Subdue them, and have dominion over them"; Gen. 1:28.

True, the human being to whom those words were originally spoken was amply equipped for the task assigned him. He lost this unimpaired vision and the adequate mental strength in the dark hour of the first disobedience and the fall. But the original order which bade him conquer the earth and its forces and make them subservient to him was never reversed. He who came to restore man to a right relation with his Maker, and by whom all things were made, in whom all things now consist, and who holds the universe in the hollow of His divine-human hand, Jesus Christ of Nazareth, Son of God and Son of Mary, restores fallen man also to his primeval task of subjugating nature and its forces to the mind and will of man.

The student who has tasted the goodness of God in the mercy and grace of the Redeemer is in all his studies carried along by that joyous fervor of which God spoke, when he said to the prophet: "Be ye glad and rejoice forever in that which I create"; Is. 65:18. The sciences are not filled with terrors and spooks and hobgoblins to his faith; for he is assured that the God who loved man when He might have cast him aside, and procured man's righteousness in the sight of God by the sacrifice of His own Son, is the God, whom the morning stars praise, to whom the ocean sings its everlasting melody in the thundering diapason of the beach, the bird warbles its song at the rising dawn, the flower sheds its fragrance on the passing breeze.

His studies yield him not only externally profitable results, but help to mold his innermost being. Wordsworth truly has said:

> "Nature—can so inform
> The mind that is within us, so impress
> With quietness and beauty, and so feed
> With lofty thoughts, that neither evil tongues,
> Rash judgments, nor the sneers of selfish men,
> Nor greetings where no kindness is, nor all
> The dreary intercourse of daily life,
> Shall e'er prevail against us or disturb
> Our cheerful faith that all which we behold
> Is full of blessings."

It is, accordingly, an amazing statement, though I fear borne out by facts, when Gamaliel Bradford in a recent magazine article described the destructive effects of scientific studies after the method of Darwin, and tells us that the impression which Mrs. Darwin first had of her husband's theory was, that it was "putting God further off," and that this has been the well nigh universal effect of his theory. It is a phenomenon too sad, too pathetic for utterance.

Where lies the fault? Plainly in the divorcement of creature study from the Creator. The original man needed no Bible to guide him in his appointed activities; fallen man does. To him the godliness which it inculcates is profitable for this life and for that which is to come. It is a matchless preparation not only for man's future but also for his present existence.

This thought the new seal of Valparaiso University seeks to emphasize: "In luce tua videmus lucem"—"In Thy light we shall see light"; Ps. 36:9. The inspired truth of God's Book shall make plain and straight whatever is perplexing to man in any study, because it keeps him close to Him who said: "I am the Light of the world; he that followeth me shall not walk in darkness, but shall have the light of life"; John 8:12. In devotion to the Sin-Bearer of Calvary, the Peace-Bringer of Easter morn, we shall pursue our allotted tasks, and lay at the foot of His cross as a votive offering the learning and skill of the ages, consecrating our every activity at this school to the spread of His glory among the children of men. By Him and in Him, sheltered in his mercy, upborne by His love we shall hope to

> "Be good, be true, and let who will be clever;
> Do noble things, not dream them, all day long;
> And so make life, death, and the vast forever
> One grand, sweet song."

Down to Business

It did not take Dr. Dau long to learn that while a university president has many opportunities to "do noble things," his life is not "one grand, sweet song." Two problems that demanded immediate attention—in spite of interruptions for good will tours, speeches, fund raising, entertaining visitors, tabulating letters of application, and directing the day-by-day affairs of the University—were 1) that of creating a specifically Lutheran way of life and thought on campus, and 2) that of achieving academic respectability through accreditation.

The first of these problems, that of refashioning the University into a truly Lutheran institution, was the more challenging and the more rewarding, but at the same time the more troublesome of the two problems. It was challenging to Dr. Dau's scholarly nature to lead a group of churchmen in exploring a philosophy of Lutheran higher education. But it was painful to have to criticize principles and practices of years' standing at the University or to have to replace members of the faculty with men more qualified to foster Lutheranism. "What makes Valparaiso University Lutheran?" became the perennial question. So far as externals went, the answers were relatively simple: Lutheran ownership and support, Lutheran administration, Lutheran faculty and student body, Lutheran traditions of worship and campus life, Lutheran religious instruction, preparation for professional service in the Lutheran Church, training to think and act as a Lutheran in one's intended calling. But difficulties arose when it became necessary to determine the quality and the quantity of these criteria. Did support and personnel have to be one hundred per cent Lutheran? [45] Was there room for disagreement with Lutheran tradition, thought, and practice? [46] What was the meaning of academic freedom on the campus of a University which was committed to a particular theological pattern? [47] What made a classroom lecture or a student entertainment distinctively Lutheran rather than merely Christian or academic? What had seemed at first so obvious became exceedingly intangible and debatable.

But however debatable the philosophical questions might be, it was obvious that a Lutheran university presupposed strong Lutheran influence in the faculty. And in view of the dispute between conservative Lutheran theology and the philosophy which at that time dominated the natural sciences, it became one of the first goals of the new administration to bring in Lutheran instructors in the natural sciences. In September of 1926, Dr. Louis F. Heimlich was persuaded to leave a promising career at Purdue to assume the headship of the departments of botany, zoology, and geology at Valparaiso. At the time of his appointment, Dr. Heimlich had the distinction of being the only Ph.D. on the faculty. He quickly gained the confidence of President Dau, was appointed Dean of the University, and had made considerable progress toward raising the standards of his departments when his activities were cut short by his sudden death, at the age of 38, on October 12, 1928.

Other branches of the natural sciences were assigned to Alfred H. L. Meyer, instructor in geology and zoology, and Dr. Albert F. O. Germann, the new head of the Department of Chemistry. Dr. Meyer later became head of the Department of Geography and Geology and Chairman of the Committee on Graduate Studies, both of which positions he still holds. In addition, he has made a distinguished record in publication and in the activities of the professional societies. Dr. Germann served as acting president of the University for a time during the summer of 1927, but he took a leave of absence the following fall and subsequently left the University. Two other veterans of these early days of Lutheran administration who have remained in the service of the University until the present are Professor Walther M. Miller, head of the Department of Foreign Languages, for many years Chairman of the Committee on Admissions and Degrees, and for a while acting registrar; and Dr. Walter E. Bauer, who later became head of the

Department of History, Dean of the College of Arts and Sciences (1946–1957), and Dean of the Faculty (since 1946). A less famous but equally faithful servant of the University who joined the staff at this time was Mr. John Lindberg, for more than thirty years janitor and bell-ringer on the Old Campus.

In the first three years of its existence under Lutheran administration, the University raised the percentage of its Lutheran faculty from almost zero to about thirty per cent, a highly satisfactory percentage in view of the short period of time involved. The percentage of Lutheran students rose from about nine per cent in 1925 to over forty-four per cent in 1928–1929. The rough beginnings of today's daily chapel exercises were made in the summer of 1926, when Acting President Baur initiated a program of voluntary services which were held several times a week. The disappointing attendance at these services made it apparent that someone was needed to direct the spiritual program of the University, and in the fall of 1927 the Rev. Henry H. Kumnick was appointed to take charge of student welfare, especially spiritual welfare. In time his assignment developed into the office of Dean of Students, a position which Mr. Kumnick held through President Kreinheder's administration and into the first year of President Kretzmann's administration.

From the outset of Lutheran administration, it had been recognized that a department of religion would be essential to the spiritual life of the campus. At its first annual meeting, the L.U.A. directed the Board to look after the matter and to encourage "men of means" to endow a chair in religion.[48] In 1928, a Jacob W. Miller Memorial Fund was set up as a part of the general drive for endowment, and money was added to this fund from the Martin Luther Fund, a few hundred dollars collected during the 1928 campaign from pastors, teachers, professors, and school children. By mid-1930, the total amount available for the establishment of a religion chair or department was $33,486.03, considerably less than was needed, but the University went ahead with plans to establish the department. The first instructors were Mr. Kumnick and Dr. Frederick William Kroencke, who had been appointed to the faculty in 1927. One of the great figures of the early days of Lutheran administration, Dr. Kroencke served as Dean of the University from 1928 until his death in 1936 and shares with President Dau and

John C. Baur the lion's share of the credit for winning accreditation for the University by the North Central Association.

Student life, too, had to be brought into conformity to the standards of the new administration, and that required, among other things, action on the matter of fraternities and sororities. The policy of the University was laid down by Dr. Dau in a talk at Altruria Hall on October 26, 1926, at which time he announced that the University would assume no responsibility for secret societies since they were inimical to democracy in student life. On the other hand, debating and honorary societies would be welcomed.[49] The University could not tolerate secret societies, furthermore, because most of the fraternities and sororities then in existence had religious rituals which brought them under the Lutheran church's definition of lodges. All fraternities and sororities were, therefore, put on probation until they would submit their constitutions and have them approved by the administration as social societies. First to receive this approval was the Sigma Theta sorority, followed soon thereafter by Gamma Phi, Alpha Phi Delta, and Alphi Xi. The fraternities preferred to hold out and a Klan-like secret society called the Koffin Klub attempted to intimidate the president into softening his policy. But Dr. Dau stood firm, and finally eight fraternities were approved.

Another aspect of student life which caused the new administration considerable concern was the pattern of social life. On practically every campus in the country, dancing was all the rage, and Valparaiso was no exception. Most of the "old" students accepted dancing as inoffensive and adult recreation. Many of the "new" students, however, believed that all dancing was sinful. Unfortunately, there was no uniformity in belief and practice among Lutherans themselves on "the dance question," and the administration confessed that it was not sure what it ought to do about the matter.[50] Pending further study, it declined, on grounds of the Lutheran doctrine of individual freedom, to ban dancing. By early 1929, campus practice allowed dancing under strict chaperonage in connection with fraternity and sorority entertainments. Dancing in public halls was, however, forbidden and led to dismissal. Over the years, the dance question continued to be a troublesome one and objections to dancing on campus were often cited as reasons for refusing to support the University.

Student government had fallen victim to the uncertainties of the transitional period between administrations, but soon after Mr. Kumnick became Dean of Students he took steps to re-establish it. Initially, the Board was wary of conceding any real power to a student organization, but after much discussion the Board, on October 25, 1930, approved a constitution for student government.[51]

As Lutheran influence became more obvious in the faculty and in campus life, feeling in the Church changed so that President Dau could speak of a "notable reversal of opinion among the former opponents of the movement to establish a Lutheran university." [52] Some frankly changed from opposition to friendship. Others, among them the president of Synod (Dr. Frederick Pfotenhauer), ceased to oppose the venture while reserving judgment as to its wisdom. A third group continued to oppose the University, either by open declaration or by "silently discounting its merit and questioning the genuineness of the efforts that are being made to build up a Lutheran University." [53]

Achieving Accreditation

As early as June 22, 1926, the Board of Directors had resolved to set March 1, 1928, as its deadline for application for accreditation by the North Central Association of Colleges and Secondary Schools. This decision was not only necessitated by the desire of the L.U.A. to maintain an excellent university; it was a life-or-death necessity. But the directors were dealing with a kind of educational octopus which required amputations and plastic surgery to conform to the pattern of the standard American college. This meant discharging faithful faculty members simply because they taught in an "unnecessary" department or because they lacked the proper degrees. The emotional strain of this unpleasant task told on President Dau and John C. Baur and exacerbated the already serious conflicts of personality and policies between them.

The College of Liberal Arts was early singled out for grooming as the nucleus of the future university. The physical plant was cleaned and renovated at a cost of about $250,000.[54] Oversize classrooms were partitioned to bring classroom size into conformity with NCA standards, the Law School was taken out of its ramshackle building on Greenwich Street and moved into the Domestic Science Building, now renamed Arts-Law, and departments were centralized as far as facilities permitted.

The most difficult task that had to be undertaken to qualify for accreditation, however, was the assembling of an educationally-qualified faculty. Of the twenty-one faculty members of the Old School who remained for the first year of Lutheran administration, only five were left in 1929. Among the new faculty appointed in the 1926–1927 academic year were seven Doctors of Philosophy: Louis F. Heimlich (botany), H. V. Fuller (chemistry), R. C. Kissling (classics), Frederick W. Kroencke (education and philosophy), R. W. Pinto (history and political science), P. E. Roller (physics), and W. J. Trjitzinsky (mathematics). There was also one Doctor of Science, A. F. O. Germann; and two Doctors of Laws, Dean Bowman and John W. Morland. Faculty additions and replacements between 1928 and 1930 strengthened the doctoral percentage and included E. M. Robinson and C. F. Abbetmeyer (English), Walter E. Thrun (chemistry), J. J. Weber (education and psychology), Frank Roy Elliott (zoology), and Arthur C. Harwood (pharmacy). By 1929, every department was headed by a professor with an earned doctorate from an institution on the NCA approved list. The College of Liberal Arts consisted of departments of biology, business management, chemistry, education and psychology, engineering, English language and literature, fine arts, foreign languages and literatures, geology, home economics, mathematics and physics, religion and philosophy, and social sciences. A health and physical education department was announced for the fall of 1929. Besides the College of Liberal Arts, there were the College of Pharmacy and the School of Law. In November of 1926, the faculty recommended the closing of the University High School, a recommendation which was put into effect by the Board of Directors in the summer of 1927.

Next to the strengthening and reorganization of the faculty, the biggest job that had to be done in preparation for accreditation was the reconstruction of the library. Mrs. Katharine Ertz Bowden, an alumna of the Old School, was appointed librarian in 1926 and given a free hand in its reorganization. Under her direction, all departmental libraries except the Law Library were consolidated into the main collection. By 1929, the library housed a collection of twelve thousand volumes and was spending close to ten dollars per student per year for acquisitions, twice the minimum NCA figure.

Early in 1928, Dr. Floyd Reeves, head of the School Service Bureau of the University of Kentucky, was employed to serve as educational adviser to the University in the final grooming for accreditation. After two visits to the campus, he assured the administration that the University was working in the right direction and could be readied for approval by March, 1929.[55]

But before the University as such could be accredited, it was necessary that each of its colleges be separately accredited. Through the efforts of Dr. Germann, the department of pharmacy had been raised to the status of a college during his term as acting president, May to September, 1927. The College had been accepted as a member of the American Association of Colleges of Pharmacy and was conforming to the Association's standards. Both a three-year and a four-year course were offered, but in 1928 John C. Baur committed the University to the action taken by other Indiana colleges of pharmacy and abolished the three-year course effective in 1930.

The Law School had begun as early as the 1927–1928 academic year to base its admission requirements on the standards of the Association of American Law Schools and the American Bar Association. Early in April, 1928, Dean Claude Horack of the University of Iowa law school, who was secretary of the A.A.L.S., had visited the University and had made recommendations for the strengthening of the school. The chief deficiency that he noted was in books of the law library. The Walther League was asked for help, and at its convention in Milwaukee in July, 1928, the League voted to collect fifteen thousand dollars for the "Walther League Library" in the School of Law.[56] League societies were subsequently asked to provide funds for two books so that the library could be increased from five thousand to 7,500 volumes. In December, 1928, the University appropriated a thousand dollars for law books.

Dean Horack was then called back for a final survey and for recommendations to the A.A.L.S. A tense situation developed when it was pointed out that the A.A.L.S. did not hold its annual meeting until May, whereas the crucial NCA meeting was scheduled for March. How to get the approval of the A.A.L.S. for the March meeting of the NCA?

Meanwhile, the College of Liberal Arts had unspectacularly received accreditation as a Class A Standard College of Indiana from the state department of public instruction. This accreditation was granted on February 2, 1929, one week before the Reeves survey was to be reported to the NCA.

In addition to the preliminary accreditation of the colleges, a major factor in NCA approval was the collection of an endowment sufficiently large to satisfy the NCA requirement on financing. In effect, Valparaiso was required to show evidence that it could count on a minimum annual income of $65,000, half of it from sources other than student fees. In addition, assuming an enrollment of six hundred students, it had to have an endowment of at least $700,000. Fortunately, income from churches or legally recognized corporations could, up to a certain amount, be figured as the five per cent income on a theoretical "living endowment" and such income could be listed as meeting endowment requirements. Thus an annual contribution of ten thousand dollars from some source within the Church could be credited as the income on a $200,000 endowment.

But even so, the amount needed was a formidable one. The half-million dollar endowment included in the 1925 campaign had melted away in campus rehabilitation. The Board of Directors therefore authorized a special endowment campaign which provided for new efforts to collect the more than $300,000 which had been pledged but not paid in the 1925 campaign; a simultaneous effort to get twenty thousand more annual L.U.A. memberships; and an approach to Synod and the synodical districts for annual support out of their budgets. The Rev. Arthur Hanser of New York was engaged on a fee basis to raise $500,000 in congregational collections and individual gifts, and the Rev. Karl H. Henrichs of Fort Wayne was appointed membership secretary of the L.U.A. with his first assignment that of increasing membership participation. In October of 1928, when Pastor Hanser's contract expired, Mr. Henrichs took over the management of the congregational collection also. For more than thirty years, except for an interval as athletic director, Mr. Henrichs has been at the job, always necessary and often discouraging, of trying to raise the money the University has needed for its operations and development.

Under Mr. Henrichs' leadership, the Endowment Appeal picked

up momentum. By December, 1928, John C. Baur could report that $275,000 had been scraped together for the endowment fund with enough more in prospect to meet the NCA minimum. The University was ready to invite the North Central Survey Committee to examine it for accreditation.

On February 9, 1929, President Dau transmitted a 208 page report to Dr. George Zook, secretary of the NCA. The report showed that the University now met the definition of the standard American college. In organization, it offered the Bachelor of Arts degree after four years of study, the first two of which continued the curricula of the secondary school and the final two of which were professional in nature and anticipated graduate work. It met the usual standards of admission. It embraced thirteen departments with eleven department heads, each department including at least one man of professorial rank (more than the NCA requirement of eight departments with one of professorial rank). It almost met the faculty training requirement which stipulated that ranking professors should have two years of graduate study and that department heads have the doctorate (three department heads did not have the doctorate). The teaching load requirement (sixteen hours) was more than met with Valparaiso's average of thirteen hours. A faculty-student ratio of 7.5 was maintained throughout the University, somewhat lower than the norm. Only two classes violated the standard of thirty or fewer students per class, while 116 of the 197 classes had fewer than ten students.

The survey committee approved the curriculum, pronounced the quality of instruction above average, and noted that "the scientific spirit" permeated teaching. It approved of the policy of not granting honorary degrees for some time. The proportion of students who remained at the University through the first two years was found to be "greater than any small denominational college." In number of library books and in library appropriations per student Valparaiso was rated as satisfactory. The accreditation of the colleges by their respective agencies and the elimination of the high school and elementary school departments were approved. An inspection of the physical plant brought commendation for the cleanliness of floors, buildings, and apparatus. Despite certain criticisms, the committee found that "conditions for accreditation are good, and it would be a shame if accreditation were not achieved."

The race to meet the endowment figure and the uncertainty of the Law School accreditation kept the University and its friends in tension through all of February. The net endowment was $294,-482.50 in early February.[57] Mr. Henrichs and John C. Baur were hopeful, however, that the needed fifty thousand dollars would materialize from the effort among Valparaiso townspeople to pay up their 1925 pledges. Mr. Henrichs and Dr. Dau were still soliciting larger givers and there was hope of more returns from the congregational collections which the Synodical College of Presidents had authorized the previous fall.

When, at the end of February, the dollars and cents of endowment were added up and the sum reported to Dr. Reeves, he pronounced it enough. In a supplementary report to the NCA, Dr. Reeves recommended that the University be accredited. The problem of the accreditation of the Law School had been taken care of by the report of an inspection committee of the American Bar Association which recommended accreditation at the May meeting of the Association.

On March 13, 1929, John C. Baur and Mr. Scribner sat outside the Chicago hotel room in which executives of the NCA were evaluating applications for accreditation. With the two men were representatives of other institutions, all anxiously awaiting the summons to appear before the committee. Periodically the door would open and an usher would ask one or another of the little group to enter and clarify a point. Baur waited impatiently, hour after hour, and received not even an invitation to enter the conference room. Finally, planning to go to his own room and catch up on work that he had brought along, he asked the usher if he could be called when needed.

"What college do you represent?" the usher asked.

"Valparaiso University."

"Why, that petition came up hours ago and was quickly passed. They only ask the representatives in when there is some doubt about the matter." "You won't have to worry about tomorrow, either," he continued. "The committee just reads the list of recommendations and the convention passes it."

That is as much as Pastor Baur remembers of the conversation. A few minutes later, he was on the phone relaying the good news to President Dau. The news touched off an enthusiastic celebration on campus and in the town and brought congratulations from every part of the country.

Approval by the NCA opened the door to further accreditation. On May 7, the Law School was approved by the American Bar Association and, a year later, was admitted to membership in the American Association of Law Schools. In June, the University was accredited by the Board of Regents of the State of New York and by the University of Illinois. Thus, within four years of its purchase by the L.U.A., the University had been raised from near death to full accreditation.

Accreditation meant that the University was no longer just a hopeful experiment. It did not, however, solve every problem. The University badly needed a gymnasium. It had to increase its endowment to at least a million dollars. It had to build up the enrollment. And it had to try to fulfill a number of the recommendations in the Reeves report. By June it was faced with the additional problem of finding a new president, for Dr. Dau felt that he could no longer serve in an office which he found more and more distasteful and which brought him into constant conflict with Pastor Baur.

The conflicts between Dr. Dau and Pastor Baur are a part of the history of the University which can not be glossed over because many who were involved in them are still emotionally involved in them. Fortunately, these conflicts do not reflect adversely upon either man. President Dau was an elderly scholar with a great appreciation of gracious living. He had accepted the presidency on the assumption that his role would be similar to that of the rector of a continental university, and he was dismayed to find that much of his time had to be spent in public relations. Pastor Baur, on the other hand, was and is a hard-driving promoter, a man who gets things done. The dual corporate structure under which the two men worked, necessitated by doubts as to the financial situation of the University at the time it was bought, divided authority and responsibility so that it was impossible for Dr. Dau, as president of the University, and John C. Baur, as representative of the L.U.A., to avoid trespassing on each other's presumed area of authority and responsibility. Thus when President Dau went on leave of absence in the spring of 1927, he learned that it was not he, but the Board through Pastor Baur, that named the acting president.

In retrospect, it can hardly be denied that the dominating figure and the man who prodded the University back to life during the first decade of Lutheran administration was John C. Baur. But it is doubtful whether even he could have done so had it not been for the association of Dr. Dau's respected name with what many Lutherans of those days considered a doubtful, if not foolish, enterprise.

Another Interim

No acting president was appointed after Dr. Dau's resignation. Instead, the Board of Directors vested the powers of the president in an executive committee consisting of Pastor Baur, Mr. Scribner, Dean Kroencke, and Dean Kumnick.[58] This committee was to meet once a week and submit monthly minutes or recommendations to the Board. Although a nominating committee was immediately appointed to recommend candidates for the presidency, the executive committee continued in office for almost a year.

While the search for a president went on, the Board addressed itself to the still-critical financial problem. In June of 1929 it authorized a new campaign which, since it set the pattern for the financial campaigns of the next twenty years, may warrant detailed explanation.

One approach was to be to potentially large givers, men who could contribute five thousand dollars or more. This part of the work was assigned to Mr. Henrichs, Pastor Baur, and President Emeritus Dau. A second approach was to be in the direction of enlarging membership in the L.U.A. with the appointment of more field men to undertake this work. The Rev. John Sohn had been serving as field man, but at this time was anxious to re-enter the parish ministry. To succeed him, the Board in 1930 appointed the Rev. Theodore Andres who, a year later, was joined by the Rev. Theophil Strieter. A third approach was to be to the "in-between" group who could not afford to contribute five thousand dollars but could do more than make a five-dollar membership contribution. A fourth approach was to be to the congregations of Synod who would be urged to hold an annual collection or to place a contribution for the University in their annual budget. And the fifth approach was to be to the alumni with the intention of asking them to take on a special project, initially a new gymnasium to replace the old wooden structure which had been burned in December, 1927.

For direction of the alumni drive, the Board turned again to Dr. O. H. Pannkoke who had helped to direct the 1925 fund campaign. Dr. Pannkoke set to work immediately, but by October he had to report that the alumni lists were in such fragmentary form that it would still take months to get the news out to the alumni. He felt also that, in view of the large numbers of uninterested alumni on the list, it would take an outstanding gift to arouse any alumni enthusiasm for the campaign. The pall of gloom which this cast over the October, 1929, meeting of the Board was dispelled, however, when John Misch of Detroit recommended that the Board should resolutely plan a substitute campaign until the alumni effort could go ahead. John C. Baur mentioned the possibility of raising funds for the gymnasium from a special list which had been compiled by Mr. Henrichs. Thereupon Misch came forward with a personal pledge of five thousand dollars if the Board would bring the total up to thirty-five or forty thousand dollars. His gesture stimulated Henry J. Neils of Minneapolis to match the pledge and to offer to get an additional five thousand from friends. Misch matched this second offer and George F. Nolde of Richmond, Va., came up with another five-thousand-dollar pledge. Harry Eberline, who had become president of the Board upon Dr. Duemling's death in 1927, promised to make a sincere effort to raise ten thousand dollars. William Boeger of Chicago offered to give five thousand dollars and to raise another five thousand. H. F. Rohrmann of Chicago promised to give five thousand dollars and to raise another ten thousand. Herbert Hackstedde of Cincinnati pledged five thousand dollars. John C. Baur now chimed in with a five-hundred-dollar pledge plus another five hundred if he could realize that much on a certain investment; and the Rev. O. C. Kreinheder promised half the returns from an investment. The result of this morale-boosting interlude was the resolve, whatever the results of the alumni campaign, to initiate a campaign for a new gymnasium costing at least $200,000.

Meanwhile Dr. Pannkoke went ahead with his campaign among the alumni. Laymen were called in to consider "Valparaiso, Our Church's Great Victory—Let Us Strengthen It," and were sent out to visit, between January and April, 1930, those in their areas who could give over two hundred dollars. At a public rally in town, Professor Walter E. Bauer told his audience that

We of the faculty came here not to build just another school. . . . There was no need for that. . . . We came inspired to undertake a great and worthwhile work—to build in Valparaiso an educational institution dedicated to the building of Christian character and helpful citizenship.[59]

Former President Horace M. Evans was quoted as observing that the general spirit of confidence and achievement seemed "like old times," and a Valparaiso attorney who had served on the Board of Trustees of the Old School, E. J. Freund, rose to congratulate the L.U.A. for continuing the ideals of Brown and Kinsey. He wished to dispel the idea, he said, that the L.U.A. had taken over only a lot of old buildings. It had taken over great prestige and many nationally and internationally famous alumni in the industrial, merchandising, and political world.[60]

Optimistic as the situation appeared on the surface, Dr. Pannkoke himself soon issued words of warning. Nevertheless, the Board proceeded with plans for the new gymnasium. In January, 1930, however, truly formidable trouble presented itself in the form of objections raised by Synodical leaders to some aspects of the campaign. The short-term effect of these objections was to limit the success of the campaign. Their long-term effect, however, was highly beneficial to the University, for out of the meetings which were held between Synodical officials and representatives of the University over these objections came a formal endorsement of the University by the Synodical College of Presidents and an arrangement for co-ordination between Synodical officials and the University administration.

By March, Pastor Baur had to report to the Board that the campaign was not going as well as had been hoped, and by April he had to report that current obligations and campaign expenses had exhausted the gymnasium fund. From then on, the campaign bogged down. By January, 1931, the University was no longer thinking of building a new gymnasium but simply of balancing its operating budget. At the time, there was much disagreement over the reasons for the failure of the campaign. Perhaps the chief reason was that the campaign was launched at about the same time the country was entering the worst years of the Great Depression. For the University as for the country, prosperity was not "just around the corner."

NOTES

1. C. F. W. Walther, *Der Lutheraner*, VII (January 21, 1851), 11.
2. W. Gustave Polack, *The Building of a Great Church*, pp. 114-16.
3. W. H. T. Dau, Remarks at a meeting of regional representatives in Recital Hall, Valparaiso University, January 19, 1927.
4. Theodore Graebner, *The Lutheran Witness*, XXXIX (Nov. 23, 1920), 366-77.
5. *Synodalbericht, Atlantischen Distrikts*, 1913, p. 76.
6. *Bericht der neunundzwanzigsten Delegatsynode*, 1914, p. 67.
7. William Schoenfeld, "The Present Urgent Call for Expansion of Synod's System of Higher Education," reprinted in *Theological Quarterly* (July 1919), p. 165.
8. Theodore Graebner, "Our Higher Education," *op. cit.*, pp. 175-77.
9. *Ibid.*, pp. 177-79.
10. Vogel and Wendt, *75 Years of Grace*, p. 67.
11. *N.L.E.A. Bulletin*, III (December 1920), 1.
12. "Articles of Incorporation of the National Lutheran Educational Association."
13. Vogel and Wendt, *op. cit.*, p. 68.
14. Frederick Lewis Allen, *Only Yesterday*, (Harper and Brothers Publishers, 1931), p. 197.
15. *Ibid.*, p. 205.
16. The first such full-time student pastor was the Rev. Adolph T. Haentzschel at the University of Wisconsin. He began work there in 1920, erected the first Lutheran student chapel on a university campus in 1926, and remained at Madison until he joined the faculty of Valparaiso University.
17. The Rev. George F. Schutes had come to Valparaiso in 1923. John C. Baur believes that the possibility of Lutherans' acquiring the University came to Pastor Schutes' attention through President Evans, his neighbor. Pastor Schutes was active in civic affairs and belonged to the ministerial association. Here he came into contact with the Rev. C. W. Wharton, pastor of the Presbyterian Church, who was on the Chamber of Commerce committee which was trying to save the University. Wharton had offered the University, unsuccessfully, to the Presbyterian Church. Pastor Schutes was prominent in the early Lutheran activity at the University. Later a dispute within Immanuel Church in which Pastor Schutes and several members of the University faculty were ranged on opposite sides of the issues led to Pastor Schutes' withdrawal of support from the University and his resignation from the Missouri Synod.
18. Interview with John C. Baur, February 4, 1950.
19. *Proceedings, 53rd Convention of the Central District*, 1925, p. 73.
20. Members of the Chamber committee were the Rev. Chester W. Wharton, chairman; W. C. Sutter, manager of the Chamber of Commerce; E. L. Loomis, superintendent of the Valparaiso Water Company; Herman E. Sievers, treasurer of the Specht-Finney Company; and the Rev. E. W. Strecker, minister of the Methodist Episcopal Church.
21. Minutes of Central District of the N.L.E.A., June 26, 1925.
22. John C. Baur recalls that the physical, spiritual, moral, and educational condition of the University on that visit made him hope that the negotiations would fail. When the L.U.A. did acquire the institution, he worked "with all determination, not knowing once whether it would succeed."

23. Minutes by J. C. Baur at Valparaiso, June 26-27, 1925.

24. Minutes of Board of Directors, Central District of N.L.E.A., July 2, 1925.

25. Synopsis: Tentative Understanding Between N.L.E.A. and Proposed L.U.A., July 19, 1925. Also Minutes of Representative of L.U.A. with Representative of N.L.E.A., July 22, 1925.

26. Minutes of First Meeting of Members of the L.U.A., July 22, 1925.

27. Minutes of Meeting between Representative of L.U.A. with Representative of N.L.E.A., July 22, 1925.

28. *Valparaiso Evening Messenger*, July 23, 1925, p. 1.

29. Interview with W. C. Dickmeyer, February 19, 1957.

30. Minutes, Board of Directors, V.U.A. and L.U.A., September 9, 1925.

31. Interview with John C. Baur, February 4, 1950.

32. Although the L.U.A. was under the auspices of the Missouri Synod, affiliation with the N.L.E.A. gave it access to Synodical Conference members and churches. Synodical Conference donors were later given L.U.A. membership certificates.

33. Otto Herman Pannkoke, born in Germany in 1887, graduated Concordia Seminary, 1908; D.D. from Lenoir College, 1920. Parish pastor, 1908-1917. Entered public relations work as secretary to the New York Quadricentennial committee, 1916-1917. (*Who's Who*, 1930).

34. *Valparaiso University Bulletin*, LIII (October 16, 1925), 2.

35. *V.U., a God-Given Opportunity*, p. 7.

36. Minutes of Executive Board of the L.U.A., December 12, 1925.

37. Interview with Walther M. Miller, February 4, 1950.

38. *Ibid.*

39. Interview with John C. Baur, February 4, 1950.

40. *Valparaiso University Catalog*, 1925, p. 13.

41. Interview with Mrs. Katharine Ertz Bowden, October 14, 1957.

42. *Valparaiso University Bulletin*, LIII, No. 2 (June 1925), 5.

43. *Ibid.*, pp. 22-24.

44. *Valparaiso Daily Vidette*, May 17, 1926; also W. M. Miller reminiscence.

45. John C. Baur vs. Dr. Frederick Pfotenhauer.

46. Cf. debate over compulsory chapel and the dance question.

47. This had been one of Dr. Theodore Graebner's most serious concerns at the time serious discussion of a Lutheran University was beginning.

48. "Record of Proceedings of First Annual L.U.A. Meeting," *L.U.A. Bulletin*, I, No. 1 (April-June 1926), 9.

49. *Valparaiso Daily Vidette*, October 26, 1926, p. 1.

50. President's Report to the Board of Directors, December 23, 1926.

51. Minutes of meeting of L.U.A., October 25, 1930, published in the *Torch*.

52. President's Report to the Board of Directors, October 5, 1926.

53. *Ibid.*

54. John C. Baur in the *Vidette-Messenger*.

55. Minutes of Board of Directors of the V.U.A., April 17, 1928.

56. *The Walther League Messenger*, August-September, 1928, p. 34.

57. Minutes of Board of Directors of the L.U.A., February 2, 1929.

58. Minutes of V.U.A., July 14, 1929.

59. *The Vidette-Messenger*, November 20, 1929.

60. *Ibid.*

CHAPTER VI

A Period of Consolidation

1930–1940

IN MAY, 1930, the Rev. Oscar Carl Kreinheder was elected President of the University. He was inaugurated on October 26. Dr. Kreinheder had been closely associated with the Lutheran University Association since its founding. Elected to the L.U.A. Board of Directors in 1926, he subsequently served as chairman of its committee on by-laws, as a member of the committee on buildings and grounds, and as a member of the committee on instruction at the time the University was seeking accreditation. As pastor of big-city churches in St. Paul and Detroit and as president of the English District of Synod from 1918 to 1928, he had earned a reputation as an excellent administrator. Reluctant at first to accept the presidency, he yielded to the persuasions of Dr. Dau [1] and to official assurances by the Board that it would stand by him and his administration.[2]

It was Dr. Kreinheder's misfortune that he came to the presidency at the worst possible time, in the midst of the Great Depression. His administration was almost wholly preoccupied with drives, campaigns, efforts, and solicitations which, despite the best efforts of the president and his staff, accomplished little more than keeping the University solvent at a low level of subsistence. This was in itself, however, no small accomplishment in those difficult days, and in spite of the financial strait-jacket, the Kreinheder administration left a record of substantial progress: the curriculum was reorganized to conform to the best accepted models, the old campus was given a general face-lifting, the present departmental structure was established, able faculty members were retained and added. The sacrifices which were made by members of the faculty and administration during these trying years prompted one of the University's supporters to describe it as "a place that consumes men." One of those whom it consumed was President Kreinheder.

The new administration began in an atmosphere of optimism and good will. In preparation for the inauguration, the town had installed new lights along College Avenue making it a kind of "white way." Enrollment for the fall semester stood at 563, an increase of a hundred over the previous year. Of the 563, almost half (252) were new and sixty-two per cent were Lutheran. Student morale was high—a new field house or gymnasium had been promised them by the Board. Students were enjoying their first taste of "freedom with responsibility" under a system of student government which had been approved by the Board at its October 25 meeting. Athletic events that fall were livened by the new "Victory March," composed and published just before the end of the school year the previous June. To music by August Bucci had been set a lyric of three stanzas written by the three student winners of a contest: Margaret Marquart, Geneva Gordon Dye, and Edward A. Anderson. The campus itself looked better than it had ever looked before.

The recommendations and resolutions of the Board at its early meetings under the new president read like a kind of table of contents to the problems of the Kreinheder administration.[3] The president was made *ex officio* member of all committees; he was authorized to establish a College of Engineering; he was asked to get a director for the Field Office as soon as possible; a National Advisory Board was to be created and the Women's Welfare Committee enlarged; bids for the proposed gymnasium were called for; and the unpaid pledges hanging over from the 1925 campaign were written off and new endowment funds properly invested.

The Ups and Downs of Engineering

The relatively small enrollment in the late Twenties and early Thirties was believed to be ascribable, in part, to the limited range of courses offered by the University. In the hope of attracting more men students, the Board authorized the president to establish a College of Engineering. Formal announcement of the opening of the College was made at a dinner on March 6, 1931, at which time a congratulatory telegram was read from the most famous engineer of that day, President Herbert Hoover.[4] Six departments were contemplated: chemical engineering and metallurgy, civil engi-

The Rev. Oscar Carl Kreinheder, D.D.
President of the University, 1930–1939.

Mr. Harry E. Eberline
*President of the Lutheran University As-
sociation, 1927–1932; Member of the
Board of Directors, 1926–1944.*

W. Charles Dickmeyer, LL.D.

President of the Lutheran University Association, 1933–1953; Member of the Board of Directors since 1926.

Mr. Ralph Richman

President of the Lutheran University Association, 1932–1933.

Alfred H. Meyer, Ph.D.

Member of the Faculty since 1926. Professor and Head of the Department of Geography and Geology.

The Rev. Karl H. Henrichs, M.A.

Veteran fund-raiser for the University, formerly Director of Athletics.

Walter Emil Bauer, Ph.D.

Member of the Faculty since 1926. Professor and Head of the Department of History. Dean of the College of Arts and Sciences, 1946–1957, and of the Faculty, since 1946.

Walther Martin Miller, M.A.

Member of the Faculty since 1926. Professor and Head of the Department of Foreign Languages.

Walter George Friedrich, Ph.D.

Professor and Head of the Department of English since 1938. Dean of the College of Arts and Sciences and Dean of the Faculty, 1938–1946. Acting President of the University, 1939–1940.

Mrs. Katharine Ertz Bowden, B.S.

University Librarian, 1928–1949. Archivist since 1949.

Mr. Fred Wehrenberg

*Member of the Board of Directors,
1926–1927, 1928–1951.*

Jacob Melius "Jake" Christiansen

*Director of Athletics, Football Coach,
Basketball Coach, Lecturer in Health
and Hygiene, 1929–1941.*

Mr. John A. Sauerman

*Member of the Board of Directors since
1934. Treasurer of the Lutheran University Association.*

Mrs. E. W. Schultz

*First President of the Valparaiso Uni-
versity Women's Guild, 1931.*

The Rev. Gustav W. Lobeck
Head of the Department of Public Relations, 1937–1942.

The Rev. Frederick Lawrence Miller
Head of the Department of Public Relations, 1943–1948.

neering, drawing and architecture, electrical engineering, mechanical engineering, and industrial arts. A capable dean was found in Dr. Howard Wilson Moody, who had been dean of engineering at Mississippi A. and M. He was assisted by Professors Carl W. Lauritzen, Herman Blickensderfer, Donald Mallory, Moses Uban, and Horace Taveira.

Enrollment in the first class in the College of Engineering, 1931–1932, was 101. By 1934–1935, however, it had declined to fifty-one, raising serious doubts as to whether the University could afford to maintain the College, particularly in view of the fact that it was the costliest of all of the schools on campus in terms of equipment and salaries. By 1936, the urgent need for retrenchment compelled President Kreinheder to recommend reducing the program to two years. The Board, fearful of the loss of prestige and of the effort it would take to reinstate the full Engineering College later,[5] decided to postpone action for one year. In 1938–1939, however, chemical engineering was omitted and in the following year only senior level engineering courses were offered. Meanwhile the University had worked out a co-operative arrangement with Purdue University, under the terms of which students could take two years of engineering work at Valparaiso, then transfer to Purdue without loss of credit. This program was later imitated by a number of the better small colleges of the country.

The Strengthening of the Liberal Arts

Many of the recommendations left with the University by the Reeves survey committee were also followed up in the years after 1930. In the natural sciences, the work in biology, zoology, and botany was organized under a Department of Biology in 1929. In 1931, Dr. Frank Roy Elliott became head of the department, a position which he retained until his retirement in 1954. His colleague throughout the decade was Dr. Fred H. Kaufmann. The Chemistry Department had been thoroughly reorganized by Dr. Germann before accreditation in an effort to bring the College of Pharmacy up to standard. Work was carried on in the following years by Dr. H. V. Fuller, head of the department from 1931 to 1933, and by his successor, Dr. Walter E. Thrun, who served as head from 1933 until his death in 1951. Mathematics and physics added Dr. Ancil Ridgeway Thomas to its staff in 1930. In 1933, he was named head of the department and served in that capacity until his resignation in 1956.

In the social sciences, economics was added to the curriculum and the title of Department of Business Management was adopted in 1930. Mr. A. M. Skinner became head of the department in 1933, serving until the appointment of Mr. Charles Ziebarth in 1937. In 1939, the department included Mr. Ziebarth; Mr. Erwin H. Goehring who had been appointed to the faculty in 1935; and Mr. Myers E. Zimmerman, a veteran of the Old School. The Department of Geology, which added geography to its title in 1937, was largely the creation of Dr. Alfred H. Meyer, instructor since 1926 and its head since 1933. History, sociology, and political science were combined under a Department of Social Science. In the fall of 1930, Dr. Ernest George Schwiebert was appointed head of this department. Dean Kroencke taught sociology in the department until his death in 1936 and Dr. Walter E. Bauer taught history throughout this decade, succeeding Dr. Schwiebert as head of the department in 1946.

Courses in the Department of English Language and Literature were largely rewritten by 1931. They included extensive work in journalism. The department head, Dr. Edna M. Robinson, was replaced in 1932 by Mr. A. C. Hartung. Upon Dr. Hartung's death at sea in 1935, Dr. Herbert H. Umbach, who had joined the faculty the previous year, served as acting head for a year until the appointment of Dr. Walter George Friedrich.

By 1930, Italian and Greek had been omitted from the offerings of the Department of Foreign Languages and Literature, but majors were offered in Spanish, Latin, French, and German. Dr. R. C. Kissling, on the faculty since 1928, became head in 1931 and was succeeded by Professor Walther M. Miller in 1933. Spanish lost favor after 1932, and the department finished out the decade with majors and minors in French or German and a minor in Latin. Miss Hazel Tallman, who had joined the staff in 1930, became a specialist in Romance languages and, as Professor Hazel Guillaumant, is still serving. Miss Elizabeth Rechenberg was transferred from botany to German in 1933 and continued to serve until her retirement.

The year 1933, which saw the major overhauling of the decade throughout the academic program, also brought the end of instruction in art until the early Forties. The Department of Fine Arts consequently became simply the Department of Music with Professor Frederick Schweppe as head. Professor Richard Schoenbohm joined the music faculty in 1936 and, the following year, succeeded Professor Schweppe as head. A veteran of the Old School, Dr. Edmund W. Chaffee, served as professor of piano and later of harmony through this decade, retiring in 1940 after forty-five years on the staff. In the 1929–1930 school year, at the suggestion of Mr. Henrichs,[6] the department had organized a touring choir. The first choir tour was made in 1930 in the interest of the endowment campaign. By the end of the decade, membership in the choir was a highly-coveted privilege, and the annual choir tour was one of the highlights of the academic year.

When President Kreinheder took office, all courses in education had just been unified under a Department of Education and Psychology. Teaching majors were offered in thirty different areas, all approved by the Indiana department of public instruction.[7] The department was headed by Professor J. J. Weber until 1932, by Dr. C. A. Serenius until 1934, and by Dr. Carl Frederick Lindberg from 1934 until his death in 1952.

Included in the Department of Education until 1929 were courses in health and physical education, taught mainly from the standpoint of teacher training. More work in physical development, athletics, and hygiene was offered beginning in 1929 under Mr. Paul R. Lankenau, instructor and director of athletics. Between 1930 and 1932, physical education courses were grouped under a new Department of Health and Physical Education. After 1931, Coach Jacob Melius ("Jake") Christiansen directed the department with the help of Mrs. Helen Gross Alderman. The University had joined the Indiana Intercollegiate Conference in 1927[8] and faithfully observed its regulations in its athletic program despite lack of facilities. When the hoped-for new gymnasium failed to materialize by 1933, however, the number of courses in physical education was reduced to four and the work was again placed under the Department of Education and Psychology. Here it remained until plans for reviving a full schedule of physical education were worked out in 1941.[9]

Curtailment of the extensive offerings in religion left just six courses in the years 1932 to 1934. Two more courses were added in 1934, and students were required to earn six credits in religion for the A.B. degree. The religion courses were a division of the Department of Religion and Philosophy, which was headed by Dean Kroencke until his death, at which time Dr. Adolph T. Haentzschel took over. Courses were taught chiefly by Dean Kumnick with the assistance of President emeritus Dau and, later, Dr. Bauer and Dr. Schwiebert.

A re-assessment of the total academic picture took place in 1935, when the faculty charged Professor Walther M. Miller and the Committee on Curriculum and Educational Planning with responsibility for maintaining a continuing scrutiny of the University's observance of N. C. A. requirements. The committee drew up a statement of the history and aims of the University which was approved by the administration and classified courses by number into upper- and lower-division courses. The committee also tightened up admission and graduation requirements [10] and enforced a policy of minimum deviation from these requirements.

Streamlining the University

The College of Pharmacy experienced declining enrollments through the Thirties but held to its accredited curriculum under Dean Frederick V. Lofgren. Other full-time members of the pharmacy faculty were Dr. Arthur A. Harwood and Dr. Fred H. Kaufmann. In January, 1938, a report by the Board's Committee on Instruction raised the question of whether the University was not probably trying to operate too broad a program in view of its size and income and by January, 1939, general agreement was reached that the College of Pharmacy should be discontinued.

By contrast with the Colleges of Pharmacy and Engineering, the School of Law maintained a satisfactory enrollment. After several years as acting head, Dr. John W. Morland became dean in 1931. Professor Virgil E. Berry, a veteran of the Old School, continued his association with the Law School until his retirement in 1957, and Dr. Marshall John Jox was added to the faculty in 1934. In 1937, Dr. Louis Albert Wehling joined the law faculty.

The library was also notably strengthened during the Kreinheder administration. Gifts such as the one hundred volumes on music from William Wade Hinshaw, a former head of the music department, and two hundred volumes from the Rev. William Moll of

Fort Wayne swelled the collection. Such gifts were the more appreciated as University finances prohibited acquisition of any but the most urgently needed books.

By 1935, the tenth anniversary of the purchase of the University by the L. U. A., the faculty considered the reputation of the University sound enough to permit the conferral of a few honorary degrees. The anniversary celebration, accordingly, was marked by the conferral of doctorates upon Pastor Paul F. Miller, the secretary of the L. U. A., and Mr. Edmund Seuel, Manager of Concordia Publishing House in St. Louis.

Footnote: An indication of the interest of the faculty in public affairs can be gotten from a letter which it sent to President Franklin D. Roosevelt on March 13, 1933, commending him for certain policies of the New Deal. The dissolution of party lines, the "shattering of hidebound precedent," the use of trained specialists as advisers, and the "bringing of the axe to bear upon the temples of the money changers" were singled out for special mention. This letter was the first and last letter addressed by the faculty to a president of the United States.

The Enrollment Problem

As the effects of the Great Depression filtered into every part of the country and every area of its economy, one of the major problems of the Kreinheder administration became the problem of maintaining enrollment. The figures for these years tell the story:

1930	. . . . .	606	1936	480
1931	. . . . .	627	1937	521
1932	. . . . .	563	1938	506
1933	. . . . .	523	1939	458
1934	. . . . .	522	1940	399
1935	. . . . .	446		

In an effort to offset enrollment losses, the University strained its resources to provide every possible cent of student aid. By 1939, fifty-four per cent of the student body was receiving some form of aid, averaging $135.14 per student. At the same time, a vigorous program of student procurement was inaugurated (1936) with the Rev. Frederick L. Miller and Mr. Frederick H. Rechlin taking on the responsibilities for building the enrollment. Their efforts probably staved off disaster, but they were unable to reverse the long-term trend. This trend was the product of conditions in the country over which the University had no control.

Among students who had enrolled at the University, however, morale was high. Practically everybody knew everybody else, student and faculty alike, and there was an awareness, real though seldom expressed, of being part of the crew of a ship in distress. Some of this awareness of being in a tight spot was reflected in the growing popularity of the militant name "Uhlans" for the athletic team and, by extension, for the student body at large. In 1934, even the yearbook, until then called *The Record*, became *The Uhlan*.

Another contribution to the solidification of school spirit was the publication, in the January 10, 1935, issue of *The Torch*, of a new Alma Mater song, "Hail to the Brown and Gold." The song appeared anonymously and there is disagreement as to its authorship. Majority opinion favors the tradition that it was written by President Kreinheder himself.

Physical Improvement

Campus improvements in the Thirties were dictated partly by the sheer necessity of creating a comfortable enough environment to attract and hold students and partly by the opportunities to add cheaply to the physical plant such properties as would have future value to the University.

In 1930, the Board authorized the purchase of the business property north of Music Hall at a price of six thousand dollars from the endowment fund. A total investment of fifteen thousand dollars made the first floor the Brown and Gold Sandwich Shop and the upper floor a residence for women. "Trouble with rodents" caused the closing of the sandwich shop in 1936 and the first floor of the building was rented to Mr. Myers E. Zimmerman to be converted into the University Book Store.

In March, 1933, the city approved a request by the University to close College Avenue south of Mound Street and the adjoining College Place to the west. The street was torn up and replaced with lawn, greatly enhancing the appearance of the campus. In August of the same year, recognizing that the gymnasium project would have to be postponed indefinitely, the Board authorized the erection of the team house on Brown Field. Townspeople pledged eighteen hundred dollars toward its three-thousand-dollar cost.

The purchase by Mr. J. C. Mandery, of Cincinnati, of an unsightly property on Mound Street behind the B and G Sandwich Shop for use or for future razing suggested the possibility that others might be interested in buying up other sub-standard structures which still cluttered up the campus. By September, 1934, Mr. Henrichs had interested six people in this program, but by June, 1935, the Board saw that its program of land additions and debt retirement would have to be slowed down in favor of simply balancing the budget.

Just before the end of the 1936–1937 school year, the president of the Student Council presented to the L. U. A. the deed to property adjacent to the Biology Building, plus a receipt for $50.60 and a check for $222.65 toward unpaid interest, back taxes, and sewer assessments—all the gift of the student body to the University. The students had bought the property with the proceeds from one of their entertainments. This was the first, but not the last, time that the student body has contributed to the expansion of the campus.

Faculty Loyalty

One of the surest evidences of the long-term strength of the University was the loyalty which its faculty demonstrated during the worst years of the Depression when salaries had to be cut twice by 10 per cent from figures that were already low. By 1936, salaries ranged between $1,200 and $1,800 for instructors, $1,800 and $2,400 for assistant professors, $2,200 and $2,600 for associate professors, and up to $3,000 for full professors. The president himself was getting around $4,000.

Partly to compensate for the low salaries, the Board on January 15, 1936, approved a faculty tenure policy which had been drawn up by a joint committee of the faculty and the Board. Under this policy, permanent tenure was offered to professors and associate professors after five years of commendable service until the age of sixty-five, with easy extension of service if desirable or advisable. In January, 1937, the Board also purchased a group insurance policy providing a thousand-dollar coverage for each of the fifty-two employees of the University.

The Development of Public Relations

Until 1930, the fund-raising department of the University was known as the Field Office and it was practically a one-man affair, the one man being John C. Baur. With the occasional assistance of Dr. Pannkoke and the aid of a secretary, a bookkeeper, a mimeograph, and an address list, Pastor Baur saw to it that literature flowed out and funds flowed in. At times, President Dau's office took over part of the work, and in the 1925 campaign a number of pastors served as solicitors. The Rev. John Sohn of Fort Wayne became a full-time assistant, and faculty members were called upon for service from time to time.

A major step toward a more definite organizational setup was taken in 1929, when a newly-appointed group of district chairmen was called to the campus for briefing. These men, pastors who had been spotted as strong supporters of the Lutheran university movement, were asked to help increase L. U. A. memberships in the 1930 endowment campaign. During 1930, a staff was assembled on campus consisting, by the end of the year, of Mr. Henrichs, the Rev. Theodore Andres, the Rev. Eric Malte, and Dr. Pannkoke.

In November, 1931, the first annual "Valparaiso Sunday" was observed in the churches of the Missouri Synod by proclamation of the President of Synod. Permission to observe this "Sunday," which was later shifted to the last Sunday in January of each year, represented a major accomplishment in the process of winning the active support of Church officials and contributed greatly to assuring a reasonably dependable source of income.

In the October, 1930, meeting of the Board, the President was asked to engage a Field Office director as soon as possible. Since he had not been able to find a suitable director by April, when Dr. Pannkoke's contract was due to expire, President Kreinheder asked Dr. Pannkoke to stay on until August. Renewals continued and finally, in August, 1931, Dr. Pannkoke was made head of the Field Office or, as it was to be known thereafter, the Department of Public Relations. He served until March, 1932.

By this time the Rev. Theophil W. Strieter had joined the staff and had become head of the department, but in May, 1933, he accepted a call into the ministry. During his year on campus, he and Mr. Henrichs made another effort to increase the number of L. U. A. memberships, but with little success. This was the very bottom of the Depression, and money was just not available.

Failure to find a new head of the Public Relations Department after Pastor Strieter's resignation resulted in a decision by the executive committee of the Board to make John C. Baur executive secretary of the L. U. A. and to move Mr. Scribner into the business managership.[11] Under Pastor Baur's direction, Public Relations then intended to launch a campaign of information through mail while Mr. Henrichs would devote his time, as endowment secretary, to securing larger gifts. At the same time, the Board approved a proposal by Mr. E. J. Gallmeyer to organize a group of "Minutemen" to "get or give" fifty dollars to the University.[12]

By the tenth annual meeting of the L. U. A. on June 15, 1935, it was necessary to report that funds were still not coming in as needed, and by August the continual strain of fighting the deficits had brought John C. Baur within inches of a nervous collapse. He therefore resigned as executive secretary of the L. U. A. and left the campus. Public relations work was taken over, pending the selection of a new director, by the Board's Committee on Public Relations and Development, headed by W. C. Dickmeyer.

In the fall of 1936, Mr. Henrichs was pressed into service as head of public relations with the Rev. Armin Born as his assistant. Mr. Henrichs served until September, 1937, when he was succeeded by the Rev. Gustave W. Lobeck. Pastor Lobeck proceeded to organize the work regionally with the Rev. Frederick L. Miller serving the Central territory, E. A. Richert in Michigan, E. Manz in Wisconsin, Henry Buchholz in Chicago, President Kreinheder in Kansas, Florida, and California, himself in central Illinois and Iowa, and Mr. Henrichs continuing his search for large givers. Whatever spare time the staff had it spent in visiting prospective students.

"It is required in stewards that a man be found faithful." Measured in terms of financial success, the various men who served in the public relations service of the University during the Thirties were not eminently successful. But if there were time to describe in detail the many ingenious approaches that were made to solving the financial problem, it would be evident that the meager success was not the result of any lack of imagination or effort. Being director of public relations at Valparaiso University during the Thirties was like being premier of post-war France: one could not hope to succeed, but one did not have to fear that he would spend a lifetime in the job.

The best comment on the financial situation was that of Ralph Richman who had succeeded Mr. Eberline as President of the Board in January, 1932. Speaking to the members of the L. U. A. at their annual meeting in 1932, Mr. Richman said: "When Valparaiso was taken over, we had a great vision of realizing an ideal in a very short time. But the Lord thought otherwise. . . . But the vision is not forgotten [as we] face the fact that the paramount task is that of balancing the budget."

Adding both to the problem of public relations and the uncertainty of the financial situation in the early and middle Thirties were a number of unhappy controversies over certain financial obligations which the University was alleged to have assumed and then failed to meet. One of these involved Mr. Henry A. Dahlen, a long-time member of the Board. Mr. Dahlen had saved the day at the time the University was scraping together funds to meet the accreditation requirement by putting $250,000 at the service of the University. Now the desperate conditions of his business compelled him to ask for the return of these bonds, in spite of the understanding that at least part of the funds from the bonds were to be a gift to the University. After a prolonged period of negotiations, painful both to Mr. Dahlen and the University administration, the situation was resolved amicably and the Board minutes of October 21, 1936, include the statement that "Mr. Dahlen has been and is a real friend of the University and arrangements should be made to adjust this liability in a manner satisfactory to Mr. Dahlen." The matter was finally settled in September, 1937, and Mr. Dahlen continued to serve on the Board of Directors until his retirement in 1943.

Less satisfactory was the settlement of a dispute which arose between the University and Dr. Pannkoke over the amount due him under the unwritten contract which had been made with him for conducting the alumni campaign. An agreement was finally reached to compromise his claim under a schedule of monthly payments, but misunderstandings continued over the size of these monthly payments and Dr. Pannkoke threatened to sue the University. The Board felt that it had dealt fairly with Dr. Pannkoke, however, and eventually the matter was dropped.

In April, 1933, the architects who had been employed to plan the new gymnasium demanded a larger fee than the University intended to pay. This matter was settled with a legal opinion by Dean Morland which found that the University was not obligated.

Finally, there had been disagreement for some time over the status of the $16,500 loan which had been secured from the National Lutheran Education Association at the time of the organization of the L. U. A. Since the time the loan had been negotiated, the N. L. E. A. had become an inactive organization, its business being run by an executive committee. This committee was, however, pressing the University for interest and for payments on the principal. President Kreinheder turned to the Synodical Board of Directors, since the N. L. E. A. had been sanctioned by Synod, to negotiate a gift of the total sum to Valparaiso. The University, he contended, was actually performing the functions for which the N. L. E. A. had been organized and which it was no longer capable of performing. Upon the legal dissolution of the N. L. E. A. on May 31, 1938, this matter, too, was settled, the N. L. E. A. giving the University a check for $683.28 which, taken together with the cancellation of the note and its accumulated interest, represented a gift of $25,000.

Organization of the Women's Guild

The tapering off and final end to payments on the 1925 pledges compelled the University to develop special groups which would commit themselves to regular annual support. Two such groups have been especially valuable to the University.

The older and stronger of the two is the women's group. In April, 1929, the Board made definite plans to include women in the work of building the University and directed the Dean of Students and the Business Manager to organize a small group of lay women who would function under the Board's Committee on Buildings and Grounds and would meet on campus several times a year to confer on current needs. The history of the present Valparaiso University Women's Guild goes back, however, only to April 13, 1931, when twenty-five women met on campus in response to an invitation by Mrs. Kreinheder, Mrs. Eberline, and the wives of other Board members. This meeting resulted in the formation of a permanent organization to further interest and financial support for the University, to increase enrollment, and to improve living conditions for the students. The first officers were Mrs. E. W. Schultz of Sheboygan, Wisconsin, president; and Miss Lily Fedder of Hammond, Indiana, secretary.[13]

By the time of the next meeting, on October 7, 1931, this new "Women's Committee" had organized chapters in Detroit, Fort Wayne, and Appleton, Wisconsin, and by the end of 1931 membership stood at eighty-six. The first project of the Committee, undertaken as early as October, 1932, was the raising of five thousand dollars toward financing the Home Economics and Physical Education Departments and the refurnishing of Altruria Hall. In 1935, the "Women's Committee" adopted a constitution and restyled itself the "Women's Auxiliary." At this time the Auxiliary consisted of chapters, besides the original ones, in Rockford, Illinois; Cleveland, Ohio; Logansport, Indiana; and St. Louis. Mrs. H. W. Bartels of Cleveland succeeded Mrs. Schultz as president at this time. In 1936, Mrs. Harry Eberline became president of the Auxiliary under its new name, the Valparaiso University Women's Guild. Mrs. W. N. Hoppe succeeded Mrs. Eberline as president in 1939.

In 1934, the Guild undertook the project of furnishing and redecorating dormitories. In 1935 it added to this project an additional project of raising funds for current support and for the gymnasium. In 1937, it originated the custom of presenting a special gift annually. And in 1938 it contributed toward funds which were being raised to make a film depicting life at Valparaiso. Already a strong organization by the end of the Kreinheder administration, the Guild really came into its own when it undertook its great building program in the next decade.

The Alumni Association

The formal organization of the Valparaiso University Alumni Association was an accomplishment of President Kreinheder in 1934. After the failure of the 1929–1930 Alumni Campaign and the meager response to the Alumni Remembrance Library Drive, the alumni of the Old School had been written off as a group which could not be called upon for any definite program. Individual alumni of the early days did, however, keep in touch with the University, and a certain number of them put in appearances at homecomings. Their addresses were kept up to date and a flourishing correspondence was carried on by Miss Catherine Corboy until her retirement in her fifty-fifth year with the University in 1940 at the age of eighty-one.

The first approach to organizing the alumni of the Lutheran administration was made at homecoming in 1933 when President Kreinheder met with about seventy-five of them. Plans were made to adopt a constitution and to elect officers the following year. As a result, Leonard Schramm, '31, was elected first president of the Alumni Association at the organizational meeting on October 27, 1934. By June, 1935, President Kreinheder reported a membership of about 275.[14] The small size of the graduating classes prevented the Alumni Association from carrying on any elaborate program until after the Second World War, when its numbers had increased to the point where it could maintain a permanent organization of its own and undertake large projects.

The Dance Question

One of the problems which the Kreinheder administration had inherited was the question of what to do about dancing on campus. "The Dance Question" was the subject of many letters addressed both to the President of Synod and the President of the University; it was the subject of paragraphs in the President's annual report to the Board; it was the theme of endless bull-sessions among students and alumni and of heated debate in pastors' studies all over the Church. It became clear to the Board in the early Thirties that some "official policy" would have to be put on record to still the clamor.

In early 1934, Dean Kumnick called the Board's attention to the fact that the University practice of permitting supervised dancing at fraternity and sorority affairs was unfair to the unorganized student. He noted also that a survey in 1930 had shown that 95 per cent of the students favored dancing and that eleven out of twelve urban pastors whom he had interviewed in 1934 recommended campus dancing under strict supervision rather than a ban which would drive students to subterfuges.[15]

A committee headed by the Rev. Louis J. Sieck, later president of Concordia Seminary, was asked to study the problem and come up with recommendations. At the meeting of the Board on April 2, 1935, this committee reported that, although it found that present regulations reduced the amount of dancing and prevented irresponsible and surreptitious dancing, it felt that it was necessary to recommend complete prohibition in order "to enjoy the full confidence and support of Synod and its members."

The Board was reluctant to carry out this recommendation and postponed final decision until its next meeting, in June. In the June meeting it voted, over the protest of some of its members (John A. Sauerman asked to be recorded) to impose a ban on dancing which, after a period of "warning and education," would become official on June 15, 1939. The effect of the ban was what University officials had expected that it would be: students who had learned to dance long before they had even heard of Valparaiso found ways to continue dancing after they came to the University.

The "official ban" on dancing, with all of its ramifications, may serve as an example of the kind of control exerted by the Church over the University in relation to support. The Board imposed the ban in order to conform to Synodical policy and thus to maintain friendly relations so that channels to the members of the Church would remain open. It is a matter of record, though, that there was a division of opinion among University officials on the subject. Dancing was forbidden on campus at University-sponsored affairs, but it continued in chaperoned student parties off campus, for which the University did not assume responsibility. Whatever support was given or denied the University during this period because of the ban or the degree of enforcement was on a purely individual basis and was not a matter of official Synodical decree. There was no subsidy from the Church to be granted or denied because of campus practice. This position of being "in the Church but not of it" became the envy of heads of publicly-supported and many other church-supported institutions. In the case of the latter, policy could be dictated by those who held the purse strings. In the case of Valparaiso, policy-making was in the hands of the University Board, but in a spirit of co-operative service to the Church. This meant that the University had to depend for support on its ability to meet the needs of the Church through the development of a needed, wanted, and accredited academic program; through the production of an able and articulate group of graduates; and through the creation of a place for itself in the life of the Church through specific services. These services ranged all the way from providing intellectual direction on problems that were troubling the membership of the Church to providing an environment where young men and women could win a Lutheran husband or wife along with, or instead of, an academic degree.

Channels of Communication

During the first fifteen years of Lutheran administration, the greatest single problem of the University was getting its message through to the laity of the Church. Local pastors were then, as now, the keys to the congregations, to congregational societies, and to individual laymen. Many of the information and fund-raising activities of the years 1930–1940 were, therefore, directed to and through the pastors. Pastoral conferences and District conventions were consulted before major moves, and were annually informed of the needs and triumphs of the University. Seminarians were invited to attend the University during the Depression years when there was a surplus of pastors. Pastors' institutes were offered each summer on campus. Directors and personnel of the Field Office until the late Forties were always clergymen. And the Board of Directors always included a number of clergymen.

Two other valuable channels of communication were the International Walther League, the young people's society of the Church, and the Lutheran Laymen's League. Both organizations went all-out in their support of the University from the earliest days of Lutheran ownership and have continued their support to the present.

The Turning Point

The academic year 1937–1938 reflected the general improvement in the national economy and the results of many years of diligent spade-work by the University administration. The renewed gymnasium fund-raising effort, spurred by an initial gift in 1935 from the late Board treasurer, Mr. L. H. Letz, had reached a pledged total of $96,500, of which $52,607 had been received in cash. In a flurry of optimism, the Board considered a campaign for a million dollars to celebrate the fifteenth anniversary of the L. U. A. and to meet current needs. This plan was never carried out, but, in the meantime, the new Board treasurer, Mr. John A. Sauerman, made steady progress in strengthening the University's financial base. One hundred fifty thousand dollars of indebtedness had been refinanced by the sale of bonds, a new accounting system was set up, and the University's credit standing was greatly improved. In September, 1937, Mr. Sauerman could report the University's assets at $1,610,530.27.[16]

Gifts seemed to pour in during the following year. The dissolution of the N. L. E. A. brought with it cancellation of the $16,500 note plus accrued interest. There was a $10,000 bequest to endowment from Mr. Henry Bokerman of Aspinwall, Pennsylvania; a $10,000 endowment-scholarship bequest from Mr. Henry Moellering of Fort Wayne; a $20,000 bequest from Miss Mollie Page of Staunton, Virginia; and a $22,612 contribution from Mr. John P. Hemmeter of Detroit, the proceeds of which were to be used for library books. In addition, Mrs. W. H. T. Dau of Berkeley, California, raised her earlier gift of $10,000 to $50,000, and suggested that it be used immediately for the badly-needed library.

Another encouraging sign, early in 1938, was the 9 per cent increase in enrollment. President Kreinheder pointed out that this compared more than favorably with the national increase of 3.6 per cent. Unfortunately, this rising trend was short-lived, for by fall enrollment had dropped again. Drab housing conditions and a poorly organized social program caused a number of students to leave for home shortly after registration, the President said.[17]

The return to more normal conditions brought with it some improvement in faculty salaries which, in September, 1937, began to be increased, especially in cases of sickness or in view of long service or to hold some members of the faculty who were receiving offers at other institutions at salaries which were very difficult for them to turn down.

Although retrenchment was still taking place in the academic departments in 1938 and 1939, this was generally regarded as a strengthening of the University's position as a strong college of the arts and sciences. Dr. Walter George Friedrich, head of the Department of English, was appointed Dean of the College of Liberal Arts and Dean of the Faculty in June, 1938, filling the vacancy which had been left by the death of Dean Kroencke in September, 1936. Dr. Friedrich began at once to act on recommendations which had been made by the Board's Committee on Instruction and by the special faculty committee which had been studying the University's adherence to N. C. A. standards. Both the College of Pharmacy and the College of Engineering were under fire by the accrediting agencies. Moreover, only 40 per cent of the forty-four students of pharmacy were Lutheran. The Engineering School was also losing enrollment and would require heavy investments of money and equipment to remain accredited. On recommendation of the President and the Dean, the Board on October 27, 1938, approved the closing of the College of Pharmacy. By March, 1939, President Kreinheder and Dean Friedrich had completed the plans for the co-operative program in engineering which was established with Purdue University.

With the University relieved of the weight of these two colleges, the Dean could proceed with the final steps in the University's academic development: 1) expansion of the departments of Religion, Business and Economics, and Music; 2) addition of a Department of Fine Arts; and 3) continued attention to the quality and accreditation of the Law School.

By the end of 1938, the University was faced with the necessity of developing another department, for the ten-year dream of a new gymnasium had become a reality on September 29 of that year with the breaking of ground for a new "health and physical education" building. The ground-breaking ceremonies were a big thing at the time for this was the first new building constructed under Lutheran administration and it was taken as the symbol of a new era that was about to begin. Mr. W. C. Dickmeyer, who had been a prime mover in the Lutheran University movement from the very beginning and had succeeded Ralph Richman as chairman of the Board in 1933, turned the first shovelful of dirt, President Kreinheder turned another shovelful, and Mr. Fred Wehrenberg, chairman of the Committee on Buildings and Grounds, made a speech which conveyed, in words easily understandable to the undergraduates, the elation which he and his colleagues on the Board felt over the accomplishment of this often-deferred goal. In fifty-four weeks, the gymnasium would be completed and ready for use.

Ironically, it was not to be given to President Kreinheder to preside over the dedicatory ceremonies. By May, 1939, exhaustion and the effects of diabetes had so weakened him that he offered his resignation. The Board prevailed upon him to accept a six-months' leave of absence, but by July his health had deteriorated so badly that he again requested the Board to relieve him of the presidency. Regretfully, the Board granted his request with the provision that when his health improved he should continue to serve the University as a representative-at-large. Dean Friedrich was asked to serve as acting president pending the election of a new president.

Walter George Friedrich, Acting President
July 1, 1939–October 1, 1940

The outstanding event of Dr. Friedrich's term as acting president was the dedication of the first new building erected under Lutheran administration. More than 2,500 friends and alumni of the University witnessed the dedicatory ceremonies on October 8, 1939. The dedicatory address was delivered by Dr. Walter E. Bauer, and honorary degrees were conferred upon Dr. Kreinheder, Dr. Dau, and Dr. Ludwig Fuerbringer, President of Concordia Seminary, St. Louis.

Deliberations over the choice of the new president led to discussions of the aims and ideals of a Lutheran university and late in August, 1940, the Executive Committee of the Board set down a directive in the form of four resolutions:

1. That in addition to making Valparaiso an outstanding Christian school energetic work should be directed toward the end that Valparaiso University become the best possible school of arts and sciences.[18]

2. That the location of the University in Valparaiso, Indiana, offers every opportunity to challenge the energies of the administration of the school to make the University a school of the highest order.

3. That its administrators consistently work to the end of coordinating the curriculum with the educational program and needs of the Synodical body.

4. That the Acting President be authorized to direct study relative to the future of Valparaiso University with the view of attaining the aforementioned objectives.

The formulators of this significant directive were Dr. Friedrich, Mr. Sauerman, W. C. Dickmeyer, and Dr. Paul F. Miller.[19]

Accordingly, Dr. Friedrich presented his study, "Valparaiso Looks Ahead," at the Board meeting of October 18, 1939. In this study, he noted that the trend was toward general education in the college years, leaving professional training to the graduate school; that at Valparaiso the requirements of the Association of American Universities with regard to faculty, salaries, endowment, books, and equipment had to be kept in mind; that the small-town location of the University was an advantage which should be preserved; and that while efforts should be made to adapt the University's program to the needs of Synod, Valparaiso should remain outside the Synodical education system. "If the Board of Directors of Valparaiso University has the courage to build slowly and soundly, if it is willing to cooperate with other groups within the Church, and if its ultimate aim is a great university rather than a large one, then," Dr. Friedrich concluded, "the future of Valparaiso looks bright, indeed!" [20]

Appropriate steps were taken in the next months. Expenses were kept within budget limitations and fund raising was devoted to decreasing the deficit and providing funds for current support and equipping the gymnasium. A committee was appointed to study the religious program. Attention was given to the program of recreation for the students so that a substitute could be found for the dancing which "truthfully did not take place where the University was concerned" but which was being done surreptitiously by the students.[21] The health service was established with Walther League funds. And efforts were made to reverse the declining enrollments.

Dr. Walter A. Maier, a member of the faculty at Concordia Seminary and the best-known radio preacher of his day, was offered the presidency in October, 1939, but declined when he found that it would be impossible for him to serve as president and continue his radio ministry simultaneously. On April 18, 1940, the Board elected the Rev. Otto Paul Kretzmann, executive secretary of the Walther League, to the presidency. For almost three months he wrestled with the question of whether he should follow his own inclination and accept or yield to the advice of his closest friends, practically all of whom felt that his greatest opportunities for service lay with the League. At commencement on June 9, 1940, Professor Kretzmann's acceptance was announced and Dr. Friedrich was relieved to learn that he would soon be able to get back to his first love, teaching. At the same time, Dr. Kreinheder was named President Emeritus.

Though many problems still existed, the position of the University had been stabilized and Dr. Friedrich was able to hand over the leadership of the University to his successor with the conviction that "now that the re-organization of the University has been completed, many of the problems that have retarded the develop-

ment of the University have been obviated. I believe the administration of the University should now be able to devote its time to
formulating a long-range program of development that will challenge the imagination of our entire Church!" [22]

NOTES

1. Statement by Edith Kreinheder Shannon, November, 1956.

2. *Minutes* of the Valparaiso University Association, May 3, 1930.

3. *Minutes* of the Lutheran University Association Board of Directors, June 24, 1930, and October 25, 1930.

4. *The Vidette-Messenger*, March 7, 1931. Mr. Hoover's message had been suggested by John Kreinheder, a son of the President, who was a student in the department of engineering.

5. *Minutes* of the Valparaiso University Association, January 15, 1936.

6. Suggestion of Karl Henrichs to the Board, February 2, 1929.

7. Report of the President in the *Minutes* of the Valparaiso University Association, 1930–1931.

8. *The Torch*, XV (December 15, 1927), 11.

9. *The Valparaiso University Bulletin*, New Series, XIV, No. 10 (May 14, 1941), 1.

10. *Minutes* of the Faculty, June 5, 1934; December 8, 1932; and February 1, 1936.

11. *Minutes* of the Executive Committee of the Lutheran University Association, September 25, 1934.

12. *Ibid.*

13. Louise Nicolay, *History of the V.U. Guild, 1931–1950*, p. 8.

14. President's Report to the Board, 1934–1935, pp. 29–30.

15. President's Report to the Board, 1933–1934, p. 9.

16. *Minutes* of the Lutheran University Association Board of Directors, September 22, 1937.

17. *Minutes* of the Lutheran University Association Board of Directors, October 27, 1938.

18. The name of the College of Liberal Arts was changed to the College of Arts and Sciences at the end of the 1939–1940 school year. (*Valparaiso University Bulletin*, February 21, 1940, p. 2.)

19. *Minutes* of the Executive Committee of the Lutheran University Association, August 15 and 29, 1939.

20. "Valparaiso Looks Ahead," p. 2.

21. *Ibid.*, p. 8.

22. Acting President's Report, March 21, 1940, p. 3.

CHAPTER VII

A Lutheran University in America

1940—

THE PRESENT CHAPTER in the history of the University begins on a damp, chilly afternoon, the afternoon of October 6, 1940. The world was once again at war, the University had become dispirited as a result of several successive years of declining enrollments, and the acoustics in the newly-completed gymnasium, where the new president was to deliver his inaugural address, were bad. Against this background, and with a diction which combined the most distinctive elements of Harvard English and the Brooklyn patois, the Rev. O. P. Kretzmann delivered his inaugural address:

Anyone who is charged with the task of speaking on an occasion of this nature in the year of our Lord 1940 must be profoundly conscious of the potential futility of anything which might be said. By this time even the most optimistic observer of the course of human events knows that the world has come to an hour of crisis in the life of man which threatens to destroy all the values of Western civilization as we have known them since the Church emerged from the catacombs. We have come now to the winter of the modern world, and there are few signs of spring. It would be relatively easy, therefore, for us to retire to our campuses, our classrooms and our sanctuaries, to admit that the important things in the world of 1940 are being said by bombs and planes and guns, and to concede the futility of saying anything at all which might be heard above the roar and confusion of a world which is now concerned with another demonstration of the ultimate futility of life without God.

But just here is the justification for a few words which are rooted in the very principles which the new barbarism is seeking to destroy. No matter how futile our words may appear at this moment, the ultimate futility is not here. This twilight hour of the world may darken down into a deeper night than man has ever known before, but the lights by which men find their way between the eternities will not die forever.

133

Once before in the history of the Western world, the lamps of Truth were kept alive by men in hidden places, in half-forgotten schools and monasteries, while the captains and the kings had their little day for almost a thousand years. And then the relentless dust of time covered the sons of the sword, as it always has and always will, and out of the darkness came the bearers of the light, the lone watchers of the lamps, the blessed and terrible Meek for whom Truth is greater than Power, and Wisdom is sharper than a sword. The Almighty is not yet on the side of the strongest battalions. He may not balance the scales of history every day, but when He does, the weight of the Universe is on the side of truth and mercy and justice and faith and hope and love. It is much too late in the time of man for God to forget these now.

It is this great, fundamental fact—a fact which lies at the very heart of my personal philosophy of life and history—which has persuaded me to speak to you today concerning

The Destiny of a Christian University in the Modern World

and to submit to you that in view of the present crisis in the affairs of men this destiny is almost inconceivably great, both intellectually and spiritually. In choosing this topic I feel that I am, in a very small way, paying a debt of gratitude to the men and women who for fifteen years have carried the vision of this destiny in their hearts, and have given this University the full measure of their loyalty and devotion. I am certain also that I am merely reaffirming the compelling influences which guided my distinguished predecessors in their difficult task of reorganizing the University and carrying it safely through one of the most trying periods in the economic and social history of America. I am dominated by the conviction that we are now privileged to enter upon the heritage which they have given us and to build here a school, a center of learning and of faith, whose destiny cannot be limited by forces outside ourselves. The measure of the future of Valparaiso University is our own measure—the measure of our courage and our willingness to sacrifice in order that the dreams of the founders of the University may come true.

Essentially a University is a voluntary association of free men and women in a community which is dedicated to a two-fold task: the search for Truth and the transmission of Truth, free and unbroken, to those who are born later in time. Its first and supreme requirement is a company of men and women who will know Truth when they meet it, no matter whence it comes or whither it leads; who will love Truth more than riches and power; who will conduct the search for Truth with radical sincerity, intellectual honesty, and a deep reverence for even its smallest and faintest gleam; and who will be able to transmit this devotion to the generation who will live long after they have joined the company of the wise and the silent in the graveyards of the world. Especially in the modern world it must be the destiny of a Christian University to cling to the reality of universal truth. There is a moral, philosophical, and scientific Truth which must be one and the same for all races and all nations. For the modern heresy of the relativity of all standards it must substitute the concept of an order of absolute Truth, of absolute ethical goodness, of absolute social justice to which all differences must be submitted, and by which they must be judged. Although we must be ready at all times to admit the partiality of our apprehension of Truth, we must also stand sharply and immovably against the unintelligent and unreasonable pretensions of the philosophies in the modern world which identify the extent of Truth with our partial apprehension of it, or confine it to a certain race or nation. In the fullest and highest sense of the words the Christian University can be and must be, the most catholic and universal and democratic institution in the modern world. It can never compromise with the moral disorder of liberalism or the dangerous heresy that Truth is a slave and not a master.

It is one of the tragedies of the modern educational world that the Church-related college or university has too often failed to recognize its profound and fundamental difference from all schools which have not been integrated by a unified and permanent philosophy of life and history. On the one hand, there can be little doubt that the contributions of the Church-related colleges and universities to the life and progress of America have been far more important and significant than the general public realizes. Since their material resources have often been pitifully limited, they have been unable to meet the American demand for magnificent buildings and great numbers. Despite these handicaps, however, the Church-related college has since the beginnings of the Republic played an important role in the progress and development of American society. On the other hand, it must be noted with regret that it has often been forgetful of its essential mission and message, particularly in the twentieth century. Overwhelmed and even dismayed by the development of education under the almost unlimited resources of the state, it has retreated from the modern world in a pitiful attempt to live by a negation which has at times degenerated into a vicious form of obscurantism. It has too often appealed to its constituency in terms that were entirely negative: We are deserving of your support because we do not do certain things, because we are not as other men are. Even the approach to prospective students has been based on the dubious appeal that in a Christian school they would be protected from the evil that is abroad in the world. Although I yield to no one in my spiritual and intellectual doubt concerning the truth and value of much of the theory and practice which has permeated the educational world for the past twenty-five years, I must reaffirm my conviction that the destiny of a Christian University does not lie in a negative approach to its problems and opportunities. Men and institutions simply can not live by saying "No" to reality. A Christian University can not fulfill its destiny by belittling or even ignoring the impact of science upon the life and thought of man, the manifest tensions in our social order, or the constant and crying need for intelligent reorientation as scholars throughout the world push back the horizons of man toward the Unknown. It must immediately and incessantly appropriate every newly discovered Truth, and place it in the permanent frame of reference which it alone possesses. A Christian University must be in the van of the progress of knowledge, not behind it.

It is this positive and aggressive approach to the problems of a changing world which enables us to face the future of this particular University with absolute confidence in its destiny. Only the school with a Christian orientation can today stand before the rising generation and say: We have something to offer you which you can find nowhere else. Others may try to make men scientific; we must do that—and make them wise. Others may give men knowledge; we must give them that—and understanding. Others may try to make men useful; we must do that—and we must make them noble. We are not asking you to come to an ivory tower to escape from the realities of life or to a market-place where the voices and minds of men are confused by the immediate and material things of life. We are able to give you the fellowship of men and women whose respect for Truth is not vitiated by doubts concerning its reality and permanence. We are able to offer you a school which recognizes the supreme dignity and worth of the individual human being. We are committed to the principle that the destiny of a Christian University lies in the quality of the men and women who are graduated from its halls rather than in quantitative production. Our future lies in the development of men and women, perhaps relatively few in number, whose quality will be so high that they will exert an influence on society which cannot be measured in terms of numbers. Above all, we are deeply committed to the recovery of the one great fact which our wayward world has forgotten: The reality of God and the individual's personal responsibility to Him, a responsibility which can be met only by the fact of the Atonement and the re-establishment of an intimate relationship with the Ruler of the Universe through Him who once entered the stream of time in order to tell men that they could know the Truth and that it would make them free. We can build here a school whose greatness is the greatness of freedom under God, the greatness of the free preservation and transmission of Truth, the greatness of an intelligent and dynamic application of a militant faith. It is our destiny "to enter into the labors and sorrows of the world in order to carry into it the flame of a faith truly free from the world."

In the development of this attitude over against the future of the University there is, of course, always the immediate danger of sentimentalizing or oversimplifying the enormous difficulties which confront us. I have no illusions about them. In the fulfillment of our destiny as a Christian University we shall run head-on into some of the most perplexing problems in modern thought. How can we train a generation which will be both open-minded and deeply committed? Is it possible to be highly intelligent and deeply religious? How much of our thinking must be in terms of the historic other-worldliness of Christianity? Is there an answer for our social problems which will avoid, on the one hand, the evasive sentimentality of many academic solutions, and on the other hand, the immediate pragmatism of those who believe that when a man has bread he has everything? These, and many other, questions will require the hard, cold, realistic processes of thought in the best sense of the word. There can be no doubt that the world of tomorrow will be the scene of two battles. One will be fought with bombs and guns on land, on the sea, and in the air; the other, and, I suspect, the far more important, will be fought in quiet classrooms, in libraries, in laboratories, and in the hidden meetings of men of thought and good will. Nor will it be a battle suspended in the thin, lifeless air of theory; the issue will be a matter of concrete living and desperate importance for the next generation. It will revolve about the great questions which must be answered in our time—our view of God, of the Church, of the State, of man, of the human mind and spirit, its origin, nature, function, and destiny, of the nature of Truth, and many other related issues. It is our destiny to throw ourselves into this battle with all the resources of body, mind, and soul, and to train here a generation which will carry the conquering spirit of a vital Christianity into the life and thought of America.

Is all this a practical program for a Christian University? I must confess that I am somewhat suspicious of the word "practical." If it means that we must always think in terms of compromise, in terms of financial support, in terms of our immediate material needs, then, I truly believe, the word should be eliminated from our thinking. Finances, endowment, enrollment—these are not the primary problems of a Christian University. Perhaps that has been the trouble with Church-related schools. To be practical only in this sense of the word means that we shall go down in defeat. There is only one way of being permanently practical. Let the University set an ideal, a vision, a dream, if you please, for itself—and I am confident that there are still enough men and women in visible Christendom who will see the glory of the dream and, with their prayers and support, help to make it a reality. The human resources of this University today are great. There is the growing body of men and women in the University Association who realize that the future of the Church in America demands the services of a great University. There are the alumni whose loyalty to the school and its mission has been one of the most striking factors in the development of Valparaiso. There are the citizens of the city of Valparaiso who have stood by the school these many years and who, I am sure, will continue to stand by it in the years to come. There are the women of the University Guild whose quiet devotion has already made tremendous contributions to the progress of the University. Perhaps there are men and women in the modern world who honestly believe that we represent a lost cause. I can only say that I am persuaded that lost causes are the only ones that are finally never lost. There is a hidden flame in them which will not die. If God is in them, they can not lose. The prayers of so many men and women for the University will not go unheard and their work will not be in vain.

Permit me to speak for a moment in more immediate terms. The fulfillment of our destiny requires the adoption of a seven-fold program for action in the very near future. I am deeply aware of the fact that I am able to present such a program only on the basis of the heroic work of my distinguished predecessors, Drs. Dau and Kreinheder, and the thoughtful administration of the affairs of the University by its Acting President during the past fifteen months, Dr. Friedrich, who today becomes the Dean of the Faculty. In large part the program of the University for the immediate future has been conceived and prepared by them. The seven concrete and tangible realities which should engage our immediate attention are:

1. The constant and intelligent interpretation of the mission and message of the University to the Church. This will require the full co-operation of the Administration, the Faculty, and the Board of Trustees.

2. The continued building of a faculty of great teachers who will exert a compelling influence on the life and thought of the student body.

3. The development of the social and spiritual life of our student body by means of a deep respect for the dignity and worth of the individual student. This will require the construction of a system of faculty counseling which will bring the students into constant personal relations with their instructors.

4. The extension of the work of the University to metropolitan centers in order to reach men and women who, for one reason or another, can not come to Valparaiso.

5. The preparation of plans for a School of Higher Studies, especially in those fields in which the life and thought of the Church are involved.

6. The periodic release of members of the faculty from other duties so that they may devote themselves more completely to research. This will result in the production of books and articles which will be a contribution to scholarship and to the life of the Church.

7. The immediate formulation of permanent and far-reaching plans for increasing the enrollment of the University. This will require an intelligent interpretation of the purposes of the school to the younger generation and increased student aid.

I am persuaded that these more immediate objectives are not only attainable, but almost desperately imperative if we are to continue the process of building this school toward the vision and dream of its founders and supporters. We shall have no time for the contemplation of possible failure. Ours is a great task. If we are to accomplish it, our spirit must be great—great in its humility, great in its devotion, great in its single-minded, relentless driving toward the realization of the will of God for Valparaiso University.

I should like to say a few words to the men and women of the student body now in residence. When all is said and done, you are the heart of the University. For almost ten years I have noted that one of the most remarkable things about Valparaiso is the spirit of loyalty and fellowship among its students. I hope you will continue to foster and develop that spirit. As many of you know, I am persuaded that the generation of men and women now enrolled in our colleges and universities is far better, both morally and spiritually, than we have been ready to admit. It has become a habit with some members of the older generation to identify the darkest corners of their own minds with the complete mind of the younger generation. This has led to much misunderstanding between the generations which must now desperately face the ultimate problems of life and living together. May I assure you that the administration of the University will always be sympathetically concerned with your problems; that we will recognize you as centrally important; that we will do everything possible to make your campus experience happy and memorable; that we shall consider you ladies and gentlemen who have joined us in this academic community to help us work out the problems of the troubled present and the clouded future. Many of you know already that I have no use for authority which is predicated on vertical relationships; that I believe, deeply and consistently, in the discipline of liberty; and that I shall join you in your impatience with all blind traditionalism; in your opposition to all sham and pretense; and in your fight against all the forces and factors which may prevent your full growth and development. In the years to come you will be the final measure of the success or failure of Valparaiso University. If you will leave this campus prepared to become thoughtful and intelligent citizens of a free and democratic America; sympathetic and understanding healers of a torn and broken society; great and courageous leaders of the Body of Christ in the world—then there is no power on earth that can stop Valparaiso University in the attainment of its destiny.

In this spirit, then, I am deeply grateful for the privilege of joining the company of men and women who have prayed and worked for Valparaiso University these many years. I know that our task is great. Our time is short. It is later now than we think. We can not wait for another time and another generation. Clearly aware of the magnitude of our problems, deeply committed to the importance of our work, humbly certain of our destiny, we may hope, under God, to prepare a growing number of men and women who will go out of this community into the darkness of a dying world as the living embodiment of the motto of this University, "In Thy light we shall see light." To that end I implore the benediction of Almighty God.

When sufficient time has passed to permit an objective appraisal of the Kretzmann administration, it may well be that this speech will be singled out as one of its most significant accomplishments. For overnight the entire atmosphere of the campus changed. The young president was obviously willing to risk his future and the future of the University in a gamble for greatness which, whether it succeeded or failed, would at least provide some excitement. There would be no more marking time. There would be action.

The President's reference in his inaugural address to the heroic work of his distinguished predecessors was not merely a polite gesture. From the Dau, Kreinheder, and Friedrich administrations he had inherited an institution which was academically highly regarded, a faculty which was competent and seasoned, and an acceptance in the Church which was remarkable in view of the fact that it had been built up almost from scratch in a period of only fifteen years. The notable successes of the Kretzmann administration would most likely never have been achieved under less able leadership. But, by the same token, they could not have been achieved had there not been a sound foundation upon which to build.

The two major sources of strength which the Kretzmann administration inherited from its predecessors were the Board of Directors and the faculty. From the beginning of Lutheran administration, the Board had played an active part in the administration of the University and it continued to do so under the new administration. Composed, as it is, primarily of business men, the Board has had the job of translating dreams into budgets. When the Board supports proposals by the President which seem beyond the resources of the University, it is called a rubber stamp. When it disapproves or postpones action on such proposals, it is called obstructionist. In any case, the lot of the Board, like that of the policeman in *The Pirates of Penzance*, "is not a happy one." Nevertheless, the members of the Board have continued to serve year after year with no compensation other than the satisfaction that they derive from helping the impossible to happen.

Upon the faculty has devolved the difficult job of giving practical, day-by-day meaning to such great but necessarily vague abstractions as "the search for Truth and the transmission of Truth," "the intelligent and dynamic application of a militant faith," and "the relevance of the Christian Gospel to the secular disciplines." The brunt of the responsibility for ensuring that these abstractions were realized in academically respectable courses and curricula has fallen upon the deans and the department heads, most of them veterans of two or three decades of service to the University. Still vividly mindful of how difficult it had been for the University to win accreditation, these men have tended to be extremely cautious about any experimentation with the curriculum. Balancing their influence, especially in the past decade, has been the influence of a younger group which has felt that the University is well enough established in the academic world to justify a reasonable amount of experimentation with curricula, course content, and teaching methods. Academic policy has, thus, tended to reflect compromises between the positions of these two groups and can perhaps best be described as progressively conservative.

The dynamic personality of President Kretzmann and the strong leadership which he has given the University through his administration have created the impression, off campus, that the University is largely a "one-man show." Apart from the fact that the University has grown far too large and complex for any one man to control it, the mind boggles at the thought of a reasonably cantankerous board and an even more cantankerous faculty meekly ratifying "front-office" decisions. One of the notable accomplishments of the Kretzmann administration has been that, as the personal prestige of the president has grown, the power of decision-making has been more widely diffused than ever before in the history of the University.

Trial Run

The three problems which the new administration singled out for immediate attention during its first year were enrollment, finances, and the possibility of extending the University's work to Chicago.

The most critical of these problems was enrollment. Speaking to the Board at its October meeting, the president stated that "another year of declining enrollment would be fatal. A school in our position with fewer students is a dying school."[1] Reasons for the decline in enrollment were not hard to suggest: the closing of the Pharmacy School meant a loss of thirty to forty students per year; the reduction of course work in engineering accounted for an additional loss; lack of sufficient funds for student aid made it impossible for some otherwise interested students to register or continue in school; a surplus of ministers in the Church reduced enrollments of pre-theological students in the synodical junior colleges and made it possible for these schools to accept non-theological students who might otherwise have come to Valparaiso; and, in spite of the best efforts of the University's public relations department during the previous decade and a half, there were still large numbers of Lutherans who had either never heard of Valparaiso University or who had no idea that it was a Lutheran university.

The detailed plan of attack upon the enrollment problem which President Kretzmann presented to the October meeting of the Board had been worked out by the registrar, Mr. Scribner.[2] It called for taking advantage of every possible means of publicity and for increasing the recruitment staff. Prior to this time, student procurement had been handled almost entirely by Mr. Henry Stoepplewerth, '31. To assist him, Mr. Frederick Rechlin, who had served as student secretary from 1936 to 1938, was brought back to the campus in February, 1941.

One of the most difficult problems in recruitment was that of assembling a list of student prospects. For this list, the University looked chiefly to the pastors, to its alumni, to members of the student body, to members of the Guild, and to its own public relations staff. It would seem that these sources should have provided pretty thorough coverage of the Church, but, as a matter of fact, coverage was quite uneven. At this time, a surprisingly large number of pastors were as little acquainted with the nature and purpose of the University as was the laity. The other groups to which the University turned for names of prospects were, at this time, still too small or too imperfectly organized to give the kind of help that was needed.

Much of the information program had to be carried out on good will and a shoe-string budget. Editors of the church publications were, by now, almost solidly behind the University and were generous in publicizing its accomplishments and its needs. In the absence of a press secretary, the staff of the *Torch* took on the job of feeding information to non-church publications.[3] The President, the faculty, and student leaders stood ready to accept any speaking dates which might bring the University a little more attention.

Persuading the student that Valparaiso was the place for him was, however, only half the job. By far the greater number of prospective students needed the assurance of some kind of financial help. The Board, accordingly, authorized a large increase in the student-aid budget. In doing so, it made one of the wisest investments it has ever made, for most of the University's student leaders and most active alumni have been "student-aid" students.

There was also considerable discussion, at this time, of the possibility of having a movie made to show prospective students what life was like on campus. Estimates of the cost of such a movie ran as high as twenty thousand dollars and the idea was almost abandoned. Finally, however, the Board voted fifteen hundred dollars for the purpose and turned the project over to Mr. Stoepplewerth for execution. A student, Donald Bohl, took the pictures; an alumnus, Lowell Thomas, did the narration; and the film, done in color and running fifty-five minutes, was issued in the summer of 1942. It proved to be a very effective means of student recruitment.

Finally, there was the handicap to recruitment imposed by the restricted social program at the University. Both Dr. Friedrich and President Kretzmann had listed the ban on dancing as one of the causes of the decline in enrollment.[4] At the very beginning of his administration, President Kretzmann had stated his personal opposition to the ban, but he promised that he would go to all lengths to exhaust the possibilities of living with it. In January, 1941, he brought Mrs. C. R. ("So") Heidbrink to the campus as social director and gave her the impossible assignment of organizing a social program which would make the students forget that they wanted to dance. The students gallantly rallied around "So," who quickly won both their affection and their sympathy, and at some personal inconvenience managed to include her parties in their social programs—in addition to the dances which were still being sponsored by the fraternities and sororities and which were reported in the *Torch* under such euphemisms as "frolics" and "socials." After about five years of this experiment, the possibilities had been exhausted. The Board, in March, 1942, rescinded the ban on dancing and defined it as a "neutral" matter, and in 1946 Mrs. Heidbrink happily took on the equally arduous job of secretary to the president, in addition to her duties as Director of Social Activities.

These various attacks upon the enrollment problem proved gratifyingly successful. Enrollment in the 1941–1942 academic year rose to 480, an increase of eighty-one over the previous year, and the largest increase, in terms of percentages, in the sixteen-year history of the L. U. A. Even more encouraging was the increase in the following year to a total of 531 students, for the general trend in college enrollments at this time was downward because of the war.

A particular concern of the administration at this time was the geographical distribution of the student body. In the academic year 1940–1941, about eighty-five per cent of the students were drawn from the five Midwestern states of Indiana, Illinois, Ohio, Michigan, and Wisconsin. While this distribution coincided rather closely with the geographical distribution of Missouri Synod Lutherans, it was felt that there was danger in permitting the University to be typed as a regional institution or, as Mr. Henrichs put it, "a freshwater college in northern Indiana." A continuing effort was, therefore, begun to cultivate certain other sections of the country more intensively, particularly the East Coast, the West Coast, and Texas, all of which had significantly large Lutheran populations.

The second of the University's most immediate problems, finances, did not lend itself as readily as did enrollment to solution by a "crash program." Every college and university in the country was feeling the effects of the Depression and Valparaiso was feeling the additional effects of its short life as a Lutheran university and its unofficial status in the Church. President Kretzmann felt that it was also suffering from the effects of an attitude which it had itself fostered in the Church by its repeated appeals for funds. "Unwittingly," he told the Board, "we have created a psychology of failure in our constituency. This process must be reversed before it is too late."[5] Instead of appealing to the constituency to come to the rescue of an institution that might go defunct if contributions did not come in, he proposed to emphasize the great promise which the future held for a university which had already laid a solid base for future development. For his own part, he undertook to travel to all parts of the constituency to tell the University's story. The Board, meanwhile, in April, 1941, approved a "Five-Year Plan for University Development" which, it was hoped, would bring in

The Rev. Otto Paul Kretzmann, S.T.M., Litt.D., D.D., LL.D.
President of the University since 1940.

Guild Hall

Memorial Hall stands just to the west of Guild Hall. The cornerstone for the Guild-Memorial Quadrangle was laid on September 28, 1946.

Herbert W. Knopp, M.A.

*Coordinator of University Relations,
1948–1955.*

Herman C. Hesse, M.E.

*Dean of the College of Engineering since
1948.*

Allen Edmond Tuttle, Ph.D.

*Dean of the College of Arts and Sciences
since 1957.*

Knute D. Stalland, LL.B.

Dean of the School of Law since 1956.

Mr. Paul F. Amling

*Member of the Board of Directors since
1938.*

Mr. Paul Brandt

*President of the Lutheran University
Asssociation since 1953.*

The President, the Deans, the Professors and the Heads of Departments in Academic Dress for the Opening Convocation of the 1958–1959 Academic Year, the First Public Event Held in the Memorial Chapel.

The Valparaiso Union

The Memorial Chapel

Showing the Chapel as it appeared while still under construction in the Fall of 1958.

Architect's Drawing of the Henry F. Moellering Memorial Library, Scheduled to be Completed in the Summer of 1959.

more than a million dollars in additional income between 1941 and 1946. Of this amount $500,000 was to go for current expenses. The balance was to go into student procurement, a public relations program, the establishment of an alumni association, a social program, faculty salaries, additions to the faculty, a Chicago extension, and campus renovation. Mr. E. J. Gallmeyer volunteered his services as director of this plan.

As it turned out, world conditions necessitated radical changes in the plan. The $500,000 needed for current expenses was raised, but even this sum lost much of its purchasing power in the wartime inflation. Land for a Chicago extension was purchased, but no building was erected. The hope for a new library remained only a hope. But the campaign was a success in terms of publicizing the University within its constituency, and this success was reflected in a notable increase in the annual congregational collections. In 1940, collections in 937 congregations totaled a little less than $25,000. By 1945, collections in more than a thousand congregations totaled more than $100,000.[6] Within the same period, total public relations income more than doubled.

The third problem which the new administration had singled out for immediate attention—that of extending its work to Chicago —was taken out of its hands by the war. The site which the University acquired, across "Bughouse Square" from the great Newberry Library, was an eminently desirable one. The site was bought jointly by the University and the International Walther League. The League built shortly after the purchase and moved into its new headquarters in 1942. The war forced the University to postpone its plans for construction and, by the end of the war, the pressing need for expansion of facilities in Valparaiso forced an indefinite postponement of plans for a Chicago campus. Meanwhile the development of Lutheran high schools in the Chicago area made it possible for the University to inaugurate an extension program which makes use of the facilities of these schools.

The rise in enrollment and the prospects of greater income made it possible for the University, in the fall of 1941, to expand its curriculum. In response to many requests for work in journalism, a co-operative program was worked out with Northwestern University's Medill School of Journalism. Dean Friedrich had had his doubts about the amount of real interest in journalism in the constituency and, as it turned out, his doubts were justified. After several years of dormancy, this program was dropped from the catalogue after the 1947–1948 school year.

Other curricular changes that were made that fall were to have more permanent significance. The completion of the new gymnasium made it possible to organize a department of health and physical education and to make courses in physical education a requirement for graduation. In the Department of Foreign Languages, courses in Spanish were introduced and immediately attracted large enrollments. The Department of Religion and Philosophy was divided, its head, Dr. A. T. Haentzschel, becoming head of the new Department of Philosophy and Sociology, and Dean Kumnick relinquishing the deanship of students to become head of the new Department of Religion. The Department of Social Science was restyled the Department of History and Political Science with Dr. Schwiebert continuing as head of the department. Work in art was also introduced at this time but not on a large enough scale to justify the establishment of a department.

In his inaugural address, President Kretzmann had expressed his distaste for "authority which is predicated on vertical relationships." His first administrative move to grant a larger measure of self-discipline to the student body was the abolition, in the fall of 1941, of the office of Dean of Students and the transfer of most of its disciplinary functions to a "Faculty-Student Council." This Council has continued to the present. The growth of the student body after the war made it impractical, however, to handle disciplinary cases under the necessarily cumbersome procedures of a council, and the council functions today chiefly as an advisory body to the Dean of Men and the Dean of Women. Informally, students were granted a far greater measure of freedom than is usual in American colleges and universities. The Student Council became very effective in student government, the publications were given full freedom of expression without any faculty censorship, fraternity and sorority presidents were given disciplinary authority in their houses, dormitories were given a large measure of autonomy under elected house councils, and the president's door was opened wide to any student who wanted to talk to him. Until his marriage in the summer of 1942 (to Miss Flora Rosenthal, an alumna of the University), the bachelor president ran a kind of informal student union in the President's House. Impressionable undergraduates, thrown into almost daily contacts with the President, were quick to adopt his mannerisms, and, for a year or two, the Valparaiso student could be identified by his habit of tugging the lobe of his right ear, dropping terminal "r's," sprinkling his conversation with such expressions as "I am profoundly persuaded" and "ultimate meaning," and substituting a "d" for "th." Some students went so far as to clutter their rooms with candles and to try to acquire a taste for Bach.

Time Out for a War

On the afternoon of Sunday, December 7, 1941, the three residents of Suite 2 of the Kappa Iota Pi fraternity house were studying with a radio playing softly over in a corner. Suddenly the program was interrupted for a special announcement, the announcement of the Japanese attack upon Pearl Harbor. One of the men slowly closed his book, laid it carefully on his desk, and said: "We won't be needing these any more." That was how World War II came to the campus of Valparaiso University. Within the next year, the three men who had been studying together that afternoon were scattered, one to the Army in the Southwest Pacific, one to the Navy on the North Atlantic run, and one to the Marine Corps. For the time being, at least, they did not need their books.

Within a month after Pearl Harbor, American colleges and universities had worked out policies and procedures designed to salvage as much as possible of education as usual while, at the same time, contributing as effectively as they could to the war effort. Valparaiso co-operated fully with the recommended practices. The school year was reorganized on a twelve-month basis with three sixteen-week semesters, final examinations were shortened to one hour, and all vacations except Good Friday were cancelled. Changes were also made in the curriculum to conform to recommendations of the National Conference of College and University Presidents on Higher Education and War. Non-credit Red Cross courses in home-nursing and first-aid were conducted on campus for interested women students. In the evening, a number of government-sponsored defense training courses were conducted by members of the faculty and others for workers and potential workers in defense plants. All men not already enrolled in a physical education course were required to attend a two-hour-per-week pre-induction physical training course, which included boxing, wrestling, calisthenics, posture, and jiujitsu. During the first months of the war, the University conducted a series of national defense convocations for students, faculty, and local citizens.

At the outset of the war, the Selective Service system announced that there would be no more blanket deferment of college students. Preference would be shown to students who were close to graduation, whose work was of acceptable quality, and who showed a willingness to complete their degree work as soon as possible. In the months that followed, the different branches of the armed services set up reserve programs for college students. By January, 1943, more than 130 men on the campus were enrolled in one or another of these programs. But, by the early part of 1943, men in all of these programs except the Navy programs were being called up and the programs were, in effect, abandoned.

By February, 1943, college enrollments in the country as a whole were down 9½ per cent from their December, 1941, figure. But thanks to the University's intensive student recruitment program, Valparaiso's enrollment showed an increase of 9½ per cent for this same period. The enrollment during the academic year 1941–1942 was 480; for the fall and winter semesters of 1942–1943 it was 531. But the spring of 1943 told a very different story. Five hundred men had left the campus for the armed services between December, 1941, and October, 1943,[7] and enrollment for the year of April, 1943, to April, 1944, was down to a low of 399. When the fall semester opened in 1943, there were 332 students on campus of whom 234 were women. The few men remaining on campus were either 4-F's or members of the navy reserve program or under eighteen years of age.

President Kretzmann recalls these years as his interlude as president of a ladies' seminary. Reconciled to the fact that the war would continue to claim practically every potential male student, the University set about making the campus and the curriculum more attractive to women. In the fall of 1943, the Lutheran Deaconess Association set up its training program on the campus with six students. A course in home management was introduced in the fall of 1943, and in the following February, a $3,000 gift was used to purchase the Mathilda Heldt Home Economics Laboratory, a small house located at the north end of the old campus. In the fall of 1944, majors were introduced in sociology and in home economics, and a pre-professional curriculum was set up in social work.

As a result of these changes, there was a large increase in the number of women on campus, and the great preponderance of women made it necessary to reorganize campus housing. By the fall of 1943, only two fraternities—Kappa Iota Pi and Sigma Delta Chi—still had enough members on campus to maintain their houses. The Alpha Phi sorority took over the Phi Psi fraternity house and the women of Gamma Phi moved into the former AE fraternity house. One wing of Lembke Hall was closed and the men were housed in the south wing. By the fall of 1944, even this male stronghold had fallen; Lembke had become a women's dormitory.

The few men who were left on campus found themselves living in a semi-benevolent matriarchy. Socially, they had things made. But so far as campus affairs were concerned they were a voiceless minority. In December, 1943, Miss Barbara Bernthal became the first woman Student Council president in the University's history. The war years and the two years that followed saw five women *Torch* editors. During one summer, a men's softball team was organized with a woman pitcher.[8] And while most of the fraternities were temporarily closed, a new sorority, Delta Chi Epsilon, was organized in November, 1944.

The exodus of men from the campus necessitated a complete reorganization of the athletic program. Intercollegiate football was dropped during the 1943 and 1944 seasons. Basketball, however, thrived as never before in the University's history. These were the days of "The World's Tallest Team," made up of men who, by reason of their remarkable heights, were ineligible for military service.

The origin of the World's Tallest Team dates back to the time when Loren E. Ellis was coaching at Michigan City High School, prior to his coming to Valparaiso University. At that time, he came across two tall and gangly players who showed little athletic promise, other than sheer height. These two boys, Don and Wally Warnke, were in their junior year of high school at that time and they already had reached the unusual height of 6'10".

Coach Ellis realized that these boys would not reach their full potential in high school because of this unusual size and, with that in the back of his mind, he decided to seek a college job where he could develop them under his supervision and take full advantage of this material, knowing that such an opportunity probably would never repeat itself.

With the two Warnkes as a nucleus, Ellis filled in the balance of his squad with "little" boys, six-feet-two and over, ending with a squad average of 6'6". Among these was 6'6" George Maddock, who later transferred to Northwestern, where he starred in football and basketball.

With this combination, Ellis was able to win seventeen out of twenty-two games in his first season with the start of what was to become the World's Tallest Team.

Then in the 1944–45 season, with several 6'10"ers added to the squad, the Crusaders really brought national and international fame to Valparaiso University as the World's Tallest Team. Sports fans all over the world saw the team in Paramount Newsreels.

Thousands of GI's read about the cagers from a small Indiana school on the front pages of STARS AND STRIPES in Germany, France, and Japan. U.S. fans saw the Ellis-coached team perform in gymnasiums in wide-spread areas across the nation and outside of the nation in Puerto Rico.

By the end of the season, Coach Ellis and his amazing Crusaders had travelled 8,800 miles through 19 states, and had met the toughest teams in the country.

During their reign as the world's tallest team, the Ellis-men won 55 and lost 16, for one of the best records in the country during that period. This record included wins over Long Island University in Madison Square Garden, Holy Cross in Boston Garden, Wyoming, Drake, DePaul, Hamline, Great Lakes and many other teams of like calibre. The Crusaders were one of three teams that could defeat the Sailors of Great Lakes on their home floor during the wartime years.[9]

The war years were a critical time for the School of Law. Its enrollment dropped from nineteen men and four women in the 1941–1942 academic year to three men and one woman in the fall of 1943. Women were urged to enroll in the Law School to enable the School to keep its charter, but during much of this period professors outnumbered students in the Law School.

The war crisis also cut deeply into the faculty. During this period, eight members of the faculty resigned, one retired, and eight took leaves of absence—a total of sixteen drop-outs from a faculty of fifty-one members.[10] The losses were, however, offset by the appointment of sixteen full-time and eight part-time faculty members during this time. But it was a real sacrifice to teach during the war. The wartime inflation sapped the purchasing power of the dollar, and salaries in industry were very attractive.

The University as a whole suffered as much as did its faculty members from the effects of the inflation. In April, 1942, President Kretzmann had to inform the Board that income was some $50,000 behind expenditures and that, while contributions from the Church were increasing, they were not increasing fast enough to keep up with the increases in costs. To meet this situation, the Board considered it advisable to put the whole responsibility for public relations, including publicity and alumni work, in the hands of one man. Dean Friedrich handled this assignment in 1942 and 1943. In 1943, the Rev. Frederick L. Miller was appointed full-time coordinator of public relations. Plagued throughout his period of service by the shortage of money occasioned by the government's appeals for funds and harassed by a succession of heart attacks, Pastor Miller nevertheless managed to narrow the gap between income and expenditures and, in the process, laid a solid base for postwar financial development.

Shortages of funds, manpower, and materials made it impossible for the University to do a great deal in the way of physical development during the war. But notable progress was made in other directions, and two of the most distinctive institutions of the University date from this period, the counseling system and the Honor Code.

After the abolition of the office of Dean of Students in 1941, it became apparent that there was need of some office to deal with student problems, personal and academic. In the fall of 1943, therefore, a personnel office was established with Dr. Marshall John Jox as personnel director. Dr. Jox recruited a staff of counselors from the faculty and organized a central file of personnel records. For several years an attempt was made to encourage students to bring not only their academic problems but their personal problems as well to their counselors. But students have a way of choosing their own counselors on personal matters and gradually the counseling system came to be restricted, in practice, to academic counseling.

The initiative for the establishment of an Honor System came from the student body. In March, 1943, the Student Council passed a resolution proposing that the honor system be instituted in all classes in which a secret vote showed at least 80 per cent of the students in favor of the system. In the months that followed, the students indicated in a series of all-campus meetings that they favored an unqualified honor system.[11] The proposition was placed before the faculty which, after much discussion, resolved that, beginning with the fall semester of 1943, the honor system would govern all matters concerning honesty in academic work. Provision was made for a faculty-student honor council to administer the system.

The system broke down temporarily under the influx of new students at the end of the war, and, during the second semester of the 1946–1947 academic year, proctoring was reintroduced in lower division courses. By the following fall, however, the system was restored after new safeguards had been built into its educational and enforcement procedures. Since that time the system has become firmly rooted on the campus and, despite the allegations of a newspaper columnist that honor systems favor the crook,[12] has proved far more effective than a proctoring system in maintaining a high level of honesty in academic work.

Although, as has been noted, building programs were out of the question during the war, the physical condition of the campus was not neglected. In 1942, the Lutheran Laymen's League donated $1,000 for campus improvement, and with these and other funds the University undertook to raze the old houses which still stood on the campus. With the razing of these houses, the singular unattractiveness of the west side of Lembke Hall stood fully revealed and this situation was remedied by the construction of a new facade. The block of College Avenue which ran from Freeman Street to the Bookstore was vacated by the city and torn up by the student body in 1946 and the former roadbed was converted into a grassy mall bordered by sidewalks. Finally, to complete the process of campus unification, the "wailing wall" was built at the Freeman Street entrance to set the campus off as an entity.

Meanwhile, the Board was anticipating a huge increase in enrollment at the end of the war and casting about for a solution to the housing problem which would accompany this increase. High on the list of necessary new buildings was a women's dormitory. Early in the spring of 1944, Edward Jansson, the University's architect, and several members of the Board were discussing a possible location for this new dormitory. Standing near the gymnasium and looking eastward toward the broad tract of land which lay between the gymnasium and Highways 30 and 49, Mr. Jansson said,

"You should have that property." His remark was taken up by Mr. Paul Amling, the chairman of the Board's committee on buildings and grounds, who gave Mr. Scribner $1,000 and told him to take options on the properties included in this tract. To keep land values from sky-rocketing, Mr. Scribner engaged a local building and loan official to make a complete survey and appraisal of the properties involved and had another local real estate agent obtain the necessary options. The asking price for the whole tract totaled $42,792.70.

Several other members of the Board were now brought into the picture. Six men—Paul Amling, John Sauerman, Robert Moellering, Fred Wehrenberg, W. C. Dickmeyer, and Paul Rupprecht—raised $22,500 among themselves. Forming a temporary corporation, they then went to a Fort Wayne bank and obtained the balance of the asking price on a mortgage. But there was one snag in the operation. One piece of land which lay in the very heart of the tract was owned by two sisters who lived somewhere in a small community in Florida. No address was available other than the name of the town. Mr. Scribner left immediately for Florida to hunt down the two sisters. Arriving at the village, he hired a cab and told the driver to start driving. Every time they passed anyone on the street, Mr. Scribner would lean out of the cab and ask about the whereabouts of the two sisters. After considerable driving and inquiring, Mr. Scribner located the sisters and closed the deal for their property.

On a set date, the owners of the various properties were instructed to come to a Valparaiso bank with their deeds and receive full payment for their land. One by one, they turned over their deeds and were paid in full. In a few hours, the University was in possession of ninety-two acres of new land at an average cost of $381 per acre. When word of the transaction was released to the local newspaper, real estate values more than doubled in the campus neighborhood.

In the April, 1944, meeting of the Board, the six men who had bought the land advised the Board of their action and offered the property to the University for $35,095.78. Naturally, the Board accepted their offer. The members of the temporary corporation were paid off in L. U. A. promissory notes, most of which were later returned to the University as a gift.[13] Of the balance, $12,000 was taken out of endowment funds and the remainder was appropriated from current funds. In the next two years, fifteen additional acres were acquired at a cost of $15,000.

Thus, at the time when it needed it most, the University got the space it had to have for the growth and development which the Board and the administration expected would follow the end of the war. Planning for the new Valparaiso now went forward more vigorously than ever before, but even as the University planned its future it took time to remember those of its sons who had paid with their lives for the right of the nation and the University to plan their own futures:

Ivar N. Anderson	Henry Kuntz
Eric Andres	William Ladwig
Thomas Auck	Steve Nobel
G. W. Bond, Jr.	John Patterson
Gilbert Butler	John Pohlman
Donald J. Finneran	William Rehwinkel
Warren G. Goetz	William Sablotny
Donald Hancock	Walter Woycik
Edward Jiede	Robert Zellen [14]
Edward Komasinski	

Readjustment and Expansion

At one time or another during the course of the war, more than seventeen million men and women were serving in the armed forces of the United States. Of this number, some 95,000 were Lutheran.[15] It was evident that the University would have to be prepared to accept its share of the large number of veterans who could be expected to return to the nation's colleges and universities at the war's end.

Most of the returning veterans had no great financial problem. Under the provisions of the Servicemen's Readjustment Act of 1944 (the "GI Bill"), the government offered to subsidize the education of any veteran at the school of his choice so long as he maintained a satisfactory level of work. But many veterans had other problems. Some of them did not have high school diplomas, although it was evident that they had the equivalent of a high school background as the result of travel, reading, and experience. Some of the veterans had taken course work through the Armed Forces Institute. Some had acquired a high level of technical or vocational competence in armed forces training programs. The University adapted its policies to meet the special needs of these veterans, permitting veterans to enter on the basis of equivalency examinations if they lacked a high school diploma, allowing credit for certain work done in the armed forces, permitting students with deficiencies in their preparation to matriculate as special students, and allowing blanket credit of eight hours for military service.

A more difficult problem to solve was the problem of housing. Campus housing was sufficient for enrollments of five to six hundred students, but it was obvious that post-war enrollments would run to two or three times this figure. Moreover, there was the special problem that a considerable number of the veterans were married. Several even had children. The University had never before needed to provide housing for married students.

Anticipating the housing problem, the University in March, 1945, purchased two buildings which had formerly belonged to the Dodge Institute of Radio and Telegraphy for $18,000 and spent $82,000 in renovating them. Eventually, it was planned to use these buildings for veterans' housing. In the fall of 1945, however, Dodge Hall became a women's dormitory and has remained that ever since. The University also purchased six other residences for use in the fall semester. Two of these were leased to sororities. The "Stoner House," across the street from Altruria Hall, was converted into a women's dormitory. Later it was reconverted into the University Health Center.

Despite these preparations, the University found itself faced with a critical housing shortage when the fall semester opened in September, 1945. The administration had anticipated an enrollment of about seven hundred students of which one-third were expected to be veterans.[16] As it turned out, enrollment that fall totaled 742 students, an increase of 273 over the spring semester. The dispossessed fraternities moved back into their houses, aggravating the already serious condition in women's housing; the Dodge Hall renovation project was not completed until several weeks after the semester opened, and promised deliveries of furniture and equipment did not materialize until the semester was well under way. The students, generally, accepted the unsettled situation philosophically, but it was difficult for some parents to leave their children in an institution which looked something like a refugee settlement. Fortunately for the University, other institutions were having the same kind of problem.

The situation became even more critical at the beginning of the second semester, when 150 new freshmen arrived to swell the total enrollment to 960, almost twice what it had been a year before.[17] Room had to be found quickly to accommodate the new arrivals. At the beginning of the year, Stiles Hall, a large privately-owned apartment and rooming house, was purchased for conversion to a dormitory and apartment building designed to house seventy-one students and eleven couples, but it would take until fall to complete its renovation. Fifteen two-room trailers were acquired for veterans' housing from the Public Housing Authority and set up at the far west end of the new campus. A number of students moved to Kingsford Heights, a war-plant community near LaPorte, and bus transportation was provided to permit them to commute to the campus. Local civic organizations found another seventy-five rooms within the city.[18]

The full impact of the post-war enrollment boom did not hit the campus, however, until the 1946–1947 academic year. In the fall semester of that year, enrollment reached a new high of 1,406, a figure which was topped by the spring semester enrollment of 1,541. Undoubtedly it would have gone even higher if there had been sufficient housing to accommodate a larger number. Three more houses were bought, three discarded barracks were acquired from the Public Housing Administration and erected on the new campus, and the inn at the Indiana Dunes State Park was leased from the State. Students lived wherever there was room for a bed and a chair, many of them in places which the University considered sub-standard. It is a tribute to the student body that, at a time when the physical fragmentation of the campus made it impossible for the University to maintain effective disciplinary control, the general level of discipline remained high.

The rapid growth of the student body required not only increased housing facilities but also greatly increased instructional facilities. In January, 1946, the old "Birkholz House," the last privately-owned building on the old campus, was purchased, named "Arts Annex," and converted into a classroom and office building. In the spring of 1946, the Auditorium was thoroughly reconditioned at a cost of $60,000.[19] An addition was built onto the library, and the original library structure was reconditioned to allow more study space and additional offices. Major improvements and repairs were made on the old Engineering Building and the Biology Building and a complex of frame buildings was erected on Mound Street, across from Lembke Hall, to provide more classrooms and a cafeteria. But even this increase in facilities only barely managed to keep pace with needs. In the fall semester of 1946, 99 per cent of all classroom space was occupied during the morning class hours.

Another immediate and pressing need at the time was for additional equipment. Two members of the faculty, Professor M. W. Uban and Dr. Raymond G. Larson, were relieved of their teaching duties and sent out in search of equipment. By the time they had completed their assignment, these two men had gathered a considerable amount of equipment, especially for the biology, chemistry, and engineering departments. The largest single lot of equipment was for the engineering department, four carloads of material worth approximately $100,000 which had been obtained from a defense plant.[20] To accommodate this new material, it was necessary to construct an annex to the engineering building. This structure, built across the alley from the old engineering building, became the engineering machine shop. This building and the equipment which it contained paved the way for the re-introduction of the four-year engineering curriculum several years later.

Much of the expansion in the years immediately after the war was necessarily makeshift. But already in March, 1946, the Board began to plan a long-range program of new and permanent housing construction. Their first concern was for additional suitable housing for women.

A fact which is not generally appreciated outside the administrative offices of a college or university is that increases in enrollment are likely to aggravate, rather than to solve, an institution's financial difficulties. Even the student who "pays his own way" pays only a little more than half of the cost of his education. The balance must be made up from other sources—State funds or private gifts. Thus at the very time that enrollment was ceasing to be a problem, the financial difficulties of the University increased. The cost of campus renovation and expansion had already run to $450,-000. Current expenses for faculty expansion and the purchase of additional equipment would require another $400,000. And the cost of two new women's dormitories was estimated at $750,000. Thus the Board faced the necessity of finding more than $1,500,000 to carry out the most immediately necessary projects that the increase in enrollment demanded. In the fall of 1946, therefore, it embarked upon another campaign—this time for $1,600,000—under the direction of the Rev. Frederick L. Miller.

Pastor Miller conducted what was probably the best-planned and most intensive campaign that the University had attempted up to that time. But the results were disappointing. But even if the campaign had succeeded it would not have accomplished the purpose for which it had been designed, for the mounting costs of labor and materials pushed the estimates on the new dormitories up from $750,000 to $1,352,300.[21] Construction went ahead, nevertheless, for the University could not afford to risk the good will of its constituency by keeping its women students in substandard living-quarters.

On September 28, 1946, in connection with ceremonies marking the fifteenth anniversary of the Valparaiso University Women's Guild, President Kretzmann laid the cornerstone for the two new women's dormitories. For five years, from 1941 to 1946, the Guild had been raising funds for the dormitories and, by the time construction began, it was able to turn over $70,617.47 to the University. In the following year, the Guild collected an additional $28,-255.80.[22] In grateful recognition of what was truly a herculean effort for such a small organization, the University named one of the new dormitories Guild Hall. In the hope that someday someone might underwrite the cost of the other dormitory, it was named Memorial Hall. At this writing it is still a memorial to an as yet undiscovered donor.

The greatest single threat posed to the University during this period of rapid expansion was the danger of losing its distinctive character. Students who could remember the small campus of pre-war years when everybody knew everybody else viewed the rising enrollment with misgivings. The administration was equally concerned, but realistically faced up to the alternatives that were presented to it. On the one hand, there was the alternative of limiting enrollment, a choice which would have meant refusing admission to large numbers of Lutheran students whose parents and congregations could hardly have been expected to continue to support an institution which would not serve them. The other alternative was to put every available penny into additional facilities and accept as many students as the facilities permitted. To President Kretzmann, it was a choice of "expand or die." [23] In the initial phases of the expansion, much of the pre-war atmosphere of the University was lost. But, by 1950 or 1951, the University had adjusted to its new size and complexity and much of the pre-war atmosphere had been restored.

An even more serious concern for the administration was that the necessity of greatly expanding the faculty might result in a weakening of the distinctively Lutheran tone of the University. From 1925 on, one of the most serious limitations under which the University had had to operate was the shortage of Lutherans who were academically qualified to teach on the college level. The first and most important assignment facing Dr. Walter E. Bauer when he succeeded Dr. Friedrich as dean of the faculty in the fall of 1946 was the recruitment of a faculty large enough to cope with the increased enrollment and Lutheran enough to maintain the Lutheran character of the University. Since there were still relatively few Lutherans with doctorates, Dean Bauer sought out promising young men who had earned the Master's degree and who intended to continue work toward their doctorates. This meant a considerable reduction in the formerly high percentage of doctorates on the faculty, but it brought in a sizable group of enthusiastic young scholars who could be expected, in the normal course of events, to serve the University for many years to come and thus give a high degree of stability to the faculty.

The curriculum was expanded during this period as new instructors were brought to the campus. A new major was offered in the Department of Religion, making Valparaiso one of the few church-related universities not offering professional work in theology to offer a major in religion.[24] In the fall of 1946, a new major was offered in psychology, and in the following spring a major was offered in government. The School of Law also participated in the general expansion of this period. Between 1946 and 1948, eleven courses were added to its curriculum, two thousand volumes were added to the law library, and enrollment grew to almost sixty.

A favorite topic of war-time viewers-with-alarm had been the probable catastrophe that would overtake the colleges and universities of the country when the veterans returned to the campus. The same type of mentality that had saddled the serviceman with the opprobrious nickname, "GI," conjured up visions of thousands of drunken, sex-starved "psychos" descending upon the campuses where they would work off their resentments against military discipline on instructors and administrators. Some even suggested it might be safer to run the veterans through some sort of emotional decontamination program before unleashing them upon society.

It is to the credit of the nation's colleges and universities that they did not share these fears. Certain problems of readjustment could be anticipated and were provided for. Lengthy interruptions of formal education cause some difficulty in getting back to the academic routine. The University provided counseling for veterans who were having this difficulty. Governmental operating procedures sometimes resulted in delays in payment of allowances to veterans. The University adjusted its deadlines for payment to meet these conditions and arranged for short-term loans to tide the veteran over his period of embarrassment. Occasionally, a veteran would show signs of unusual difficulty in readjusting to civilian life. Many members of the faculty gave long hours of informal counseling to these students.

The few problems which the veteran posed were more than offset by his contribution to the life and work of the campus. The more inane campus traditions which had survived from the raccoon coat and hip flask era held no attractions for mature young men who had been engaged in the serious business of fighting a war. Classroom discussions reflected the broader background and the greater maturity of the veteran group. Three new fraternities were organized with predominantly veteran membership—Rho Lambda Tau (now a chapter of Lambda Chi Alpha) and Omega Chi Beta in 1946, and Kappa Phi Tau (now a chapter of Sigma Phi Epsilon) in 1947.

Veterans also played a leading role in student affairs. For a number of years they supplied the major student officers, and they took the initiative in developing new campus activities. Two important activities which profited greatly from veteran leadership were the intramural athletic program and the University Youth Council. The intramural program held a great appeal to veterans who had learned to enjoy vigorous physical exercise but who did not feel inclined to take time from studies or family responsibilities to participate in intercollegiate athletics. The formation of the University Youth Council in 1947 reflected the social concern which many of the veterans had developed in war-ravaged lands where their generosity to distressed children has become legendary.

Back to Normal

By the beginning of the 1947–1948 academic year, a semblance of normality had returned to campus. Enrollments continued to grow—to 2,067 in 1947–1948, to 2,099 in 1948–1949, and to 2,203 in 1949–1950—but the University was in a much better position to handle them. Students and instructors had become accustomed to their new and more complex environment, the war became more and more of an unreal memory, and attention came to be focused more and more upon questions of the long-range future.

The small enrollments of the war years and the expansion of the post-war years had left the University with an uncomfortably large debt which threatened to grow larger unless new sources of income could be found to offset the cost of new buildings that would be needed to house students who were living in temporary dormitories and classes that were meeting in war-surplus buildings. Any expansion of the University's curriculum seemed to be out of the question until finances and facilities had caught up with the expansion that had already been authorized.

But with the increase in the number of men on campus there developed a growing demand for restoration of four-year work in engineering. This demand was reinforced by pressure from the constituency. Registration in the pre-engineering courses grew from 78 in 1945–1946 to 245 in 1946–1947 and to 280 in 1947–1948. Studies showed also that the engineering department was turning away more potential students than any other department on campus. In 1946, therefore, the Board engaged Professor Carl A. Muhlenbruch of the Carnegie Institute of Technology to survey the University's facilities and to give his opinion on the possibility of re-establishing a College of Engineering. In January, 1947, Professor Muhlenbruch reported to the Board that he felt that a four-year program in engineering could be instituted with a minimum expenditure of funds.[25] The Board thereupon appointed a committee to look into the matter and, in October, 1947, resolved to go ahead with re-establishing the College as soon as possible.[26]

Late in April, 1948,[27] President Kretzmann discussed the possibility of resuming four-year work in engineering with the Engineering Society. He pointed out that the program would have to wait for a while, though, because the University had no funds to go ahead with the necessary building project at that time. Thereupon the students took over. If the University would furnish materials and technical direction, they would provide the labor and solicit funds for a new building.[28] Eleven different unions were persuaded to allow the building to be built with student labor, a student working crew was organized for the following summer, and a committee was organized to approach the Board of Directors for permission to go ahead with the project.

The Board was understandably reluctant to authorize such an unconventional project; but the enthusiasm of the students was contagious, and the Board not only gave its approval but set up a committee to work with the students on matters of construction and financing.[29]

As the Board had anticipated, even with student labor the cost of the new building came to considerably more than the students, in their optimism, had anticipated. By the time the building was dedicated on May 15, 1949, construction costs had run to about $138,000,[30] approximately what it would have cost if the building had been built with professional labor. But there was no way of estimating the value of the favorable publicity which the student engineers had won for the University by their project nor the value of the morale which they had built on campus by this demonstration of loyalty to their University and confidence in her future. People who had never heard of the University before contributed to the building fund, and industrial concerns went out of their way to ensure delivery of scarce materials. A film account of the project, produced in 1951 by T. G. Eggers of the Lutheran Laymen's League under the title, "Venture of Faith," won a Freedom Foundation award.

As the new engineering building began to take shape early in 1949, the administration made plans for the establishment of a College of Engineering. Formal action establishing the college was taken by the Board at its meeting in January, 1949,[31] and at that same meeting President Kretzmann announced the appointment of Professor Herman C. Hesse, for fourteen years head of the department of mechanical engineering at the University of Virginia, as dean of the College.

Two additional buildings have been constructed for the College of Engineering since the completion of the Engineering Laboratory Building. In 1950, two students decided to construct a heat pump for their senior project. However, they needed a laboratory in which to test it. Mr. Leonard C. Heine contributed the $4,050 needed for this building, and the two students spent their summer constructing it.[32] Then, in the summer of 1956, a new drafting laboratory, Graland Hall, was constructed on a site east of the Engineering Laboratories Building.

The optimism of the Student Engineering Society of 1948 has been more than justified by the history of the College of Engineering during the past decade. From the outset, its growth was rapid and sound. The College has been particularly careful to avoid becoming a mere trade school. Its students are required to balance their technical training with a broad background in the liberal arts. On October 21, 1958, the College received full accreditation by the Engineers Council for Professional Development.

In 1947, the Lutheran Laymen's League had voted to raise half a million dollars for the construction of a much-needed administration building on the new campus.[33] Fund-raising efforts did not, however, turn out as well as expected, and of the $165,000 that was raised the University borrowed $75,000 to complete payment on the new engineering building. By 1951, additional classroom space was needed for engineering classes and for classes in the newly-established Department of Speech and Drama. The University therefore requested the L. L. L. to loan it the balance of the $165,000 for a new classroom building, with the provision that the whole amount would be repaid to the L. L. L. when the League should have accumulated enough funds for the proposed administration building.[34] A hundred thousand dollars was added to the L. L. L. loan, and the cornerstone of the new building was laid on Founders Day, May 19, 1951. Upon completion of the building in October of that year, it was named Kroencke Hall in honor of the late beloved Dean Kroencke and immediately became one of the most used buildings on campus. It now houses the Departments of Speech and Drama, Art, and Geography and Geology, and is used by several other departments. The agreement with the L. L. L., under which it had been built, was subsequently abrogated by mutual consent and the building may, therefore, be considered essentially a gift from the Lutheran Laymen's League.[35]

Meanwhile, the successful completion of the Engineering Laboratory had aroused discussion in the student body of the possibility of providing another much-needed building through student initiative. As early as 1942, President Kretzmann had emphasized the importance of having some central meeting place on campus where students could get together.[36] In an attempt to provide such a meeting-place, the University had converted a number of small stores at the corner of College Avenue and Freeman Street into a small student union. These quarters served for a short time but the student body soon outgrew them, and in 1948 the rooms were converted into offices for the Student Council and the student publications. In the fall of 1947, the Independents Organization proposed that consideration be given to the construction of a new and adequate Student Union,[37] and in the 1948–1949 academic year the Student Council adopted the project. After much discussion of ways and means, the Council voted on March 22, 1949, to accumulate a building fund by raising Student Council fees from seven dollars to ten.[38] The story of the successful culmination of this project in 1955 will be told later.

Academically, this period was a time of notable progress. In 1948, the Department of Sociology and Philosophy was divided, Dr. Haentzschel remaining as head of the Department of Philosophy and Mrs. Margaretta Sackville Tangerman joining the faculty as head of the Department of Sociology and Social Work. At the same time, a major was introduced in social work. The next fall, 1949, the Department of History and Government was divided, Dean Bauer retaining the headship in history and Dr. L. Albert Wehling becoming head of the Department of Government. The Department of Foreign Languages was expanded at this time. For the first time, courses in Greek were offered, and the number of courses in Latin was increased from six to fourteen. The Music Department, which had long been one of the strongest departments on campus, expanded its program notably under its new head, Professor Theodore Hoelty-Nickel.

An important innovation in the fall of 1950 was a curriculum in elementary education leading to the degree of B.S. in Education. The University had been losing many potential students because of the absence of such a program, and the introduction of elementary education immediately increased enrollment in the Department of Education. In 1950, also, the University announced two new co-operative programs with Wagner College of Staten Island, New York, one in engineering and one in nursing. Under the engineering program, students could transfer to Valparaiso's engineering program after two years at Wagner and receive the engineering degree from Valparaiso in two additional years. Under the nursing program, students from Valparaiso could transfer after two years to Wagner and receive the R.N. and B.S. degree from that college in two additional years.

Other developments of this period can be only briefly mentioned:

In 1948, two new sororities were founded, Kappa Tau Zeta and Pi Delta Chi (Deaconess).

In 1949, the School of Law invited the Supreme Court of the State of Indiana to visit the campus and hear arguments in a student moot court. This was the first of the annual Supreme Court Days which have since become a tradition in the School of Law. This year also saw the organization of the Faculty Senate, a body composed of senior faculty members which was organized to transact routine business on behalf of the faculty which had, by this time, grown too large to serve as an effective forum for the discussion of policy. In this year also, a student credit union was formed, the first to be chartered on any campus in the country.

In 1950, a student literary magazine, VU, was founded. The "Lumen Christi" medal was instituted to recognize distinguished service by laymen to the Lutheran Church in America. Its recipients have been John A. Sauerman, long-time treasurer of the L. U. A. (1950); W. H. Schlueter, for many years treasurer of The Lutheran Church—Missouri Synod (1951); Emil C. Jacobs, president of the Lutheran Laymen's League (1952); Fred Wehrenberg, veteran member of the Board of Directors (1954); and Mrs. W. N. Hoppe, a leader in the University Women's Guild (1956). On the athletic scene, the football team enjoyed its first undefeated season since 1932 and the University joined with four other Indiana colleges to form the Indiana Conference. On the not so happy side, the debt accumulated by expansion reached $2,545,850.

One of the most significant and far-reaching developments of this period was the reorganization of the University's public relations program. In June, 1948, Pastor Miller resigned the headship to accept a call into the parish ministry. Instead of appointing a successor to Pastor Miller, the Board resolved to engage the St. Louis public-relations firm of Kelly, Zahrndt, and Kelly to direct the University's public relations program. The firm then placed Mr. Herbert W. Knopp, a well-known Lutheran layman, on the campus as full-time director of the department.[39] Mr. Knopp was a happy combination of public-relations man and lay theologian who knew the "gimmicks" of advertising and the limitations of their proper use by a church-related institution. Working from the sound base which he had inherited from Pastor Miller, Mr. Knopp greatly increased both the base of support and the amount of support. His most notable accomplishment was the establishment of a Patron Program which assured the University of a predictable minimum annual income. This program and the congregational collections have become the two most important sources of income for the University.

As the University entered its tenth decade of service, it was large, respected, and optimistic that such problems as it still confronted would eventually be solved. The question was no longer one of how to gain accreditation or how to solve the enrollment problem but the much more basic question of what the University was all about. The old question, "Why a Lutheran University?" was being asked with more seriousness than ever before. To President Kretzmann, the function of any Christian university was to speak relevantly from the vantage point of the Christian Gospel to the problems and issues that arise out of scholarly work in the secular fields. But what is the relevance of the Gospel to, say, the theory of numbers or the doctrine of judicial review? For that matter, does the Gospel provide any specific directives even in such fields as sociology or history or government? The debate on these questions raged hot and furiously on campus during this period, particularly among the younger members of the faculty, to whom it was important for their own professional futures to know whether the Gospel and secular knowledge were two realms that did not touch or overlap or whether they were Siamese twins that could not be detached from each other without danger to both. Time and a growing competence in both the Scriptures and the secular fields have provided more and more insights into this problem, but it has remained a live problem. Between the unacceptable extreme of a Bible college on the one hand and the equally unacceptable extreme of a completely secular institution on the other, the road which a truly Christian university should follow has not been easy either to define or to pursue. But the search itself imposes a stern spiritual and intellectual discipline which makes the work of the student and the instructor on the campus of a Christian university as rewarding in the long run as it is frustrating in the short run.

A Time of Stabilization

During the six years following the end of the Second World War, the University had expanded more rapidly than ever before in its history. Enrollment had grown from a mere six hundred students to more than twenty-two hundred. Four major buildings had been constructed, and many more had been purchased. In the process of this expansion, the University had accumulated a debt of more than $2,500,000. This debt, plus prospects of declining enrollment, made it necessary for the Board of Directors to call a halt, temporarily, to further expansion and to study means of maintaining the operations of the University at its new level of activity.

The decline in enrollment, which began in 1950, was easily explainable but, nevertheless, troublesome. The number of eighteen-year-olds in the United States in 1951 (approximately 2,100,000) was the lowest since 1938,[40] reflecting the low birth rates of the depression years. World War II provisions for the education of veterans were terminated in July, 1951. And the "police action" in Korea, which had begun in 1950, cut into the male enrollment. During the first semester of the 1950–1951 academic year, a hundred men left the University for the armed forces.[41] By 1951, enrollment was down to its post-war low of 1,657, and the University entered a short period of retrenchment.

In view of the nation-wide decline in enrollments, the administration was not unduly concerned about Valparaiso's decline, but it took immediate steps to ensure that the University would participate in the expected upswing in enrollment in future years. In 1951, President Kretzmann established an office of New Student Services, directed at first by Mr. E. H. Ruprecht and later by Mrs. Byron Ferguson and Mr. Frederick Rechlin, which was given the job of recruiting students and allotting scholarships and aid. The aid program itself was greatly strengthened, partly to build up the enrollment and partly to ensure that qualified students would not be denied a college education at a time when the costs of education were rapidly increasing. This program has been continued to the present, and comparative figures for recent years show how large an investment the University has made in students who, had it not been for this aid, might not have been able to meet the costs of a college education:

	1946-1947	1950-1951	1956-1957
Scholarships	$24,846.58	$ 53,432.50	$116,555.50
Grants-in-Aid	26,014.07	44,342.70	42,752.50
Employment	48,860.69	61,578.24	87,761.00
	$99,721.34	$159,353.44	$247,069.00

Aid on this scale imposes obvious strains on the University budget. Of the 433 scholarships given in the 1955–1956 academic year, for instance, only thirteen were endowed and only fifty-five were donated. Thus, out of a total scholarship expenditure of $93,000, more than $60,000 had to be supplied out of current operating funds.

Another kind of assistance offered by the University to its students from about this time onward was help in finding employment after graduation. As early as 1940, the Alumni Association had set up a placement bureau, but it was not until after the war that it was fully organized. Dr. Oliver Graebner did much to get the present placement service underway in the years immediately following the war. Then, in 1948, Mr. Alfred Looman returned from naval service to serve as alumni secretary and to help in placement. Since 1952, Mr. Looman has served as director of the Valparaiso Union and director of placement, and the placement service has developed into one of the most successful areas of University activity.

The catalogues for the years 1950 to 1953 indicate few changes in the curriculum, but in the fall of 1953 the University opened a division in Fort Wayne, taking over the instruction of academic courses which were offered at the Fort Wayne Lutheran Hospital.[42] Extension work was later introduced in Chicago, in LaPorte, and in Crown Point.

Financially, the University during these years began to enjoy a notable increase in support, but much of this increase was offset by rising costs which resulted from the post-war inflation. In 1951, for instance, 22,553 persons contributed a total of $539,499.01 for current support. Of this number, more than 15,000 contributed $5.00 or less. In that same year, a new and very generous source of assistance was found in the Lilly Endowment of Indianapolis. Following a survey of the University, the Lilly Endowment made a grant of $75,000 for current support with the promise to continue its support as long as its resources and the condition of the University permitted. During each of the following five years, the Lilly Endowment contributed $50,000 toward current funds, and in 1957 increased this amount to $65,000. These grants were especially significant because they were made solely on the basis of the University's merit as an educational institution.

In July, 1951, the University acquired, as a gift from the Walther League, *The Cresset*, a monthly review of literature, the arts, and public affairs. President Kretzmann, its founding editor, continued in that capacity.

Building programs had to be held in abeyance during these years because of the size of the University debt. But the student body was bringing all of its considerable ingenuity to bear on the Student Union project which it had undertaken back in 1949. At that time, it had offered to raise the funds for a Union by increasing Student Council fees, and, by December, 1951, it had accumulated a fund of $30,000. In a referendum on April 17, 1952, the students voted another increase in Student Council fees,[43] and two days later student representatives appeared before the Board of Directors with a report on the referendum and a request for permission to proceed with plans for the new Union. The Board approved the increase in fees and authorized a committee composed of students and University officials to proceed with the project. On May 19, 1953, a stake-driving party was held on the site of the new building, but it was not until a year later that construction actually began. It took that long to solve the problem of financing which, despite the generous assistance of the student body, was a formidable one.

Finally, on May 28, 1955, the new Union was dedicated and immediately became the center of campus life.

It would be hard to overestimate the importance of the Union to the life and development of the University. For years, the University had been seriously limited in its extra-curricular program by the lack of adequate facilities for conferences, institutes, seminars, and conventions. Student activities had had to be housed in ramshackle structures. Dining facilities, since the war, had been inadequate. The Union was a place that the whole campus community could be proud of, the students especially, for it was largely their creation.

But the greatest significance of the Union was that it effectively shifted the center of the campus from the Old Campus to the New. Its striking modern lines, designed by Michael F. Hare, were prophetic of the New Campus which the University would build away from the clutter and confusion of the Old Campus. Its location helped to settle the future lay-out of the New Campus. And its facilities provided the student body with a center around which they could organize their extra-curricular interests and activities.

These years of stabilization, annoying as they were to the administration and the faculty, which were eager to see plans for the New Campus materialize in actual construction, were also years of sound but unspectacular accomplishment. Somewhere along the line in the early Fifties, the University ceased to be an experiment and became an established and recognized fact. More than a decade of strong leadership had established the fact that the University knew where it was going and that it would ultimately get there. One indication of this recognition was the acceptance, after 1951, of the formerly local fraternities into membership by national fraternities. Hot as the debate was over "going national," it was recognized that the approval of the University by national fraternity headquarters implied recognition of the fact that the University was able to meet the demanding criteria of these organizations. Similar recognition was given to the University in 1953 when it was accepted into membership by the American Association of University Women.

The Church, too, took notice of the new measure of stability which the University had achieved when, in October, 1952, the Synodical Board of Directors met with the University Board for what was to be the first in a series of annual joint meetings. Out of these meetings has come a new awareness of the mutuality of interest between the University and the Church.

Symbolic of the new maturity of the University was the election, in January of 1953, of a new chairman of the Board of Directors. After almost thirty years of devoted service to the Lutheran University movement, twenty of them as president of the L. U. A., Mr. W. C. Dickmeyer asked to be relieved of the presidency. Mr. Dickmeyer, like most of his colleagues in the early days of Lutheran administration, had not enjoyed the advantages of a university education and, perhaps just for that reason, appreciated the value of higher education more than most people who have experienced it. At much personal sacrifice, he had championed a cause which, at times, seemed a forlorn one. It was therefore singularly appropriate that the new president of the L. U. A. should be a product of the University which the Association had built. Mr. Paul Brandt is the first alumnus of Valparaiso under the Lutheran administration to serve as chairman of the University's Board of Directors.

Building for Tomorrow

The bulldozer which cut the foundations for the new Valparaiso Union was, in a sense, paving the way for a new era of expansion whose terminal date lies somewhere in the still unpredictable future. The completion of the Union building and the installation of a new concrete street which led to it pointed to the new Valparaiso University which would rise on the New Campus.

Early in January, 1955, construction began on two new dormitories east of the gymnasium. Designed for ultimate use as women's dormitories, these new dormitories, subsequently named Dau Hall and Kreinheder Hall, were opened as men's dormitories in the fall of 1955 and did much to relieve the acute housing shortage for men students.

With this construction out of the way, the administration turned its attention to the next most pressing problem, a chapel-auditorium. By the fall of 1954, the enrollment had become so large, and classes were held in such widely scattered buildings on campus, that it was necessary to hold two separate chapel services, one in the old Auditorium and one in the little theatre of Kroencke Hall. This created a distinct problem, for morning chapel exercises had always played an important part in unifying the life of the campus and President Kretzmann had frequently noted, in reply to suggestions that the University might be growing too large to maintain its "small campus" character, that the tone of the campus could be maintained so long as it was possible to assemble at least the greater part of the campus community in some one spot at least once a day.

In January, 1954, therefore, the Board of Directors formulated a request to the Synodical Board of Directors for a grant of $2,000,-000 to meet the financial needs of the University, among them the construction of an adequate chapel. The following summer, the Synodical Board authorized a $5,000,000 campaign, to be conducted the following spring, on behalf of five non-official agencies within the Church: Lutheran World Relief, which was to receive $400,000; the Lutheran Deaconess Association, which was to receive $250,000 for the erection of a new dormitory on the campus of the University; the Lutheran Home for the Deaf, $150,000; Bethesda Lutheran Home, $1,700,000; and Valparaiso University, $2,500,000.[43] This campaign (which was directed by John C. Baur) was a resounding success.

In anticipation of the funds which it would receive from this campaign, the University went ahead with plans for the new chapel-auditorium. And since the location and design of the new chapel would largely determine the pattern of the whole New Campus, the Board engaged Professor Jean Labatut, director of graduate studies of the Princeton University School of Architecture, to serve as planning consultant for new campus development. Professor Labatut and Mr. Charles F. Stade, who had been engaged as architect for the new chapel, chose an elevated site in the very heart of the New Campus for the chapel, and work began on October 9, 1956.

Hardly had construction of the new chapel got underway when history took one of its ironic turns. On the cold night of November 27, 1956, flames whipped through the old Auditorium and, by morning, only the shell of the old building was still standing. Only the grace of God and the exertions of the student body prevented the tragedy from turning into a catastrophe, for strong winds scattered sparks as far as three blocks northward from the Auditorium and, for several hours, seemed certain to engulf the old library. Students stationed on the roofs of the library, Arts-Annex, and Arts-Law played streams of water on these buildings and threw burning embers off the roofs with their bare hands.

During the course of the night, student leaders met with President Kretzmann and worked out plans for recovery and clean-up. The idea of a student disaster fund was conceived, and, within forty-eight hours after the fire had started, students had written to more than three thousand friends, relatives, and public figures. Responses poured in from all parts of the country and even from overseas. By the end of the academic year, the disaster fund amounted to more than $100,000, small enough by comparison with the $600,000 loss which the University had sustained in the fire, but far larger than anyone except the students had expected that it would be. Taken with the $300,000 collected from insurance companies, the fund added up to a substantial amount that could be applied toward a new administration building.

But the immediate concern of most people on campus was not for a new administration building, necessary as that obviously was, but for a new library. After the first shock of the loss of the Auditorium had passed, there was a general feeling of relief on campus that it had been the Auditorium, rather than the much more inflammable library, that had been lost. For much of the loss sustained in the Auditorium fire could eventually be replaced. The loss of the library would have been irreparable.

Once again, the Lilly Endowment proved a good friend to the University. Shortly after the fire, it announced a grant of $125,000 to the University toward the construction of a new library.[44] This grant, later increased by $125,000, plus a gift of $375,000 by Mrs. Margaret Moellering in 1956,[45] brought the library fund to a level which made it possible for the administration to make plans for immediate construction. Mrs. Moellering had sought to make her gift anonymously but the size of the gift and the long record of support which the Moellering family had given the Lutheran university movement through all of the days of Lutheran administration could not be allowed to go unrecognized. The new library, which was begun in early June, 1958, and will be completed during the centennial year, will be known as the Henry F. Moellering Memorial Library.

The early months of 1958 saw the beginning of another large

construction project, a new $1,000,000 men's dormitory which is being constructed on the easternmost corner of the New Campus. When completed, this dormitory will house 303 students and will permit the conversion of Dau and Kreinheder Halls into women's residences.

In the fall of 1956, another major contribution to the future physical development of the University was made when the Alumni Association announced plans for a centennial gift of $100,-000, the larger part of which will go toward the purchase of a large tract of land directly across from the New Campus on the south side of U.S. Highway 30. This new tract will be used primarily for athletic facilities, for playing fields, for a new stadium or bowl, for a National Guard armory which the University will use for intramural sports, and for a larger fieldhouse. The balance of the fund will pay for construction of an alumni memorial narthex in the University Chapel.

The $100,000 goal which the Alumni Association has set for itself in this campaign is one indication of the progress which the Association has made since it was reorganized in 1946. In August of that year, the Board of Directors appointed Alfred Looman Alumni secretary. Under his direction, alumni work was greatly expanded and, in 1948, an alumni fund was established. After Mr. Looman's recall to naval duty in the Korean "police action," Mrs. Alsie Larson, who had long been active in alumni work, carried on until the appointment, in 1955, of Mr. Marcus T. Young, '50, as Director of Alumni Affairs. Among Mrs. Larson's many contributions to alumni work were the organization of the Alumni Council and the initiation of a project, carried on for several years, of alumni assistance to faculty salaries.

Physical expansion and improvement has continued during these years not only with the construction of new buildings but also with renovation of some of the old but still serviceable buildings of the Old Campus. In the spring of 1954, the second and third floors of the Commerce Building (neé Bogarte's Book Store) were renovated for use as classroom and office space. In the spring of 1955, the cafeteria was moved into the new Union Building, and the former cafeteria in the Greenwich Group was converted into four classrooms and two seminar rooms. In the summer of 1956, Science Hall was completely renovated to make room for new facilities necessitated by the expansion of the physics department.

All of this expansion has placed a greater financial burden upon the University. In the 1956–1957 academic year, for the first time in the history of the University, the operating budget moved above the $2,000,000 mark. But as its needs grew, the University was fortunate enough to receive an unprecedented number of large gifts. From the Synodical "Building for Christ" campaign, the University received almost $2,500,000 of which $1,000,000 was allocated to construction of the chapel and $1,500,000 toward debt reduction. In December, 1954, the Ford Foundation announced a grant of $332,200 as a ten-year endowment, the interest on which was to be used for increasing faculty salaries. In 1956, this grant was increased to $509,000. Almost simultaneously with the Ford grant, the University received Mrs. Moellering's gift for the library. In 1953, the University received a collection of paintings from the trustees of the estate of Junius and Sarah L. Spencer Sloan, and in 1955 a $180,000 endowment fund for the maintenance of the collection. In the fall of 1956, the University received $51,000 from the estate of Mr. Guy N. Scovill and, the following June, a gift of $284,000 from the executors of Mrs. Scovill's estate. Gifts from the Lilly Endowment in December, 1956, and January, 1958, totaled $250,000. During one year, 1955, the assets of the University nearly doubled. More recent large gifts include those of Mr. and Mrs. H. J. W. Niehaus, $40,000; the Neils family, $70,000; and the Minnie E. Scheele estate, $75,000.

It is always a happy experience to be able to announce gifts and grants of these proportions. For the Department of University Relations, however, such gifts create a problem. Most of the large gifts which the University receives are ear-marked either for capital improvements or for special projects. They do not cover the large operating costs that must be met, today as always, by tuition, fees, and small gifts. Thus, despite the many large gifts which the University has received in recent years, it still has to scrounge for funds to meet payrolls, utility bills, maintenance costs, and equipment costs. For these funds it still depends primarily upon congregational collections, patron income, and gifts from alumni and friends.

Academically, also, the years since 1954 have seen notable progress. In the fall of 1956, the Department of Mathematics and Physics was divided into a Department of Mathematics under the chairmanship of Dr. Kermit Carlson and a Department of Physics under the co-chairmanship of Dr. Manuel M. Bretscher and Professor Armin W. Manning. In 1958, the physics department became one of the first in the nation to receive a sub-critical nuclear reactor from the Atomic Energy Commission. In the summer of 1957, the Department of Education and Psychology was divided into a Department of Education with Professor Dana B. Schwanholt as chairman and a Department of Psychology with Dr. Oliver E. Graebner as chairman. In the fall of 1954, the Department of Government was invited to participate in the Washington Semester Program under which three students each semester spend one semester of their junior year at the American University in Washington, D.C. In the fall of 1955, the University established a group of combined curricula in cooperation with the School of Natural Resources of the University of Michigan under which the student spends three years at Valparaiso and his fourth and fifth at Michigan, receiving the A.B. from Valparaiso and the M.S. from Michigan. In the fall of 1956, the University inaugurated a new co-operative program in nursing with the Lutheran Hospital School of Nursing in St. Louis, and in the spring of 1958 a similar program was worked out with the Lutheran Hospital School of Nursing in Cleveland. And in the fall of 1956, a Youth Leadership Training Program was established in co-operation with the Walther League, the Lutheran Laymen's League, and the Synodical Board for Young People's Work.

One other development in the academic picture deserves special notice. In 1956, the University engaged Dr. Ronald Thompson, registrar of Ohio State University, as consultant to assist in the planning and implementation of graduate study at Valparaiso. After a preliminary survey, Dr. Thompson noted that there were several important, but not insurmountable, obstacles to the introduction of graduate work, and advised the University to make a self-survey of its total program in order to determine whether it felt ready for graduate work. In January, 1957, President Kretzmann appointed a committee under the chairmanship of Dr. Alfred H. Meyer to direct this self-survey and to make recommendations concerning the establishment of a program of graduate studies.

It is in the midst of this period of physical and academic development that the University celebrates its centennial. What began as a small Methodist college has become the largest Lutheran university in the United States—Lutheran not only in name but in reality, for most of its faculty and over 80 per cent of its student body are Lutheran. What began as an institution designed to serve one Congressional district has become a national institution. But certain things have not changed. The Rev. Charles N Sims, Mr. Henry Baker Brown, and the Rev. O. P. Kretzmann would have no trouble at all agreeing that the basis of all higher education must be moral. The student today, like his counterpart in 1859 or 1909, takes pride in the fact that he is meeting at least a part of the cost of his education through his own work. The instructor in the classroom still expects to be judged primarily by the effectiveness of his day-to-day job of teaching. Twice in the history of the University its administrative continuity has been broken, in both cases as the aftermath of a great war. But the University has survived and, after each near-collapse, has become greater than before.

The two streams which converged in September, 1925, have, by now, merged so completely that they could never again be separated. The Perry County, Missouri, fathers of the Lutheran Church—Missouri Synod might be shocked to find their descendants taking German as a foreign language requirement, but they would feel instantly at home in the daily chapel exercises. Mr. Brown might be surprised at the number of German names in the faculty and student body, but he would undoubtedly approve of the democratic atmosphere, the emphasis upon close faculty-student relations, and the insistence upon hard work, which are as characteristic of the Lutheran administration as they were of his own.

President Kretzmann has often observed that the history of American education has been one of institutions begun under the sponsorship of the Church which have gradually drifted from the Church into the vast sea of secularism which has engulfed the life and thought of the past century. No one who is engaged in the work of the University in its centennial year can be unaware of the danger that Valparaiso might follow this same dreary course in its second century. But offsetting this fear is a lively hope that perhaps the world, especially the Western world, has been called back to sanity by the threat which has been posed to its survival by the great and widening gap between man's capacity to make things and his ability to control the things which he can make. All over the country, the years since Hiroshima have seen a return of religion to campuses from which it had been exiled, and the quality of the religion which has returned has been notably strengthened by its years of self-examination in the wilderness.

Valparaiso's centennial year will see the dedication of a new chapel which will serve as the center around which the New Campus will be built. Physically, this new chapel will make it possible for the University to maintain its small-campus atmosphere by allowing the entire University community to assemble daily in one place. But far greater than its physical value is its symbolic value. Built in the very heart of the campus and towering above all of the instructional and residential buildings, it will serve as a constant reminder of the work to which the University has dedicated itself and which has been made all the more urgent by the needs of an age of nuclear weapons and space travel: the work of adding to knowledge wisdom and to wisdom the fear of God.

"The place of high religion in a nuclear age," President Kretzmann has said, "is greater than ever before. We are riding a rising tide. Our contemporary religiosity can really become religion. Our emphasis upon 'Conscience and Competence' is increasingly relevant. And there is really no miracle about this. This is God working in history. And all that we have to do—in intelligence and goodness—is to try to keep up with Him."

NOTES

1. President's Report to the Board of Directors, Oct. 30, 1940, p. 5.
2. Appendix to the Report of the President to the Board of Directors, Oct. 30, 1940, pp. 15-25.
3. *The Torch*, October 24, 1940, p. 1.
4. Walter G. Friedrich in minutes of the Executive Committee of the Board of Directors, June 18, 1940; and President Kretzmann in the President's Report to the Board of Directors, Oct. 30, 1940. Cf. also *The Torch*, Feb. 9, 1939, p. 2.
5. President's Report to the Board of Directors, Oct. 30, 1940, p. 9.
6. President's Report to the Board of Directors, Oct., 1945, p. 3.
7. President's Report to the Board of Directors, Nov. 17, 1943, p. 1.
8. Interview with Mr. Frederick H. Rechlin, August, 1957.
9. Richard Koenig, *op. cit.*, p. 11.
10. President's Reports to the Board of Directors January 30, 1942; April 15, 1942; Jan. 22, 1943; April 1, 1943; July 1, 1943; Nov. 17, 1943; April 14, 1944.
11. *The Torch*, June 17, 1943, p. 2.
12. George W. Crane, *The Chicago Daily News*, Apr. 7, 1958.

13. There was apparently no public announcement of this gift. The minutes of the Board meeting of April 14, 1944, indicate a price offered to the Board of $42,000. However, the report of the committee on finance and investment shows a total sale price of $22,792.70.

14. *The Beacon*, 1945. It is possible that this list is incomplete.

15. President's Report to the Board of Directors, October 19, 1944, p. 21.

16. *Ibid.*, pp. 11, 21.

17. Enrollment Report, Spring, 1946.

18. *The Torch*, January 25, 1946.

19. *The Torch*, October 4, 1946.

20. *The Torch*, April 5, 1946. Also interview with Dr. Marshall J. Jox.

21. President's Report to the Board of Directors, January 29, 1949.

22. Louise Nicolay, *op. cit.*, p. 65.

23. O. P. Kretzmann in conversation with the author.

24. President's Report to the Board of Directors, August, 1946, p. 8.

25. *The Torch*, April 5, 1946.

26. Minutes of the Board of Directors, October 30, 1947, p. 2.

27. Letter in the President's Report to the Board of Directors, May 8, 1948, says that the date of this meeting was April 21. *The Torch*, May 13, 1949, says it was April 28.

28. President's Report to the Board of Directors, May 8, 1948. Cf. *The Torch*, May 13, 1949.

29. *Minutes* of the Board of Directors, May 8, 1949, p. 2.

30. Report of the Treasurer of the Lutheran University Association, Schedule "A," April 29, 1950.

31. *Minutes* of the Board of Directors, January 29, 1949, p. 1.

32. *The Torch*, Sept. 21, 1950; also *Minutes* of the Board of Directors, November 3, 1950, pp. 23, 81.

33. President's Report to the Board of Directors, October 30, 1947, p. 2.

34. *Minutes* of the Board of Directors, January 20, 1951.

35. The report of the Committee on Buildings and Grounds, November 1, 1952, p. 59, states the final cost of Kroencke Hall at $213,692.16.

36. President's Report to the Board of Directors, January 30, 1942.

37. *The Torch*, March 25, 1949. Also recollection of Mr. Paul Zehner, president of the Independents' Association at the time this proposal was advanced.

38. *The Torch*, March 25, 1949.

39. President's Report to the Board of Directors, May 8, 1948, p. 3.

40. *Nature and Needs of Higher Education* (New York: Columbia University Press, 1952), pp. 77-84.

41. President's Report to the Board of Directors, January 20, 1951.

42. *The Torch*, October 7, 1952.

43. President's Report to the Board of Directors, June 26, 1954, pp. 8-17.

44. Public Relations Release, December 31, 1956.

45. *Minutes* of the Board of Directors, December 9, 1955, p. 1.

Appendix A

OFFICERS OF THE UNIVERSITY

Presidents of the Valparaiso Male and Female College,
the Northern Indiana Normal School and Business
Institute, Valparaiso College, and
Valparaiso University

1859–1860	The Rev. Francis D. Carley, M.A. (acting)
1860–1862	The Rev. Charles N Sims, M.A.
1862	The Rev. Erastus Herman Staley, M.A.
1863–1867	The Rev. B. Wilson Smith, M.A.
1867–1869	The Rev. Thomas Bond Wood, M.A.
1869–1871	The Rev. Aaron Gurney, M.A.
1871–1873	(The presidency vacant, no acting president)
1873–1917	Henry Baker Brown, A.B.
1912–1919	Oliver Perry Kinsey, A.M. (acting)
1919–1920	Henry Kinsey Brown, M.A.
1920–1921	Daniel Russel Hodgdon, A.B., LL.D.
1921–1922	John Edward Roessler, A.M., Litt.D.
1922	Milo Jesse Bowman, A.M., LL.B., LL.D.
1923–1926	Horace Martin Evans, M.D.
1926	The Rev. John C. Baur (acting)
1926–1929	The Rev. William Henry Theodore Dau, D.D. Albert Frederick Ottomar Germann, Ph.D. (acting, 1927) The Rev. John C. Baur (acting, 1927–1928)
1929–1930	Executive Committee (The Rev. John C. Baur, Mr. Albert Frank Scribner, Dean Frederick William Kroencke, and Dean Henry Herman Kumnick)
1930–1939	The Rev. Oscar Carl Kreinheder, D.D.
1939–1940	Walter George Friedrich, Ph.D. (acting)
1940–	The Rev. Otto Paul Kretzmann, S.T.M., Litt.D., D.D., LL.D.

Officers of the University Who Have Held the Position
Equivalent to Dean of the Faculty

1881–1917	Oliver Perry Kinsey, A.M., Vice-President of the University
1920	Daniel Russel Hodgdon, A.B., LL.D.
1927–1928	Louis F. Heimlich, Ph.D., Dean of the University *ad interim*
1928–1936	Frederick William Kroencke, Ph.D., Dean of the University

1938–1946   Walter George Friedrich, Ph.D., Dean of the Faculty
1946–   Walter Emil Bauer, Ph.D., Dean of the Faculty

*Officers of the University Who Have Held the Position
Equivalent to Dean of the College of Arts and Sciences*

1913–1915   Harrison N. Carver, A.M., Dean of the Classical Department
1915–1919   Oliver Perry Kinsey, A.M., Dean of the Department of Liberal Arts
1920   Daniel Russel Hodgdon, A.B., LL.D., Dean of the College of Liberal Arts
1920–1921   Rollo Anson Talcott, A.M., Dean of the College of Liberal Arts
1921–1924   Berton Arthur Howlett, S.M., Dean of the College of Liberal Arts
1924–1927   Alpheus Americus Williams, A.M., Sc.D., Dean of the College of Liberal Arts
1927–1928   Louis F. Heimlich, Ph.D., Dean of the College of Liberal Arts *ad interim*
1928–1936   Frederick William Kroencke, Ph.D., Dean of the College of Liberal Arts
1938–1946   Walter George Friedrich, Ph.D., Dean of the College of Arts and Sciences
1946–1957   Walter Emil Bauer, Ph.D., Dean of the College of Arts and Sciences
1957–   Allen Edmond Tuttle, Ph.D., Dean of the College of Arts and Sciences

Deans of the School of Law

1880–1907   Mark L. DeMotte, M.A., LL.B., LL.D.
1907–1927   Milo Jesse Bowman, M.A., LL.B., LL.D.
1928–1955   John Wallace Morland, J.D.
1955–1956   Otto Paul Kretzman, S.T.M., Litt.D., D.D., LL.D. (acting)
1956–   Knute D. Stalland, LL.B., LL.D.

*Officers of the University Who Have Held the Position
Equivalent to Dean of the College of Engineering*

1881–1909   Martin Eugene Bogarte, A.M., Instructor in Charge of Engineering
1914–1918   Ray C. Yeoman, C.E., Dean
1919–1923   Frank R. Theroux, C.E., Dean
1923–1925   Harry Townsend Fisher, C.E., Dean
1925–1927   Howard Dayton Harvey, B.S., C.E., Dean
1927–1930   Harry Edmund Bilger, M.S., Professor of Engineering
1930–1942   Howard Wilson Moody, Ph.D., Dean (head of department after 1939)

1942–1947 Donald D. Mallory, M.S. in E.E., head of the department
1947–1948 Moses W. Uban, A.B., B.S. in M.E., acting head of the department
1948–   Herman C. Hesse, M.E., Dean

Deans of the College of Pharmacy

1895–1913 Jasper Newton Roe, A.M., Sc.D.
1914–1918 George D. Timmons, B.S., Ph.G.
1919–1925 Hugh C. Muldoon, B.S., Ph.G.
1925–1926 George Charles Schicks, Ph.C.
1928–1929 Harry V. Fuller, Ph.D. (acting)
1929–1939 Frederick V. Lofgren, Ph.D.
1939   Fred Henry Kaufmann, Ph.D (acting)
           (The College of Pharmacy was discontinued in 1939)

Librarians

1881–1898 Oliver Perry Kinsey, A.M.
1898–1919 Luella F. Porter, A.M.
1919–1928 Helen Kull, A.B.
1928–1949 Mrs. Katharine Ertz Bowden, B.S.
1949–1950 Walter Emil Bauer, Ph.D. (acting)
1950–   Herman Carl Grunau, M.A., B.S. in L.S.

Members of the Board of Directors of The Lutheran University Association and the Valparaiso University Association, *1926–1959*

Herman A. Duemling, M.D.	1926–1927
The Rev. John C. Baur	1926–1929
William Charles Dickmeyer, LL.D.	1926–
Martin H. Luecke	1926–1932
The Rev. Paul F. Miller	1926–1951
Harry E. Eberline	1926–1944
The Rev. L. A. Linn	1926–1928
Peter W. Meyn	1926–1931
W. D. Holterman	1926–1928
O. C. Lembke	1926–1928
Fred Wehrenberg	1926–1927; 1928–1951
The Rev. Oscar Carl Kreinheder	1926–1930
H. D. Mensing	1926–1927
Ralph Richman	1926–1932
F. C. Heckel, M.D.	1926–1927
Henry A. Dahlen	1927–1943
Edward W. Jaeger	1927–1958
Ludwig H. Letz	1927–1929
George F. Nolde	1927–1933

William F. Boeger	1928–1943
Herbert H. Hackstedde	1928–1934
The Rev. Louis J. Sieck	1928–1938
Henry J. Neils	1928–1934
Henry F. Rohrman	1928–1934
Rudolf Eckert	1928–1929
Otto Misch	1929–1932
Robert A. Schiewe	1929–1931
The Rev. Walter A. Maier, Ph.D.	1930–1943
George H. Letz	1931–1936
The Rev. G. Christian Barth	1932–1948
Henry F. Moellering	1932–1936
Ernest J. Gallmeyer	1932–1937; 1945–
Henry L. Ulbrich, M.D.	1933–1941
William H. Kroeger	1934–1936
The Rev. Otto A. Geiseman, S.T.D.	1934–1946
The Rev. Louis Nuechterlein	1934–1940
John A. Sauerman	1934–
Paul Klitzke	1936–1940
Charles J. F. Staerker	1936–1944
Robert C. Moellering	1936–
Martin A. Salvner	1938–1939
Paul F. Amling	1938–
E. W. Marquardt, M.D.	1939–1948
The Rev. E. T. Bernthal	1940–1950
Herbert F. Lichtsinn	1940–
Werner Duemling, M.D.	1940–1944
Paul E. Rupprecht	1942–
Alex O. Benz	1943–1952
Henry W. Graebner	1943–1946
Otto A. Dorn	1944
E. F. Dittmer, M.D.	1944–
John A. Fleischli	1945–
Leo L. Hardt, M.D.	1946–
A. E. Horst	1946–1952
Walter H. Gross	1948–
Fred Strieter	1948–1952
Richard E. Meier	1950–
Mrs. Walter A. Hansen	1950–1951 *
The Rev. Richard A. Jesse	1951–1957
Dean Arnold	1952–
Paul Brandt	1952–
Mrs. E. T. J. Birner	1951–1954 *
Gilbert Krause	1950–1951 **; 1952–

* *ex officio* during term of office as president of the Women's Guild.
** *ex officio* during term of office as president of the Alumni Association.

Walter R. Schur, M.D.	1951–1953 **; 1959–**
Raymond A. Wolff	1953–1955 **
Mrs. William A. Drews	1954–1957 *
Fred A. Reddel	1955–
Herbert Steinbach	1955–1958 **
The Rev. Bernard Hemmeter	1957–
Mrs. Roy C. Frank	1957– *
Paul Nieter	1958–1959 **

* *ex officio* during term of office as president of the Women's Guild.
** *ex officio* during term of office as president of the Alumni Association.

APPENDIX B

STUDENT LEADERS

Presidents of the Student Council

1916–1917 E. H. Miller
1917–1918 J. W. Larrew
1918–1919 No Record
1919–1920 D. W. David
1920–1921 Jack Pierce
1921–1922 "Spike" Payne
1922 Judson Wetherby
1922–1923 E. E. Morris
1923–1924 Vernon C. Mossman
1924–1925 H. Orders
(Council Suspended 1925–1930)
1930–1931 Roland Kahnert
1931–1932 Allan Nierman
1932–1933 Oscar H. Mehl
1933–1934 Walter Christopher
1934–1935 Clements Gremel
1935–1936 Leonard Gotsch
1936–1937 Robert C. Peper
1937–1938 Donald Tewes
1938–1939 Milton Ackenhausen
1939–1940 Harold C. Helbling
1940–1941 Harold C. Helbling

1941–1942 Alfred R. Looman
1942–1943 Elmer Simon
 Robert Stapleton
1943–1944 Robert Stapleton
 Theodore Wambsganss
 Barbara Bernthal
1944–1945 Phyllis Graebner
1945–1946 Louis F. Bartelt
1946–1947 Ernest R. Vierk
1947–1948 John Bolgert
1948–1949 Robert Groth
1949–1950 Arthur W. Gray, Jr.
1950–1951 William H. Boltz
1951–1952 Marvin H.
 Rammelsberg
1952–1953 Russell C. Zschoche
1953–1954 Walter E. Thielhart
1954–1955 David Snyder
1955–1956 Peter Krentz
1956–1957 Douglas Seltz
1957–1958 Robert Moellering
1958– Dieter Nickel

Editors of The Torch

1914–1915 A. Lincoln Yerex
1915–1916 Arthur E. Lankenau
1916–1917 Chapman Reynolds
1917–1918 Frederick J. Marston
1918–1919 J. W. Larrew
1919–1920 Frank W. Thomas
 Arthur F. Bayles
1920–1921 F. Orlin Tremaine
1921–1922 J. H. Hutchinson
 G. A. Wasserberger
1922–1923 Beatty R. Julien
1923–1924 Elwin E. McCray
1924–1925 Roy E. Wagner
1925–1926 Roy E. Wagner

1926–1927 Frank C. Bryant
1927–1928 John G. Roof
1928–1929 Clarence J. Fiting
1929–1930 Clarence J. Fiting
1930–1931 Richard E. Weiss
1931–1932 Alfred E. Soldwish
1932–1933 Robert Allett
1933–1934 Herbert Steinbach
1934–1935 Kenneth Wunsch *
1936–1937 John H. Schuth
1937–1938 Charles S. Stowers *
1938–1939 Ruth A. Miller
1939–1940 Raymond L.
 Scherer **

1940–1941	John Strietelmeier **	1948–1949	Carlton H. Ihde **
1941–1942	Richard Haratine	1949–1950	Melvin Doering
1942–1943	Charles W. Kern *	1950–1951	David Michel
1943–1944	August Bernthal	1951–1952	William Haeseler III
	Dolores Busse *	1952–1953	Galen Gockel
1944–1945	Adele Sohn **	1953–1954	Arthur Muchow
	Hildegarde	1954–1955	Ernest H. Kanning III
	Herfurth **	1955–1956	Crome R. Dollase
1945–1946	Lorraine Bruening	1956–1957	Loren Korte **
1946–1947	Marjorie Hausrath *	1957–1958	Donald McGibbon
	Egon Guba	1958–	Mark Ludwig and
1947–1948	Robert Raddatz		Alan Graebner

* First-Class Honor Rating
** All-American Honor Rating

Editors of the Yearbook
Founded 1911 as *The Record*, renamed *The Uhlan* in 1934,
The Beacon in 1941

1911	Arthur W. Smith	1936	Harry Little
1912	Edward D. Gallager	1937	Arthur Griep
1913	George Pierce	1938	Luella Ansorge
1914	Adolph Goldberg	1939	Joseph Berkowitz
1915	L. J. Hoeschen	1940	Edwin A. Kurtz
1916	J. W. Parker	1941	William Schlender
1917	No Record	1942	Janet Steben
1918	J. W. Smith	1943	Anna Zink Springsteen
1919	No Record	1944	Roberta Ihde
1920	Christian Miller	1945	Josephine Luecke
1921	Frank W. Thomas	1946	Ruth Ellen Haertel
1922	Joseph B. Herschman	1947	Elinor Muntzinger
1923	Warren E. Emerson	1948	Lucile Novak
1924	J. V. Hines	1949	Marianne Baerwald
1925	L. G. Tubbs	1950	Carlton H. Ihde
1926	None published	1951	Ralph H. Skov
1927	None published	1952	Lois Jane Schweppe
1928	Floyd R. Cunningham	1953	Shirley Ann Groh
1929	Herbert Graebner	1954	David Snyder
1930	Leonard Schramm	1955	George W. E.
1931	Allan Nierman		Nickelsburg, Jr.
1932	M. A. Ahlbrand	1956	Marlou Marie Seehausen
1933	Walter A. Christopher	1957	Thomas F. Schutte
1934	Gerald L. Stoetzer	1958	Shirley Nelesen
1935	Earl F. Reinke	1959	Duane Noerenberg

Appendix C

ATHLETIC RECORD OF THE UNIVERSITY

Football

Season	Coach	Captain(s)	Won	Lost	Tied	
1919	George E. Keogan	Thomas Dandelet	5	3	0	
1920	George E. Keogan	Kenneth Conley	5	3	0	
1921	Earl J. Goheen	Rossman Sawyer	2	2	1	
1922	Earl J. Goheen	John Cook	2	2	2	
1923	William P. Shadoan	Harold H. Harris	4	2	1	
1924	William P. Shadoan	Peter Christiansen	4	3	2	
1927	Earl Scott	James Doran, Luther Reiser	1	5	0	
1928	Earl Scott	James Doran	1	6	0	
1929	J. M. Christiansen	Joseph Demyan	1	7	0	
1930	J. M. Christiansen	LeRoy Shimek	4	5	0	
1931	J. M. Christiansen	Rudy Smatlak, Lester Hale	8	1	0	
1932	J. M. Christiansen	Joseph Kowalski	7	0	0	*
1933	J. M. Christiansen	Joseph Kowalski	7	1	0	
1934	J. M. Christiansen	Rudy Smatlak	6	2	0	
1935	J. M. Christiansen	George Krampien, Albert Anhold	4	4	1	
1936	J. M. Christiansen	William Drzewicki	1	6	1	
1937	J. M. Christiansen	Richard Evans	4	4	0	
1938	J. M. Christiansen		2	3	1	
1939	J. M. Christiansen	John McGinnis, Donald Finneran	2	6	0	
1940	J. M. Christiansen	Fred Mueller, Sulo Siekkinen	3	2	2	
1941	Victor Dauer	Fred Mueller, Arnold Barth	0	7	1	
1942	Loren E. Ellis	Robert Rehling	4	4	0	
1945	Loren E. Ellis		6	1	0	*
1946	Emory G. Bauer	Godfrey Heinecke	1	7	0	
1947	Emory G. Bauer	Donald Findling	2	5	1	
1948	Emory G. Bauer	Donald Trampski	4	5	0	
1949	Emory G. Bauer	Donald Findling	7	2	1	
1950	Emory G. Bauer	Harold Mack, Gene Gobreski	9	0	0	
1951	Emory G. Bauer	Joseph Pahr	9	0	0	
1952	Emory G. Bauer	Neil Montour, Norman Arnold	5	3	1	*
1953	Emory G. Bauer	Jerome Karstens	5	2	1	
1954	Emory G. Bauer	Rod Poppe	6	2	1	*
1955	Emory G. Bauer	Fred Thurston	6	3	0	

* Conference Champions (1952, tied with Butler University for championship)

187

1956 Emory G. Bauer	Charles Dhooge,			
	Kenneth Schreiber	6	4	0
1957 Emory G. Bauer	Walter Schaw,			
	Richard Melcher	4	2	2
1958 Emory G. Bauer	Max Roegge	6	3	0

Outstanding Players

James Doran—twice captain of the football team, captain of the basketball team
William Karr—Little All-American
Joseph Pahr—Little All-American
William Tatman—1941 College All-Star Team
Fred Thurston—Williamson All-American

Basketball

SEASON	COACH	CAPTAIN(S)	Won	Lost
1917–18	Sidney Winters	Allen L. Dalrymple	7	2
1918–19		Allen L. Dalrymple	1	2
1919–20	George E. Keogan	Richard Bradley	13	7
1920–21	George E. Keogan	Walter Gilbert	19	5
1921–22	Earl J. Goheen	Millard Anderson	15	8
1922–23	Earl J. Goheen	Walter Hiltpold	15	5
1923–24	William P. Shadoan	Millard Anderson	24	4
1924–25	William P. Shadoan	Earl Scott	9	5
1925–26	Andy Anderson	James Doran	6	13
1926–27	Conrad S. Moll	Austin Parker	10	10
1927–28	Earl Scott	Robert Blaese	11	4
1928–29	Earl Scott	Robert Blaese	11	10
1929–30	J. M. Christiansen	Ralph Mertz	4	11
1930–31	J. M. Christiansen	Thomas Winebrenner	16	2
1931–32	J. M. Christiansen	Emory G. Bauer	12	12
1932–33	J. M. Christiansen	Pete Rucinski	14	2 *
1933–34	J. M. Christiansen	Edward Barnekoff	9	9
1934–35	J. M. Christiansen	Vernon Giessing	2	13
1935–36	J. M. Christiansen	John Baran	8	8
1936–37	J. M. Christiansen		9	9
1937–38	J. M. Christiansen		13	6 *
1938–39	J. M. Christiansen	Carl Ruehr	5	10
1939–40	J. M. Christiansen	Edward Krenzke	6	14
1940–41	J. M. Christiansen	Harold Kenney	4	12
1941–42	Loren E. Ellis	Arlo Mueller	4	13
1942–43	Loren E. Ellis		17	5
1943–44	Loren E. Ellis	Donald Warnke	17	8
1944–45	Loren E. Ellis	Robert Dille	21	3
1945–46	Loren E. Ellis	John Janisch	17	11

* Conference Champions

1946–47	Loren E. Ellis		11	20
1947–48	Emory G. Bauer	Theodore Bean	8	15
1948–49	Donald Warnke	Theodore Bean	8	17
1949–50	Wilbur Allen	Robert Metcalf	15	8
1950–51	Wilbur Allen	William Schroer	12	10
1951–52	Kenneth G. Suesens	Willard Doehrman	12	12
1952–53	Kenneth G. Suesens	Thomas Plinke	9	15
1953–54	Kenneth G. Suesens	James Howard, Chester Meisberger	10	13
1954–55	Kenneth G. Suesens	James Howard	13	11
1955–56	Kenneth G. Suesens	Thomas Sittler	12	14
1956–57	Kenneth G. Suesens	Edward Eckart	11	14
1957–58	Kenneth G. Suesens	John Neil Reincke	7	14
1958–59	Paul Meadows	Richard L. Schroer		

Outstanding Players of Recent Years

Robert Dille—Helms Foundation All-American—all-time highest record of points per game through college career (14.0 for 77 games in 3 years)

Robert Metcalf—all-time record for total points (1175 in 4 years)

James Ove—Helms Foundation All-American—all-time single-season scoring record (469 points for an average of 21.3 per game in 1951)

APPENDIX D

OFFICERS OF THE ALUMNI ASSOCIATION

YEAR	PRESIDENT	VICE-PRESIDENT(S)	SECRETARY	TREASURER
1934	Leonard G. Schramm	Mrs. Floyd Vance	Esther Kirkhoefer	Robert C. Moellering
1935	Leonard G. Schramm	Mrs. Floyd Vance	Esther Kirkhoefer	Robert C. Moellering
1936	Walter Christopher		Esther Kirkhoefer	Robert C. Moellering
1937	Walter Christopher	Florence Schulte	Mildred Schulte	Robert C. Moellering
1938	Walter Christopher	Florence Schulte	Jane Kreinheder	Norma Luekens
1939	Robert C. Moellering	Florence Schulte	Jane Kreinheder	Norma Luekens
1940	A. John Briel	Fred Hesterman		
1941	A. John Briel	Earl Dawald	E. Alsie Bolte	
1942	Walter Christopher	Lorain Rentner	E. Alsie Bolte Larson	
1943	Clarence Ott	James Karsten	Aline Tigar	
1944	Clarence Ott		Lois Sohn	
1945	Robert Peper		Esther Biederman	
1946	Herbert Freise	Alice Becker	Esther Biederman	
1947	Vernon Reich	Marjorie Claudon Anderson	Norma Christensen Coiner	
1948	Vernon Reich	Walter W. Wieggel	Margaret Moellering	
1949	Gilbert Krause	Karl Stodden	Margaret Moellering	
1950	Gilbert Krause	Theodore Kretzmann	Margaret Knoll	
1951	Walter Schur	Theodore Kretzmann	Margaret Knoll	
1952	Walter Schur	Carleton Ihde	Constance Bruegman Felten	
1953	Ray Wolff	Carleton Ihde	Constance Bruegman Felten	
1954	Ray Wolff	Robert Peper / Carleton Ihde	Esther Foelber Kruger	
1955	Herbert Steinbach	Robert Peper / Carleton Ihde	Betty Kelly Schwan	
1956	Herbert Steinbach	Paul Nieter / Alwin Koenig	Betty Kelly Schwan	
*1958	Paul Nieter	Alwin Koenig / W. J. Karsten	Josephine Luecke Ferguson	Janet Stoner Sievers
1959	Walter Schur	Oscar Boock / Marvin Rammelsberg	Josephine Luecke Ferguson	Janet Stoner Sievers
		Marvin Rammelsberg / Robert Storbeck	Leona Plotz Kirschenmann	Richard H. Lanbe

* Beginning January 1, 1958, terms of office were made concurrent with the calendar year.   President-elect for 1960 is Oscar Boock.

Executive Officers of the Alumni Association

1937–1938	Fred H. Rechlin, Alumni Secretary
1944–1946	E. Alsie Larson, Alumni Secretary (part-time, 1944–1946)
1946–1950	Alfred R. Looman, Alumni Secretary
1950–1951	Joseph Bradley, Alumni Secretary
	E. Alsie Larson, Assistant
1951–1952	Robert Bartz, Alumni Secretary
	E. Alsie Larson, Assistant
1952–1955	E. Alsie Larson, Acting Alumni Secretary
1955–	Marcus T. Young, Director of Alumni Affairs

NATIONAL OFFICERS OF THE VALPARAISO UNIVERSITY WOMEN'S GUILD

TERM	PRESIDENT	VICE-PRESIDENT	SECRETARY	TREASURER
1931	Mrs. E.W. Schultz	Mrs. H.A. Eberline	Miss Lily Fedder	
1932	Mrs. E.W. Schultz		Miss Lily Fedder	
1933–36	Mrs. H.W. Bartels	Mrs. W.O. Bohnsack	Mrs. Walter Wolf	
1936–39	Mrs. H.A. Eberline	Mrs. A.A. Taube	Mrs. O.A. Kampe	
1939–42	Mrs. W.N. Hoppe	Mrs. A.F. Scherer	Miss Louise Nicolay	
1942–45	Mrs. A.A. Taube	Mrs. E.J. Gallmeyer	Mrs. E.G. Schwiebert	Miss Louise Nicolay
1945–46	Miss Louise Nicolay	Mrs. E.F. Stegman	Mrs. W.A. Hansen	Mrs. G.E. Penson
1946–47	Miss Louise Nicolay	Mrs. E.T.J. Birner	Mrs. W.A. Hansen	Mrs. G.E. Penson
1947–48	Miss Louise Nicolay	Mrs. E.T.J. Birner	Miss Emily Doell	Mrs. G.E. Penson
1948–49	Mrs. W.A. Hansen	Mrs. E.T.J. Birner	Miss Emily Doell	Miss Vivian Kossman
1949–50	Mrs. W.A. Hansen	Mrs. Karl Kurth	Miss Emily Doell	Miss Vivian Kossman
1950–51	Mrs. W.A. Hansen	Mrs. Karl Kurth	Mrs. E.V. Bartholomew	Miss Vivian Kossman
1951–52	Mrs. E.T.J. Birner	Mrs. L.A. Oehmke	Mrs. E.V. Bartholomew	Mrs. W.A. Steinfeldt
1952–53	Mrs. E.T.J. Birner	Mrs. R.C. Frank	Mrs. F.J. Schumm	Mrs. W.A. Steinfeldt
1953–54	Mrs. E.T.J. Birner	Mrs. R.C. Frank	Mrs. F.J. Schumm	Mrs. W.A. Steinfeldt
1954–55	Mrs. W.A. Drews	Mrs. Chas. St. Clair	Mrs. F.J. Schumm	Mrs. W.J. Kraus
1955–56	Mrs. W.A. Drews	Mrs. Chas. St. Clair	Mrs. F.J. Schumm	Mrs. W.J. Kraus
1956–57	Mrs. W.A. Drews	Mrs. Chas. St. Clair	Mrs. Edwin Busse	Mrs. W.J. Kraus
1957–58	Mrs. R.C. Frank	Mrs. Cyril Wismar	Mrs. Carl Blomstrand	Miss Charlotte Kirchen
1958–59	Mrs. R.C. Frank	Mrs. Cyril Wismar	Miss Ethelyn Baade	Miss Charlotte Kirchen

Executive Secretaries of The Women's Guild

Jan. 1, 1945 – Jan. 11, 1947	Gayle Tustin (Mrs. E. G.) Schwiebert
Jan. 11, 1947 – Dec. 1, 1952	Sophia D. (Mrs. C.R.) Heidbrink
Dec. 1, 1952	Bernice (Mrs. E.H.) Ruprecht